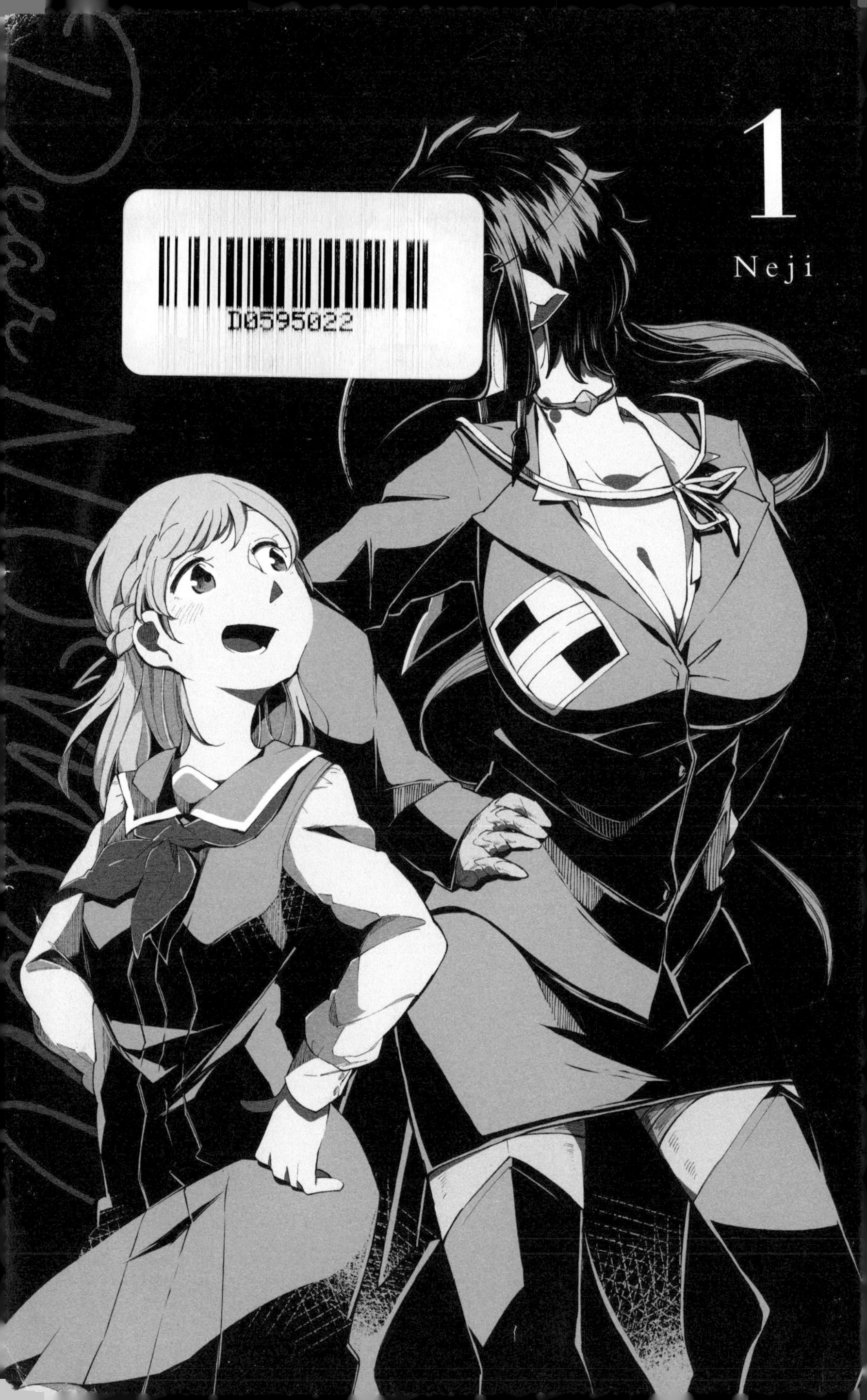
1
Neji

WITHDRAWN

Contents

LETTER 1

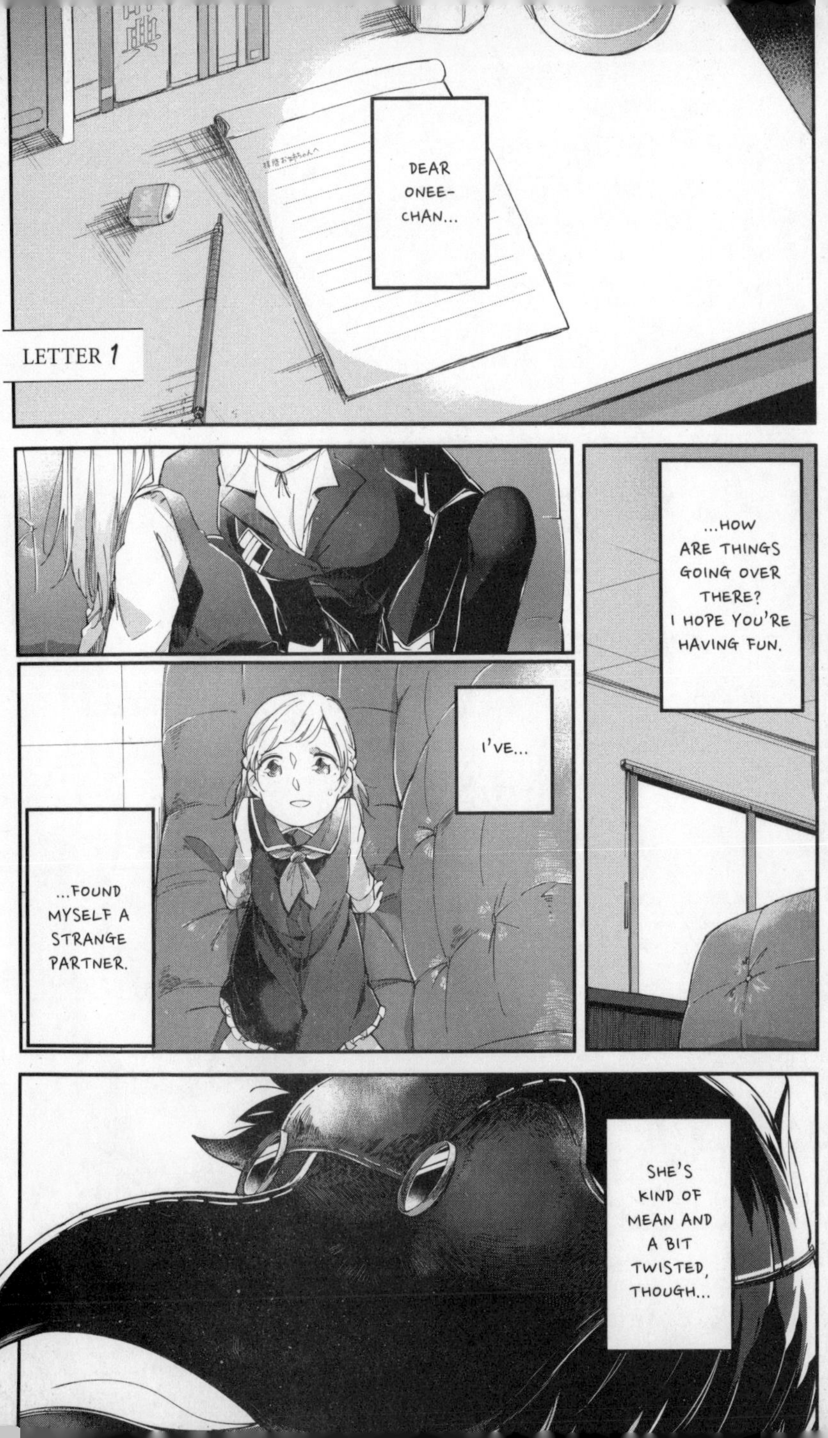
DEAR ONEE-CHAN...
...HOW ARE THINGS GOING OVER THERE? I HOPE YOU'RE HAVING FUN.
I'VE...
...FOUND MYSELF A STRANGE PARTNER.
SHE'S KIND OF MEAN AND A BIT TWISTED, THOUGH...

LETTER 1

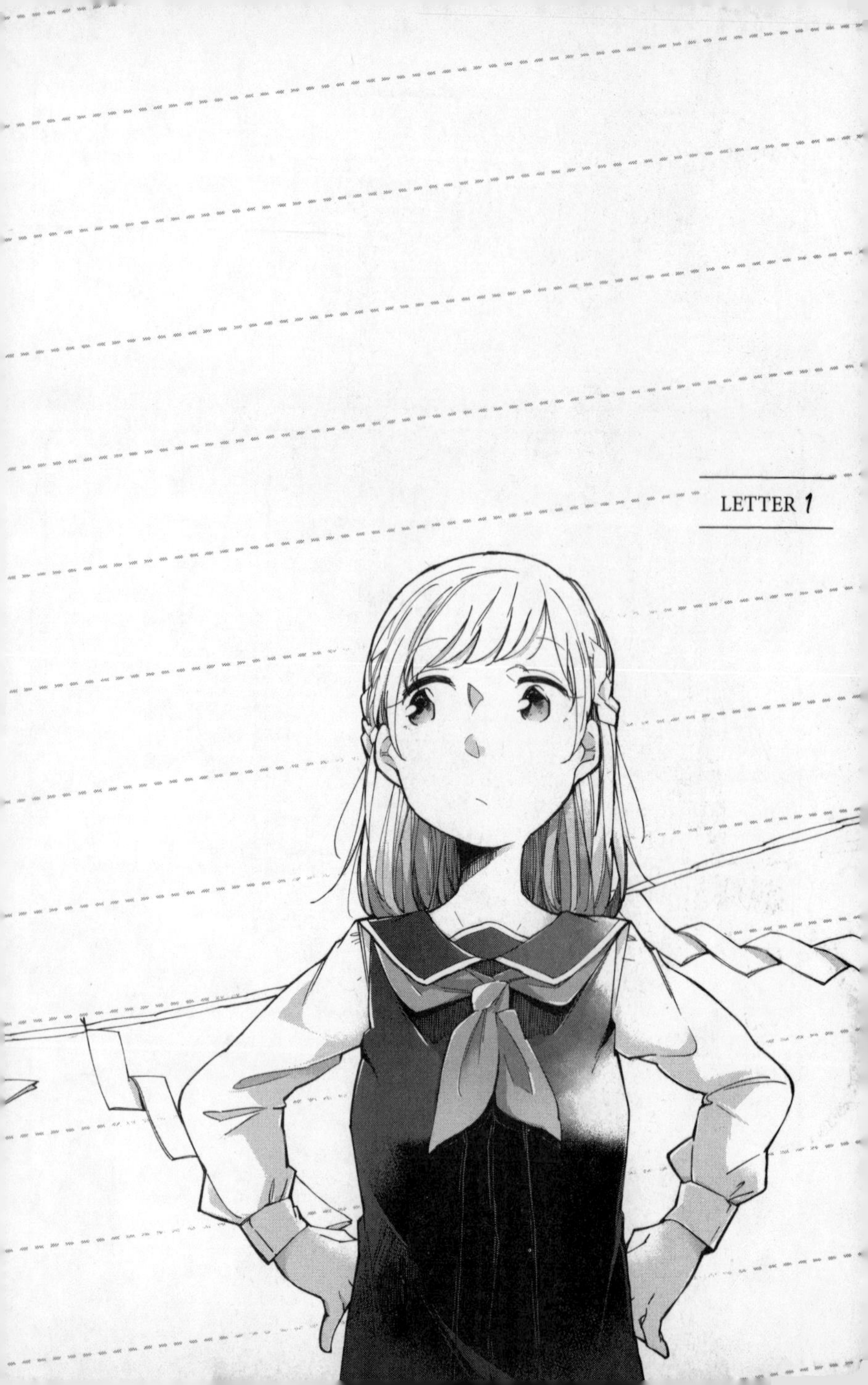

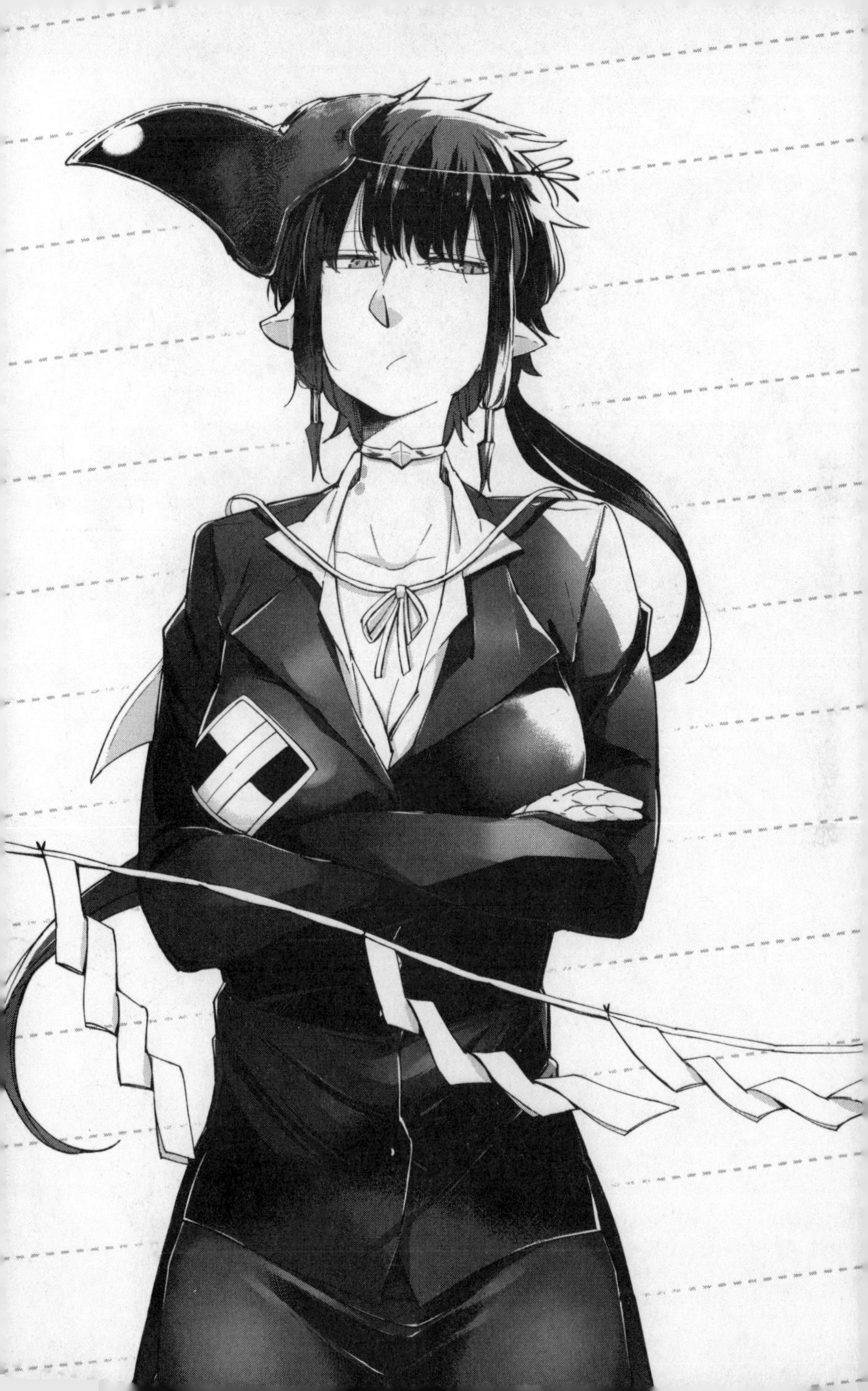

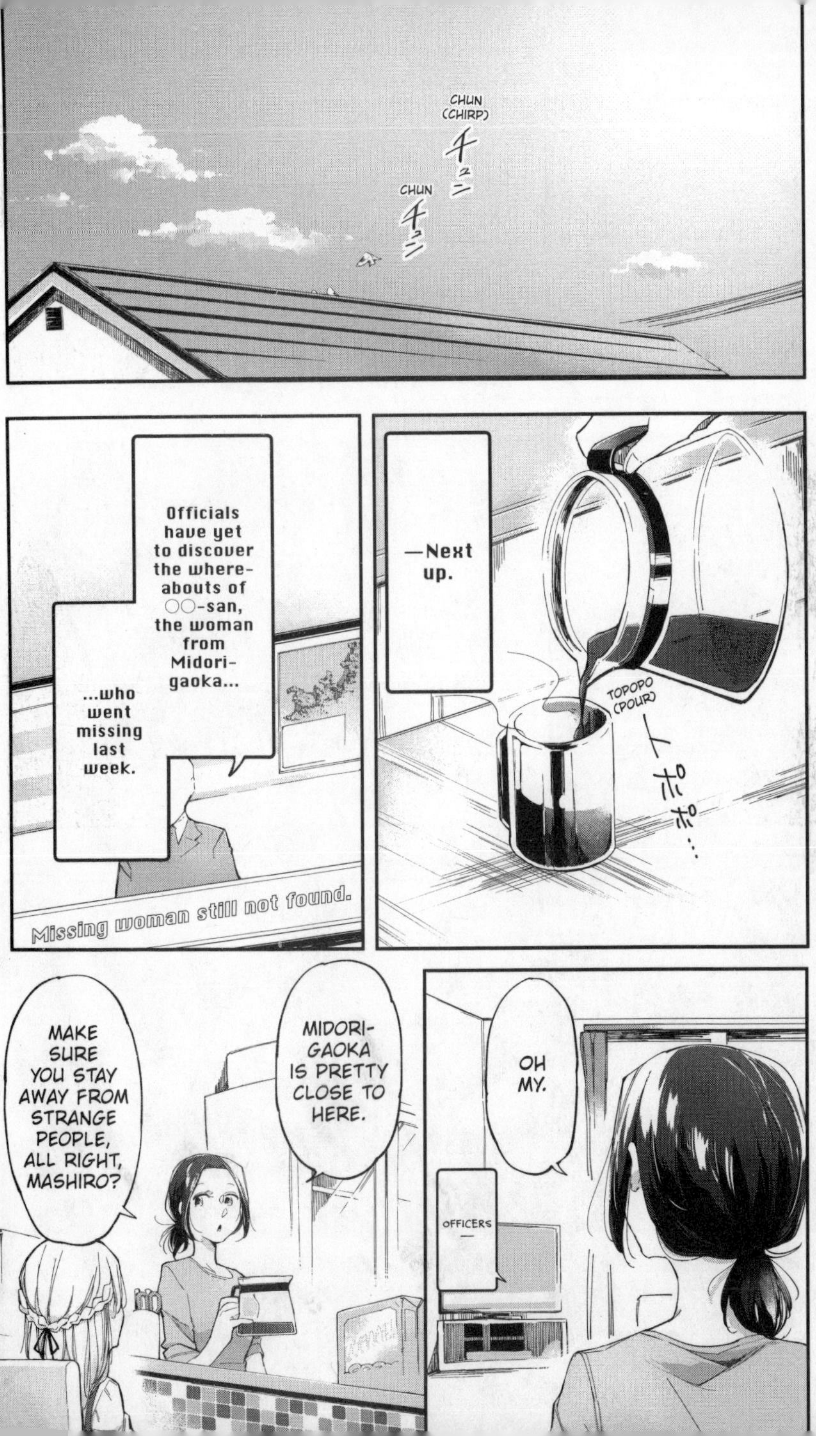
CHUN (CHIRP)
チュン
CHUN
チュン
—Next up.
TOPOPO (POUR)
トポポ…
Officials have yet to discover the where-abouts of ○○-san, the woman from Midori-gaoka...
...who went missing last week.
Missing woman still not found.
OH MY.
OFFICERS —
MIDORI-GAOKA IS PRETTY CLOSE TO HERE.
MAKE SURE YOU STAY AWAY FROM STRANGE PEOPLE, ALL RIGHT, MASHIRO?

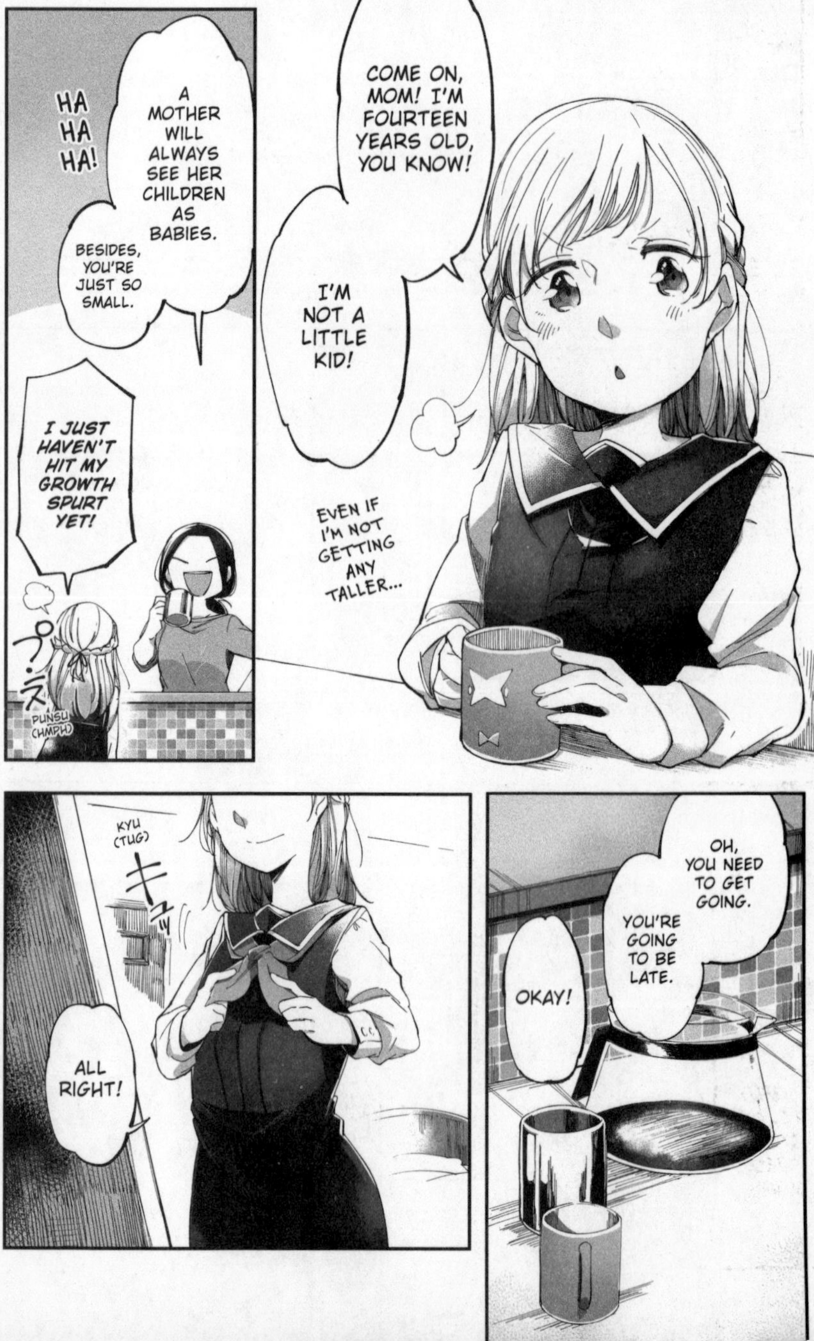
COME ON, MOM! I'M FOURTEEN YEARS OLD, YOU KNOW!
I'M NOT A LITTLE KID!
EVEN IF I'M NOT GETTING ANY TALLER...
A MOTHER WILL ALWAYS SEE HER CHILDREN AS BABIES.
HA HA HA!
BESIDES, YOU'RE JUST SO SMALL.
I JUST HAVEN'T HIT MY GROWTH SPURT YET!
PUNSU (HMPH)
OH, YOU NEED TO GET GOING.
YOU'RE GOING TO BE LATE.
OKAY!
KYU (TUG)
ALL RIGHT!

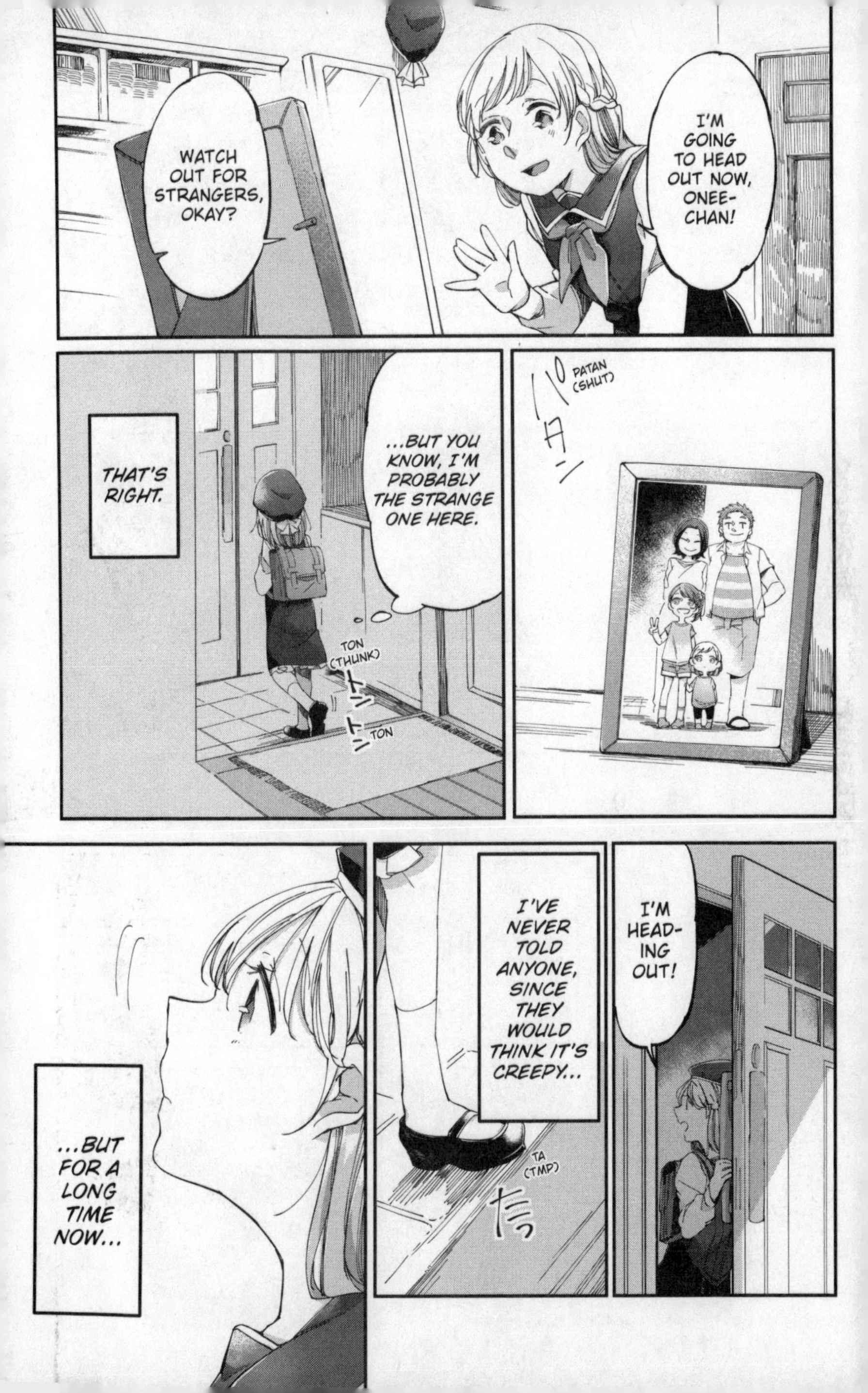
I'M GOING TO HEAD OUT NOW, ONEE-CHAN!
WATCH OUT FOR STRANGERS, OKAY?
PATAN (SHUT)
...BUT YOU KNOW, I'M PROBABLY THE STRANGE ONE HERE.
THAT'S RIGHT.
TON (THUNK)
TON
I'M HEAD-ING OUT!
I'VE NEVER TOLD ANYONE, SINCE THEY WOULD THINK IT'S CREEPY...
TA (TMP)
...BUT FOR A LONG TIME NOW...

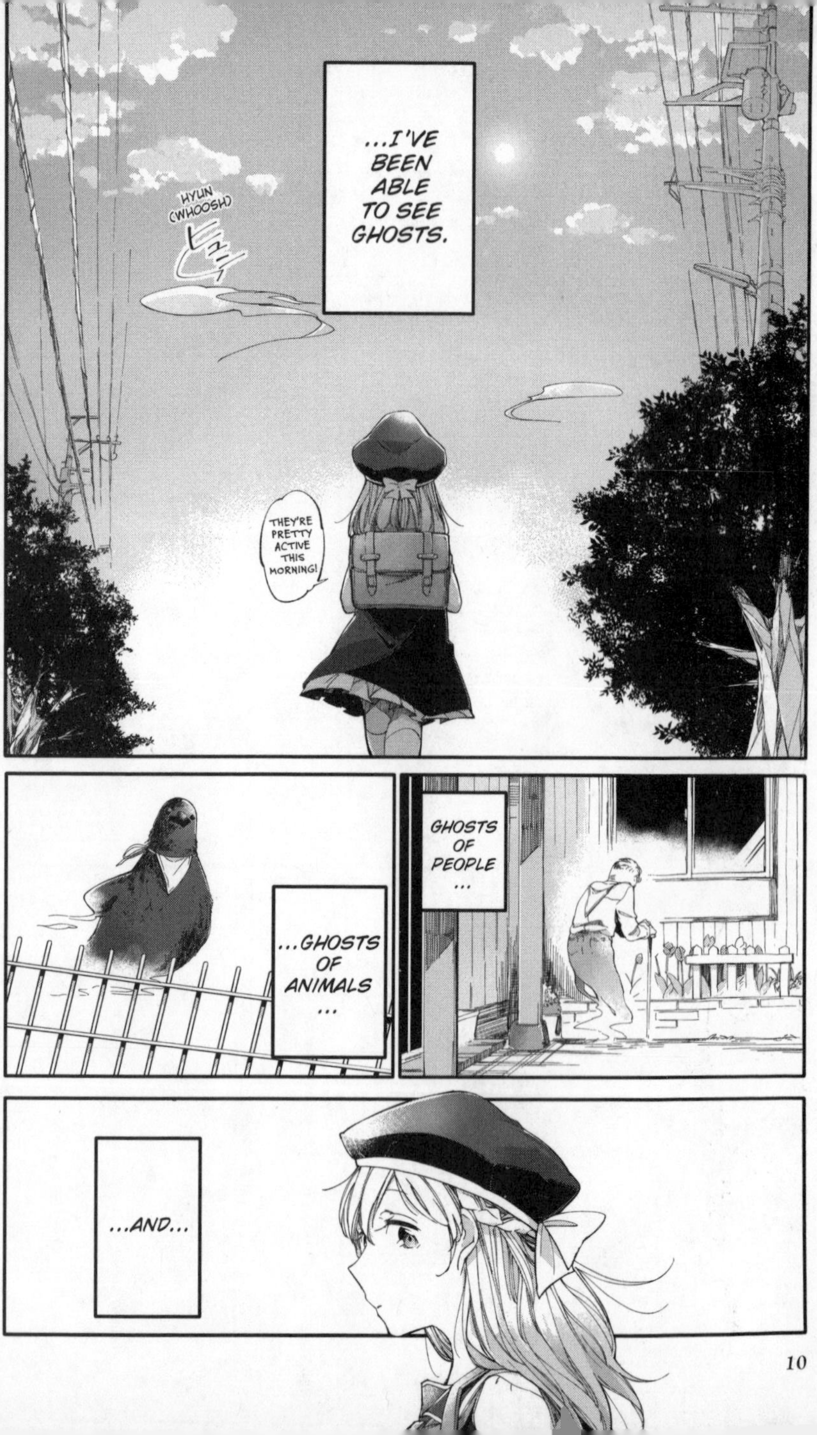
...I'VE BEEN ABLE TO SEE GHOSTS.
HYUN (WHOOSH)
THEY'RE PRETTY ACTIVE THIS MORNING!
GHOSTS OF PEOPLE...
...GHOSTS OF ANIMALS...
...AND...

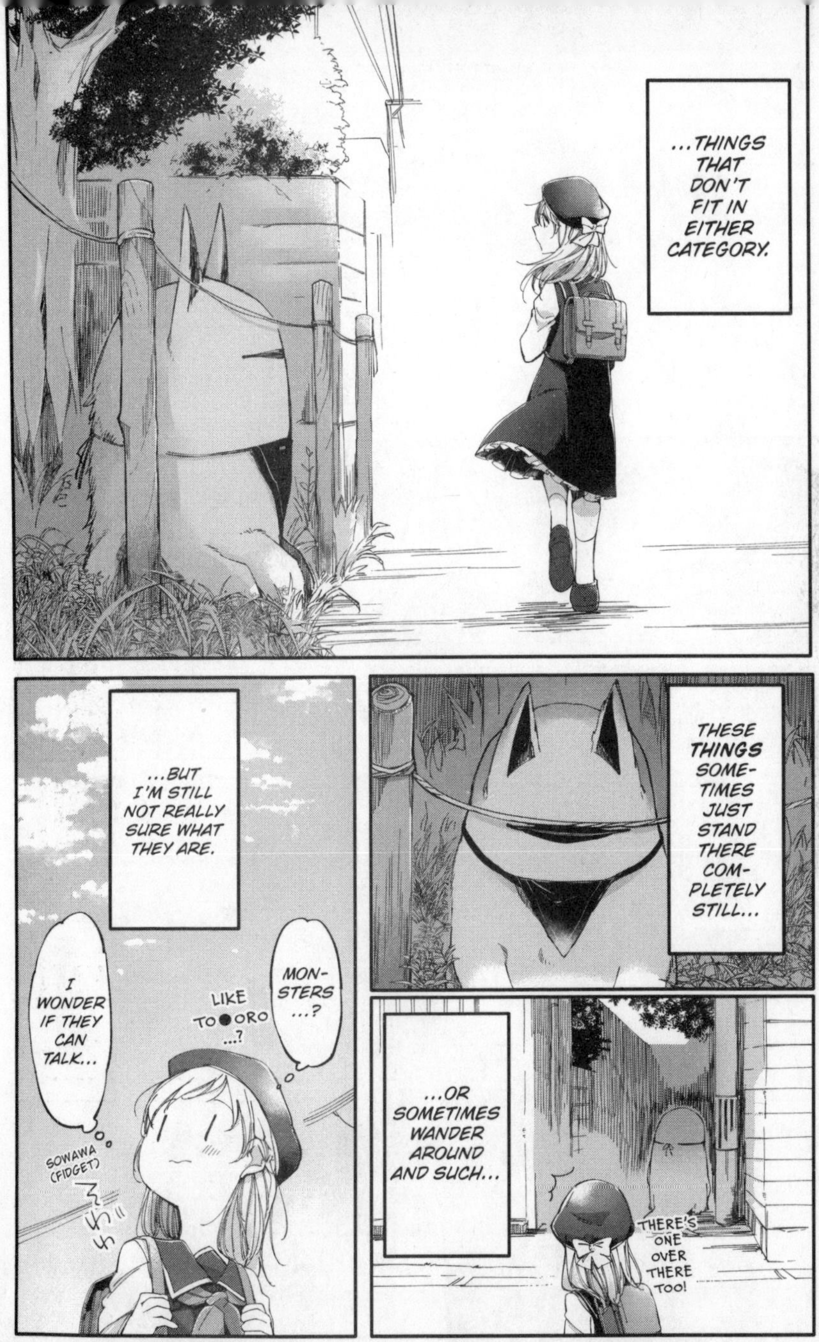
...THINGS THAT DON'T FIT IN EITHER CATEGORY.
THESE THINGS SOME-TIMES JUST STAND THERE COM-PLETELY STILL...
...OR SOMETIMES WANDER AROUND AND SUCH...
THERE'S ONE OVER THERE TOO!
...BUT I'M STILL NOT REALLY SURE WHAT THEY ARE.
MON-STERS ...?
LIKE TO●ORO ...?
I WONDER IF THEY CAN TALK...
SOWAWA (FIDGET)

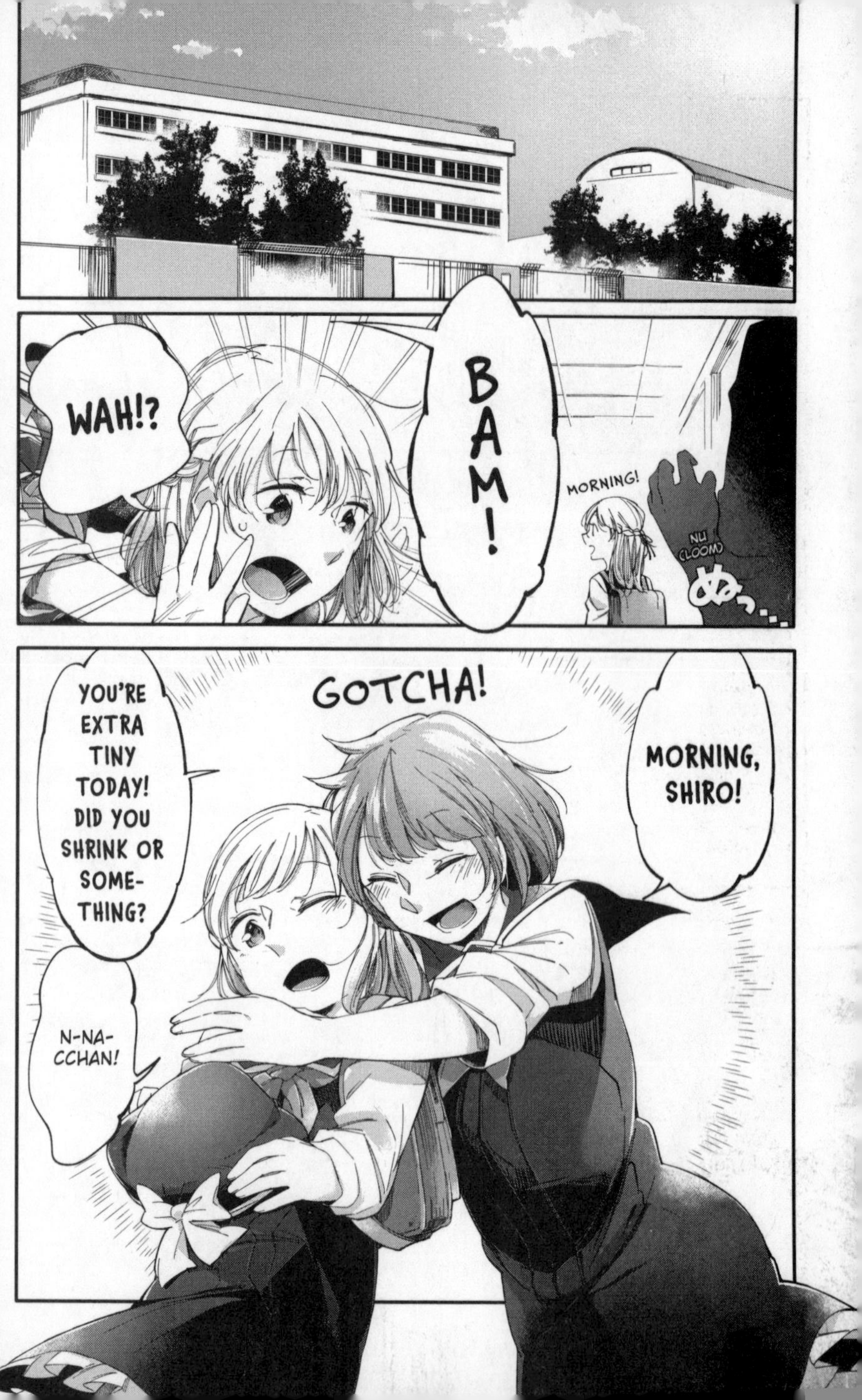
NU (LOOM)
ぬっ...
MORNING!
BAM!
WAH!?
MORNING, SHIRO!
GOTCHA!
YOU'RE EXTRA TINY TODAY! DID YOU SHRINK OR SOME-THING?
N-NA-CCHAN!

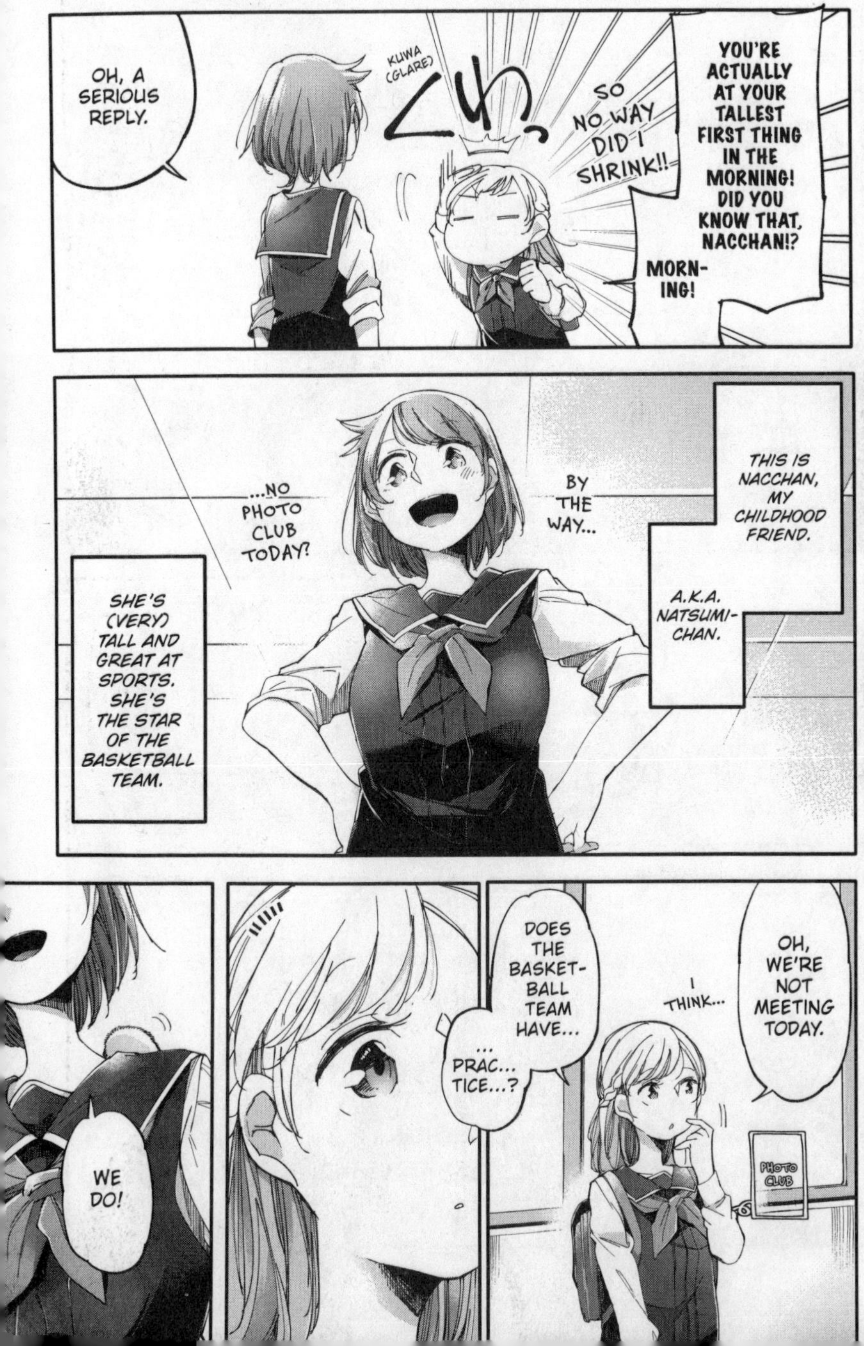
YOU'RE ACTUALLY AT YOUR TALLEST FIRST THING IN THE MORNING! DID YOU KNOW THAT, NACCHAN!?
MORN-ING!
SO NO WAY DID I SHRINK!!
KUWA (GLARE)
OH, A SERIOUS REPLY.
THIS IS NACCHAN, MY CHILDHOOD FRIEND.
A.K.A. NATSUMI-CHAN.
BY THE WAY...
...NO PHOTO CLUB TODAY?
SHE'S (VERY) TALL AND GREAT AT SPORTS. SHE'S THE STAR OF THE BASKETBALL TEAM.
OH, WE'RE NOT MEETING TODAY.
I THINK...
PHOTO CLUB
DOES THE BASKET-BALL TEAM HAVE...
... PRAC... TICE...?
WE DO!

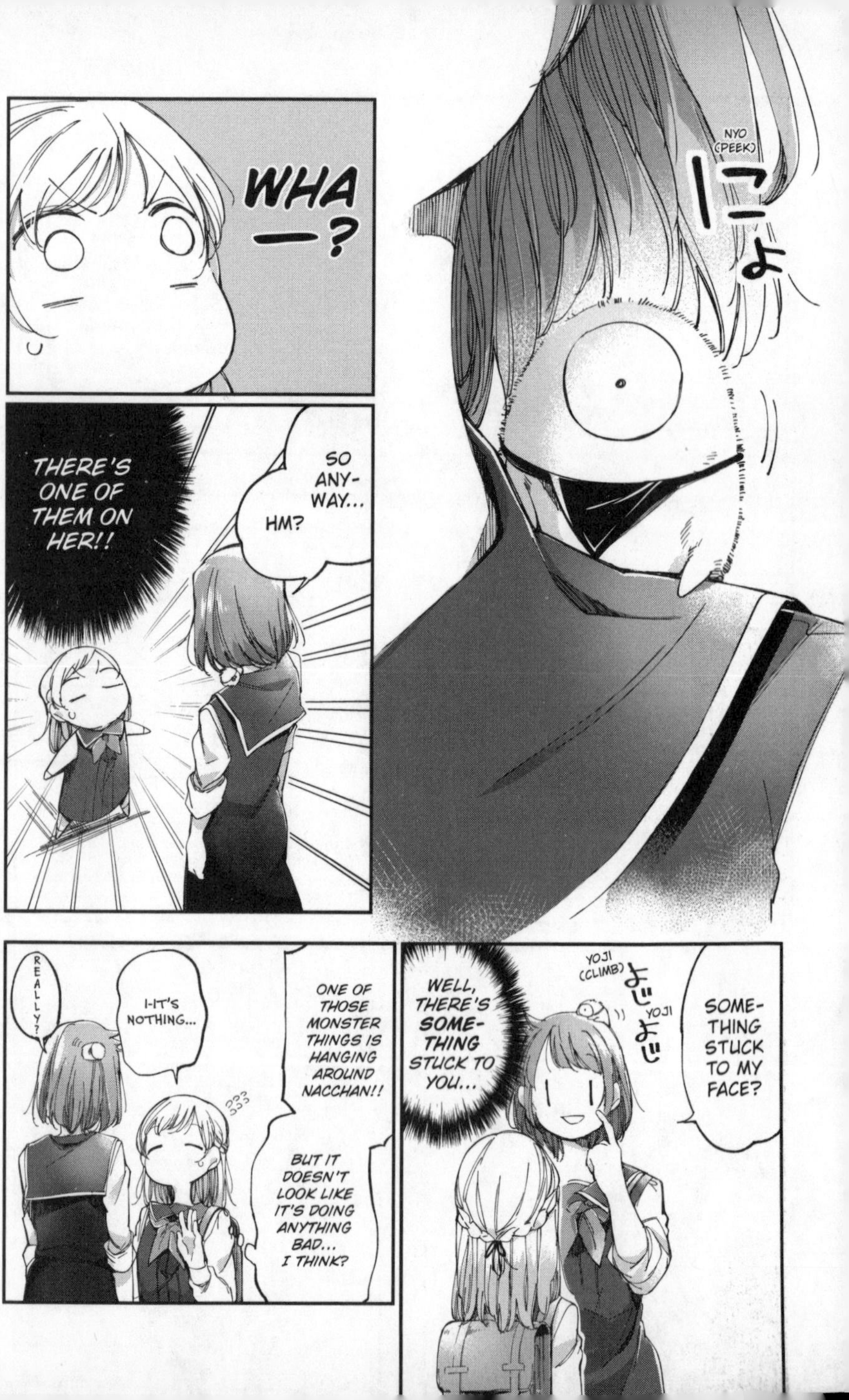

NYO (PEEK)
ニョ
WHA—?
SO ANY-WAY...
HM?
THERE'S ONE OF THEM ON HER!!
SOME-THING STUCK TO MY FACE?
YOJI (CLIMB)
よじよじ
YOJI
WELL, THERE'S SOME-THING STUCK TO YOU...
ONE OF THOSE MONSTER THINGS IS HANGING AROUND NACCHAN!!
BUT IT DOESN'T LOOK LIKE IT'S DOING ANYTHING BAD... I THINK?
I-IT'S NOTHING...
REALLY?

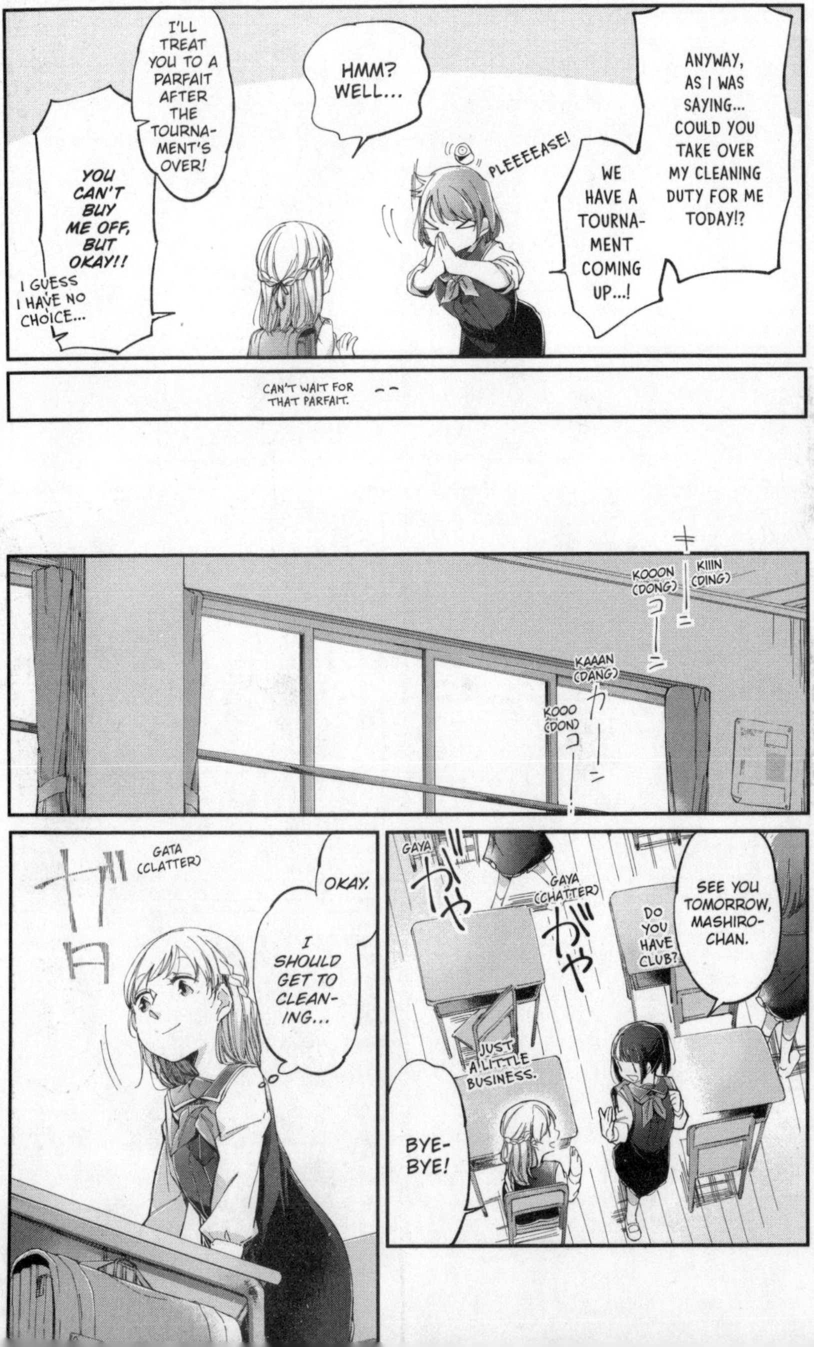
ANYWAY, AS I WAS SAYING... COULD YOU TAKE OVER MY CLEANING DUTY FOR ME TODAY!?
WE HAVE A TOURNAMENT COMING UP...!
PLEEEEASE!
HMM? WELL...
I'LL TREAT YOU TO A PARFAIT AFTER THE TOURNAMENT'S OVER!
YOU CAN'T BUY ME OFF, BUT OKAY!!
I GUESS I HAVE NO CHOICE...
CAN'T WAIT FOR THAT PARFAIT.
KIIIN (DING)
KOOON (DONG)
KAAAN (DANG)
KOOO (DON)
SEE YOU TOMORROW, MASHIRO-CHAN.
DO YOU HAVE CLUB?
GAYA (CHATTER)
GAYA
JUST A LITTLE BUSINESS.
BYE-BYE!
GATA (CLATTER)
OKAY.
I SHOULD GET TO CLEANING...

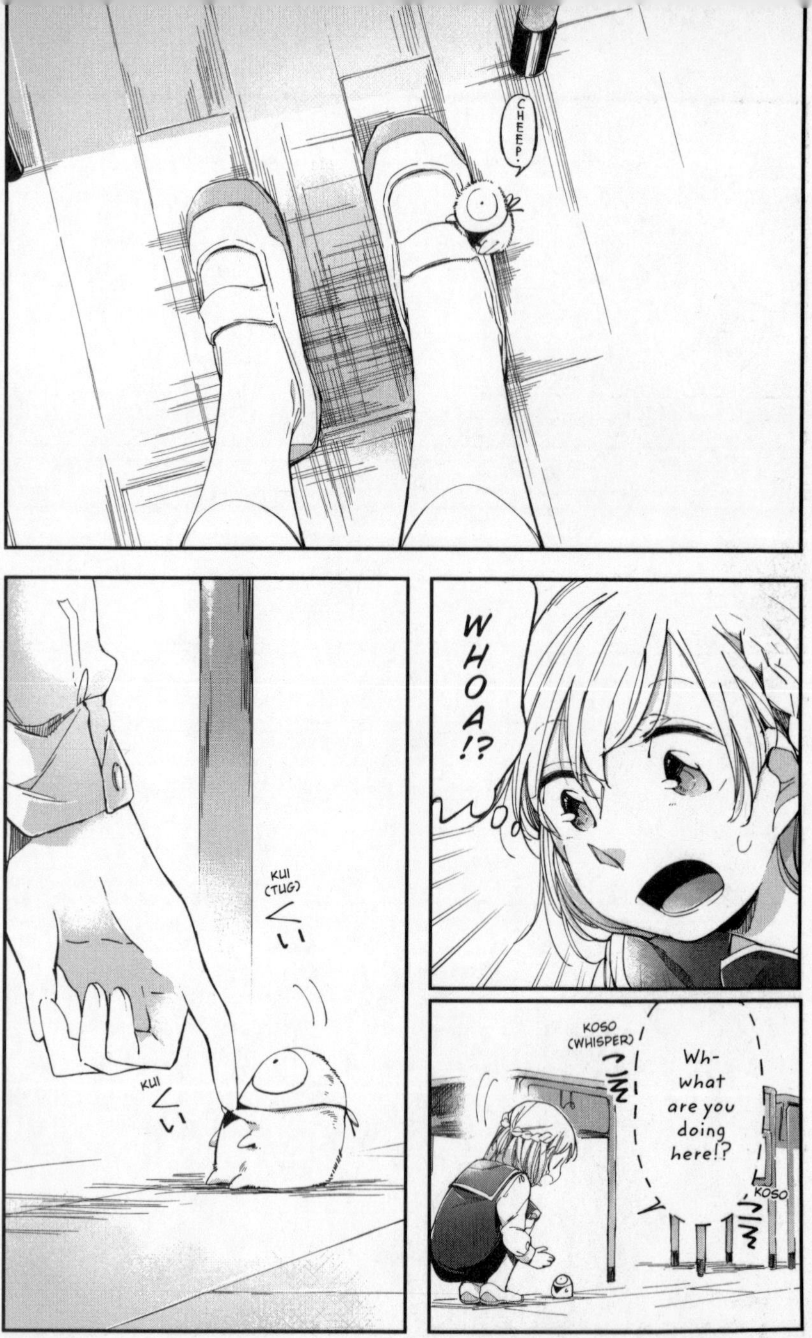
CHEEP.
WHOA!?
KOSO (WHISPER)
こそ
Wh- what are you doing here!?
KOSO
こそ
KUI (TUG)
くい
KUI
くい

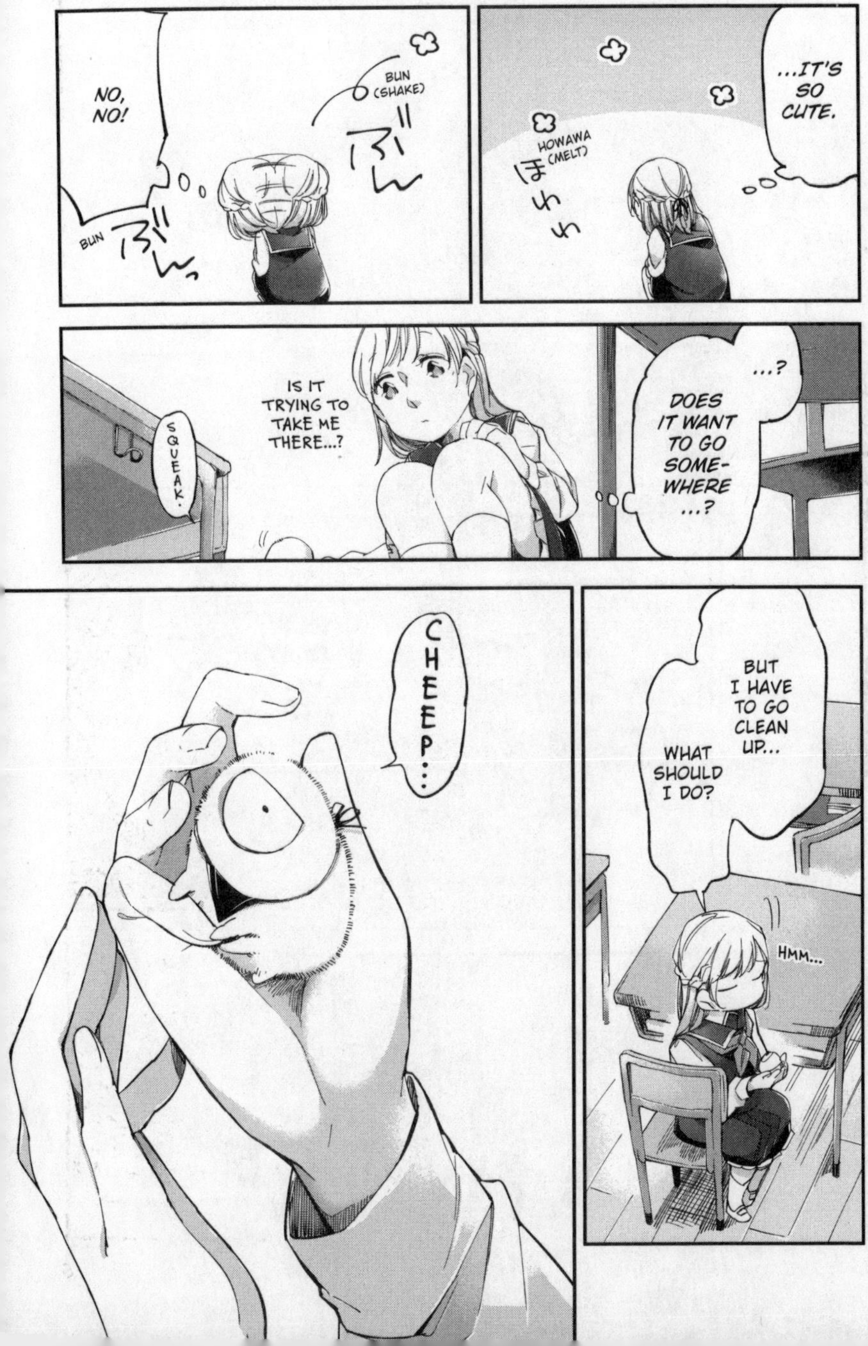
...IT'S SO CUTE.
HOWAWA (MELT)
ほわわ
BUN (SHAKE)
ぶん
NO, NO!
BUN
ぶんっ
...?
DOES IT WANT TO GO SOME-WHERE...?
IS IT TRYING TO TAKE ME THERE...?
SQUEAK.
BUT I HAVE TO GO CLEAN UP...
WHAT SHOULD I DO?
HMM...
CHEEP...

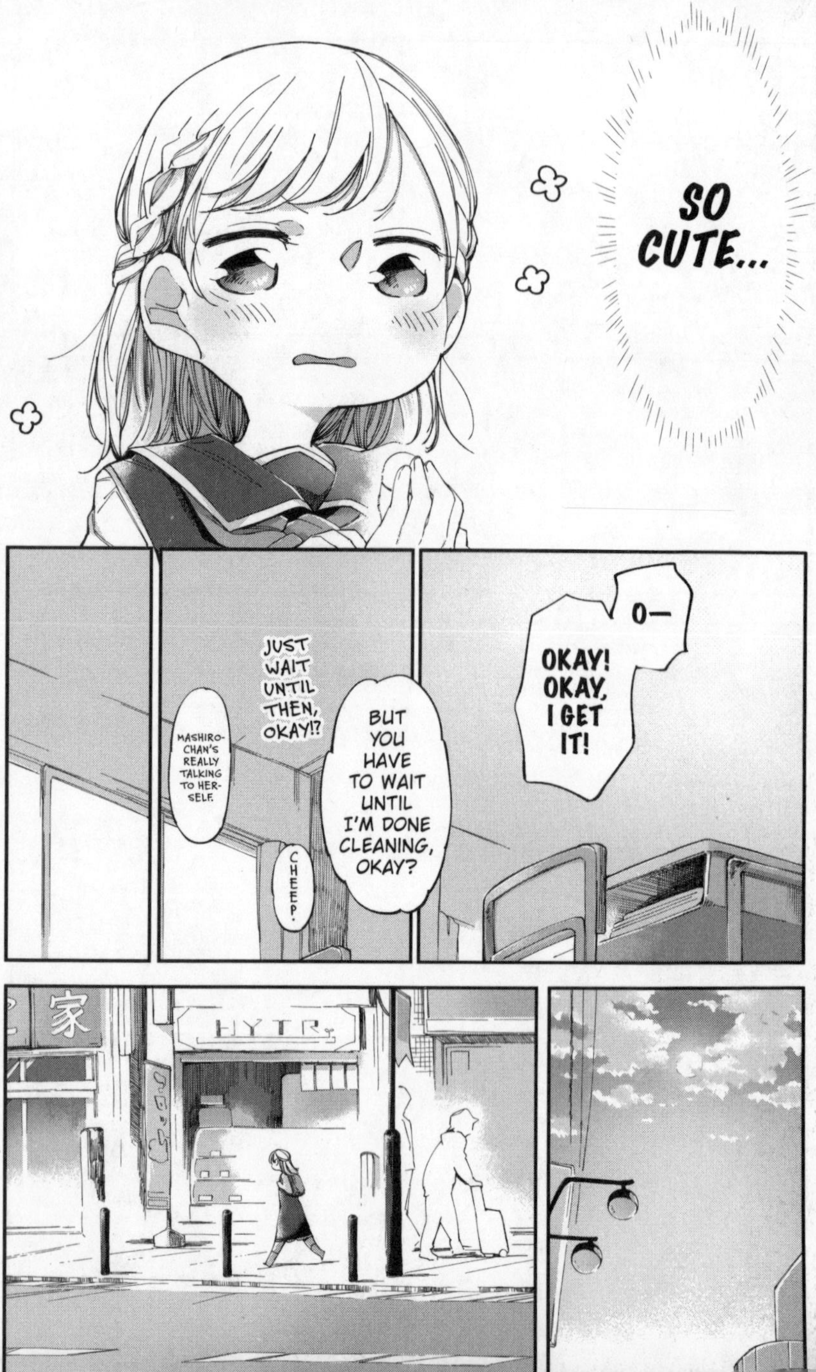
SO CUTE...
O—
OKAY! OKAY, I GET IT!
BUT YOU HAVE TO WAIT UNTIL I'M DONE CLEANING, OKAY?
JUST WAIT UNTIL THEN, OKAY!?
MASHIRO-CHAN'S REALLY TALKING TO HER-SELF.
CHEEP.
家
HYTR

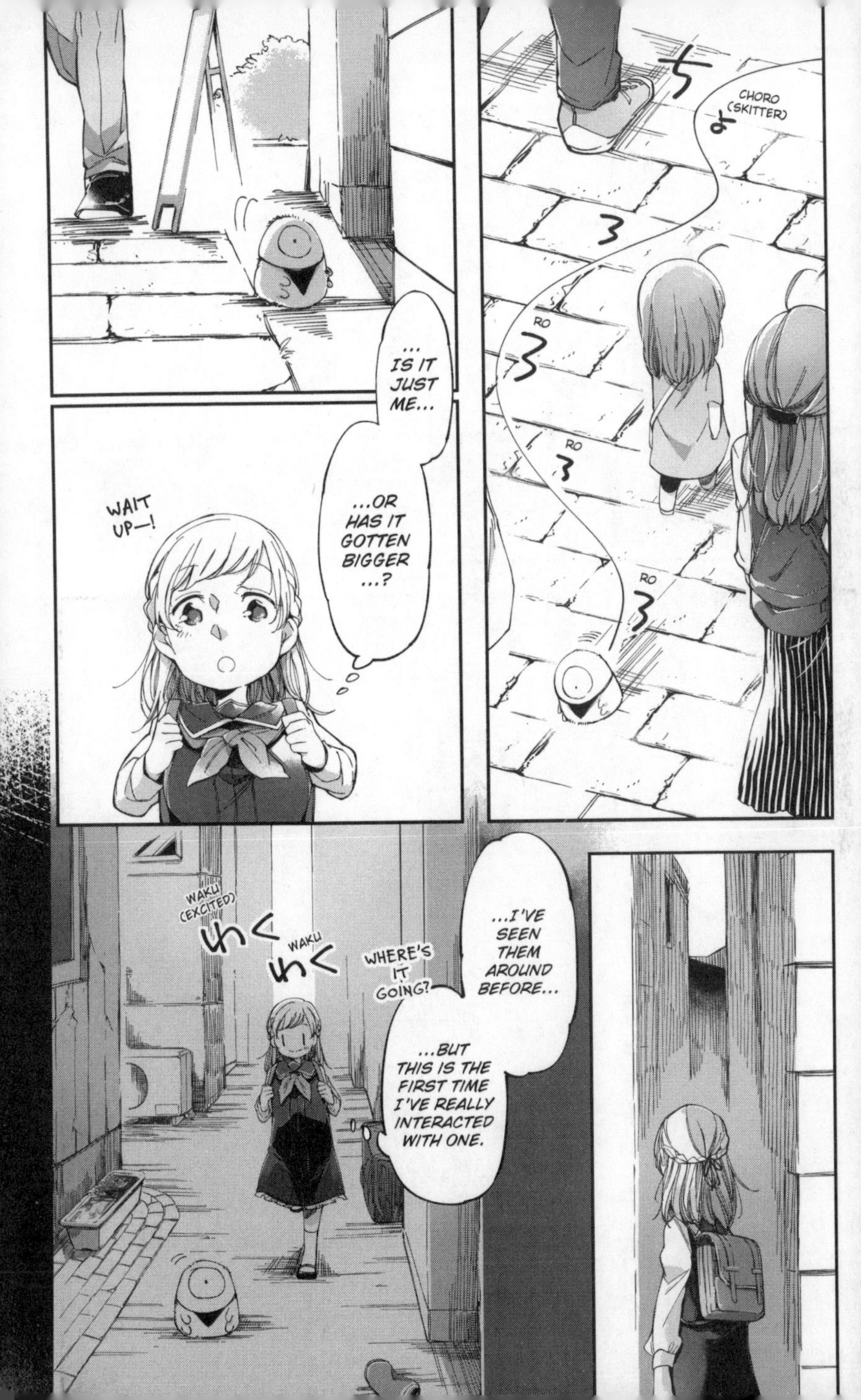
ちょ
CHORO (SKITTER)
RO
ろ
RO
ろ
RO
ろ
...IS IT JUST ME...
...OR HAS IT GOTTEN BIGGER...?
WAIT UP—!
...I'VE SEEN THEM AROUND BEFORE...
...BUT THIS IS THE FIRST TIME I'VE REALLY INTERACTED WITH ONE.
WAKU (EXCITED)
わく
WAKU
わく
WHERE'S IT GOING?

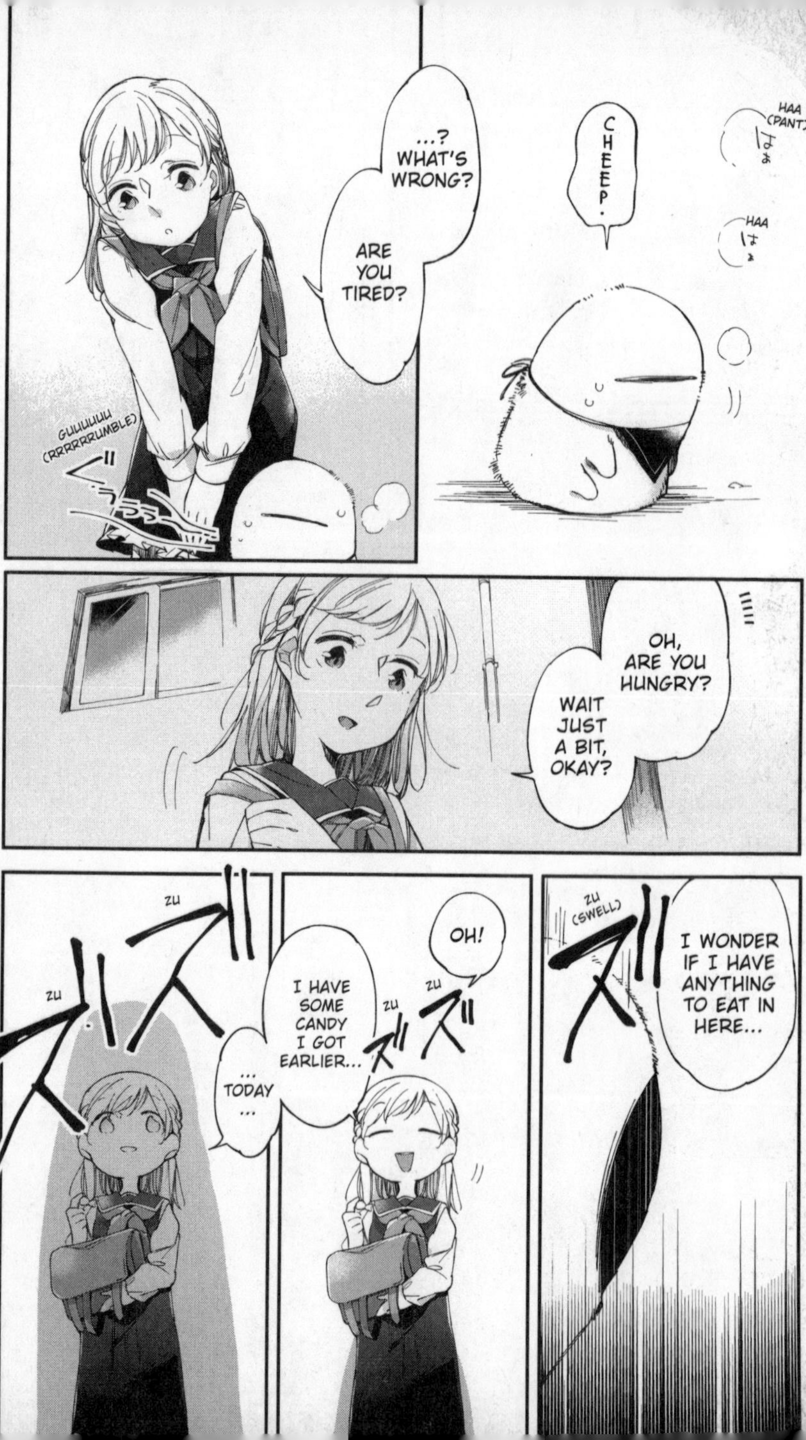
HAA (PANT)
はぁ
HAA
はぁ
CHEEP.
...? WHAT'S WRONG?
ARE YOU TIRED?
GUUUUUU (RRRRRRUMBLE)
OH, ARE YOU HUNGRY?
WAIT JUST A BIT, OKAY?
I WONDER IF I HAVE ANYTHING TO EAT IN HERE...
ZU (SWELL)
OH!
I HAVE SOME CANDY I GOT EARLIER...
ZU
ZU
... TODAY ...
ZU
ZU

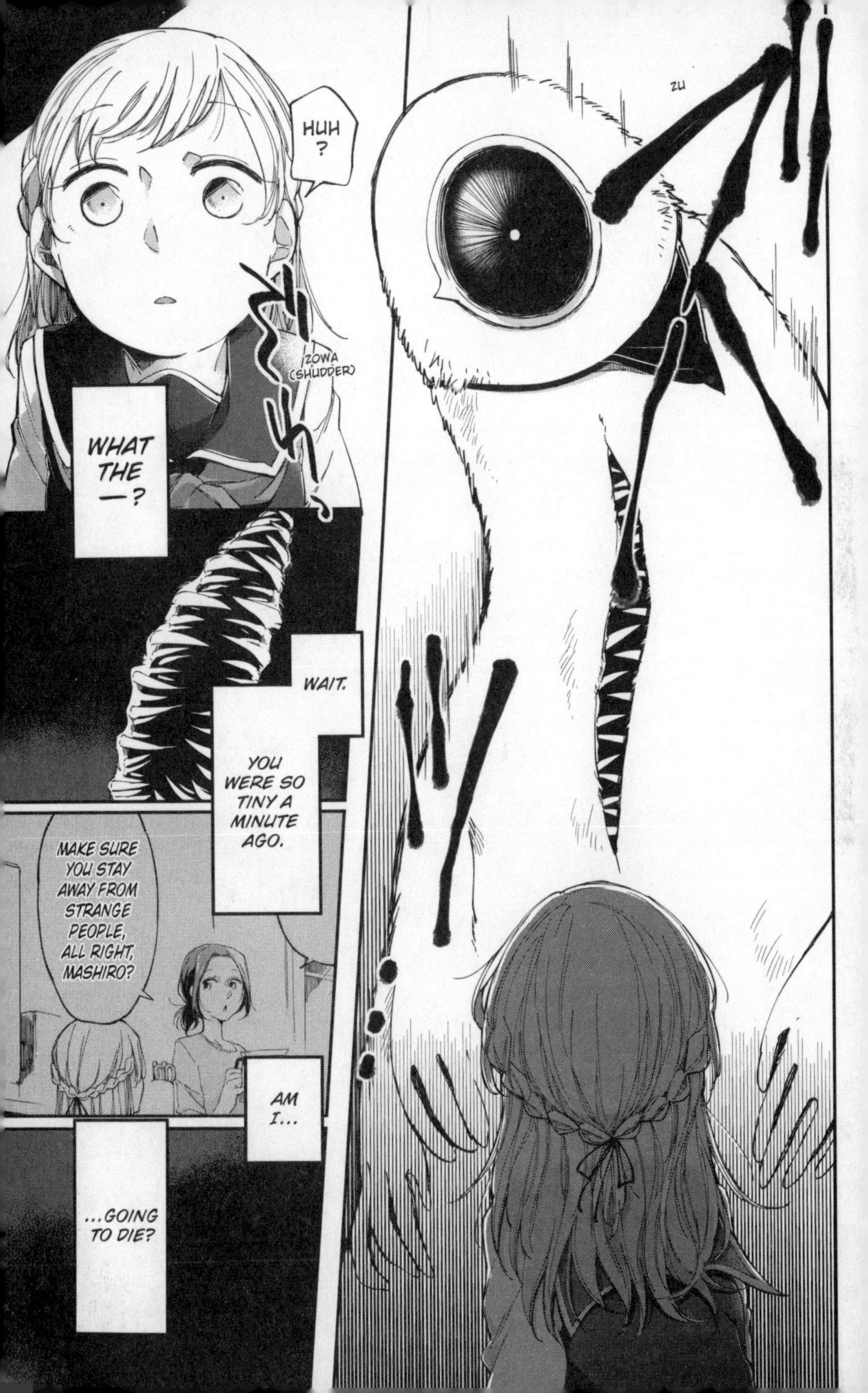
ZU
HUH?
ZOWA (SHUDDER)
WHAT THE—?
WAIT.
YOU WERE SO TINY A MINUTE AGO.
MAKE SURE YOU STAY AWAY FROM STRANGE PEOPLE, ALL RIGHT, MASHIRO?
AM I...
...GOING TO DIE?

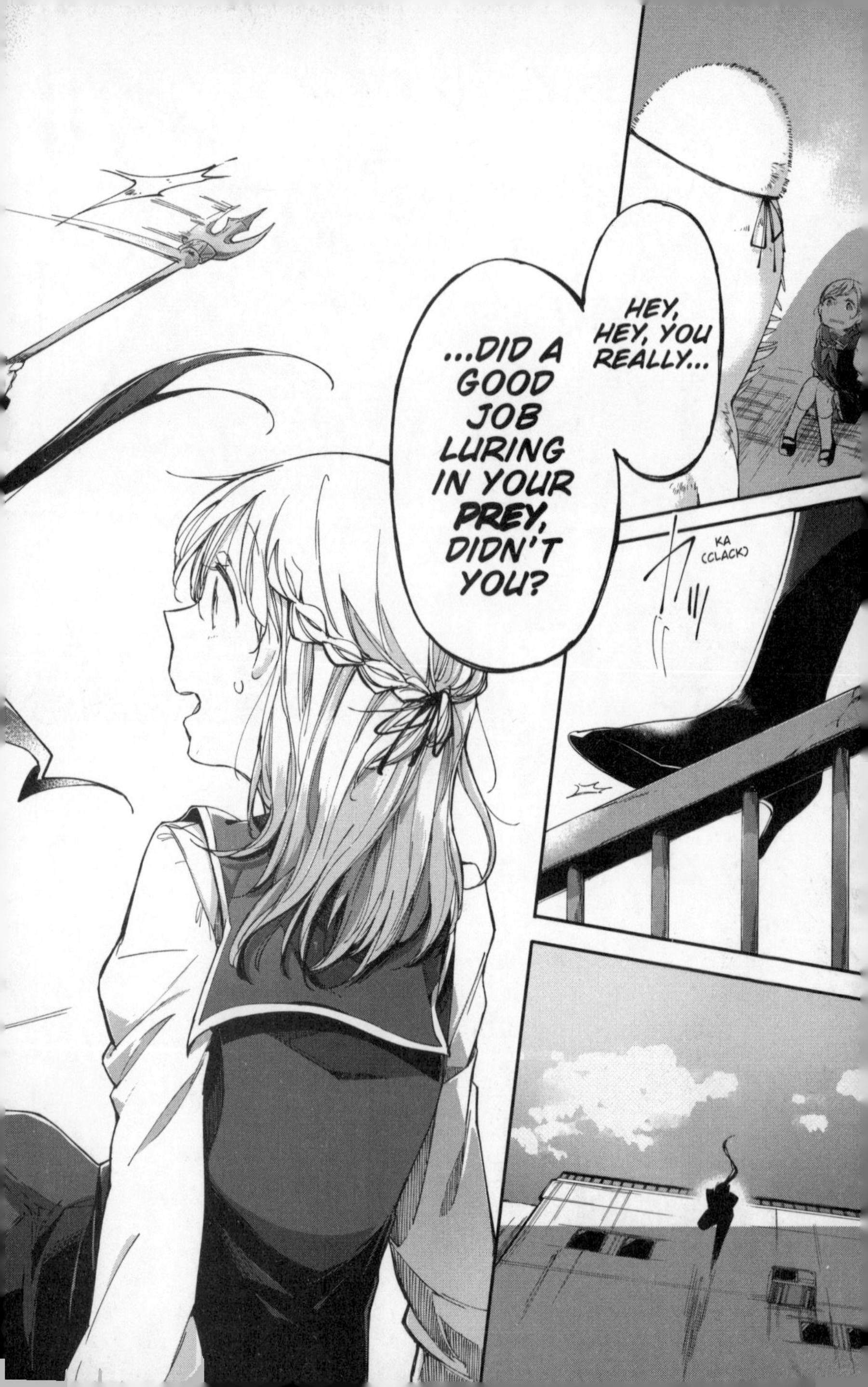
HEY, HEY, YOU REALLY...
...DID A GOOD JOB LURING IN YOUR PREY, DIDN'T YOU?
KA (CLACK)

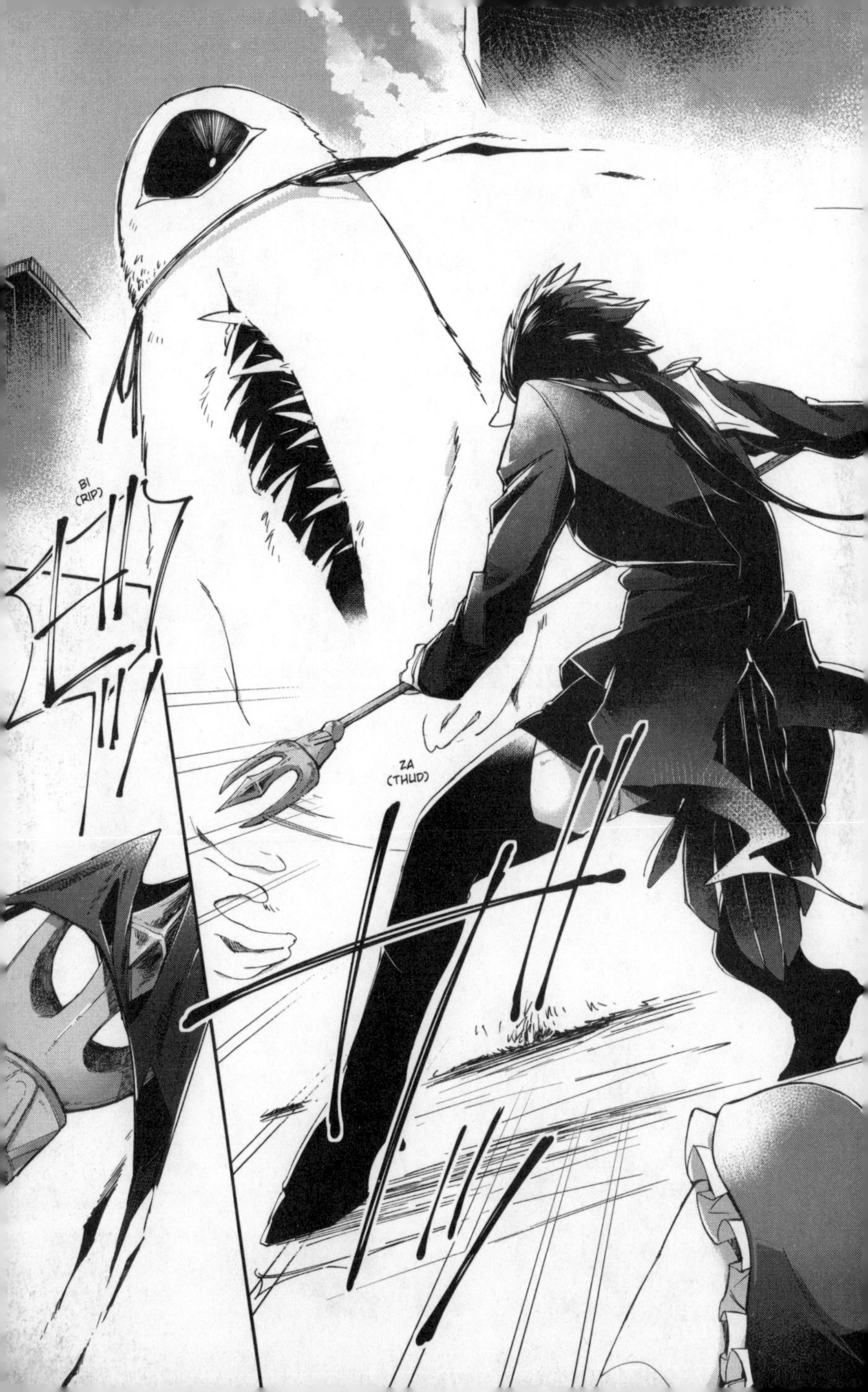
ZA
(THUD)
BI
(RIP)

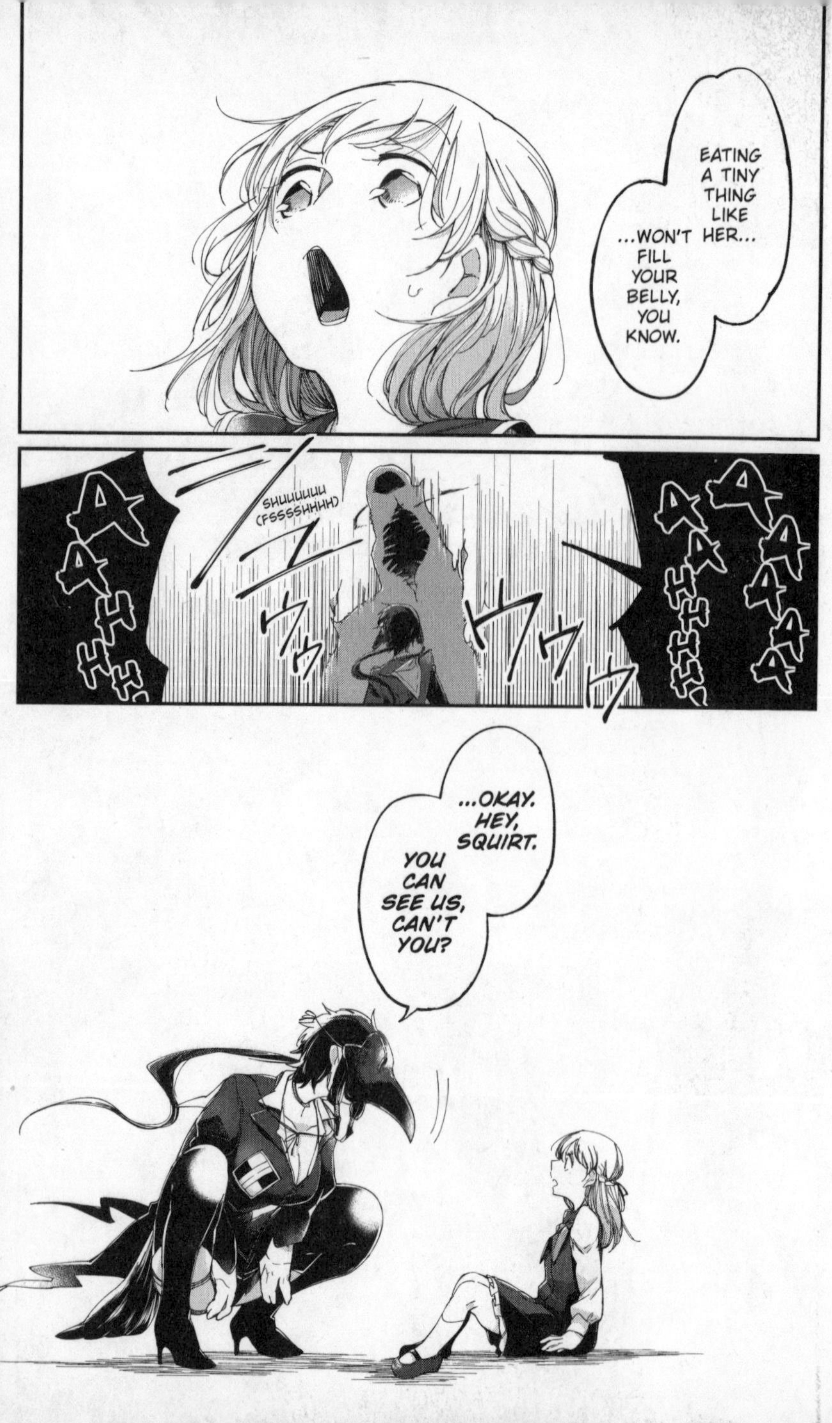
EATING A TINY THING LIKE HER... ...WON'T FILL YOUR BELLY, YOU KNOW.
SHUUUUUUU (FSSSSHHHH)
...OKAY. HEY, SQUIRT. YOU CAN SEE US, CAN'T YOU?

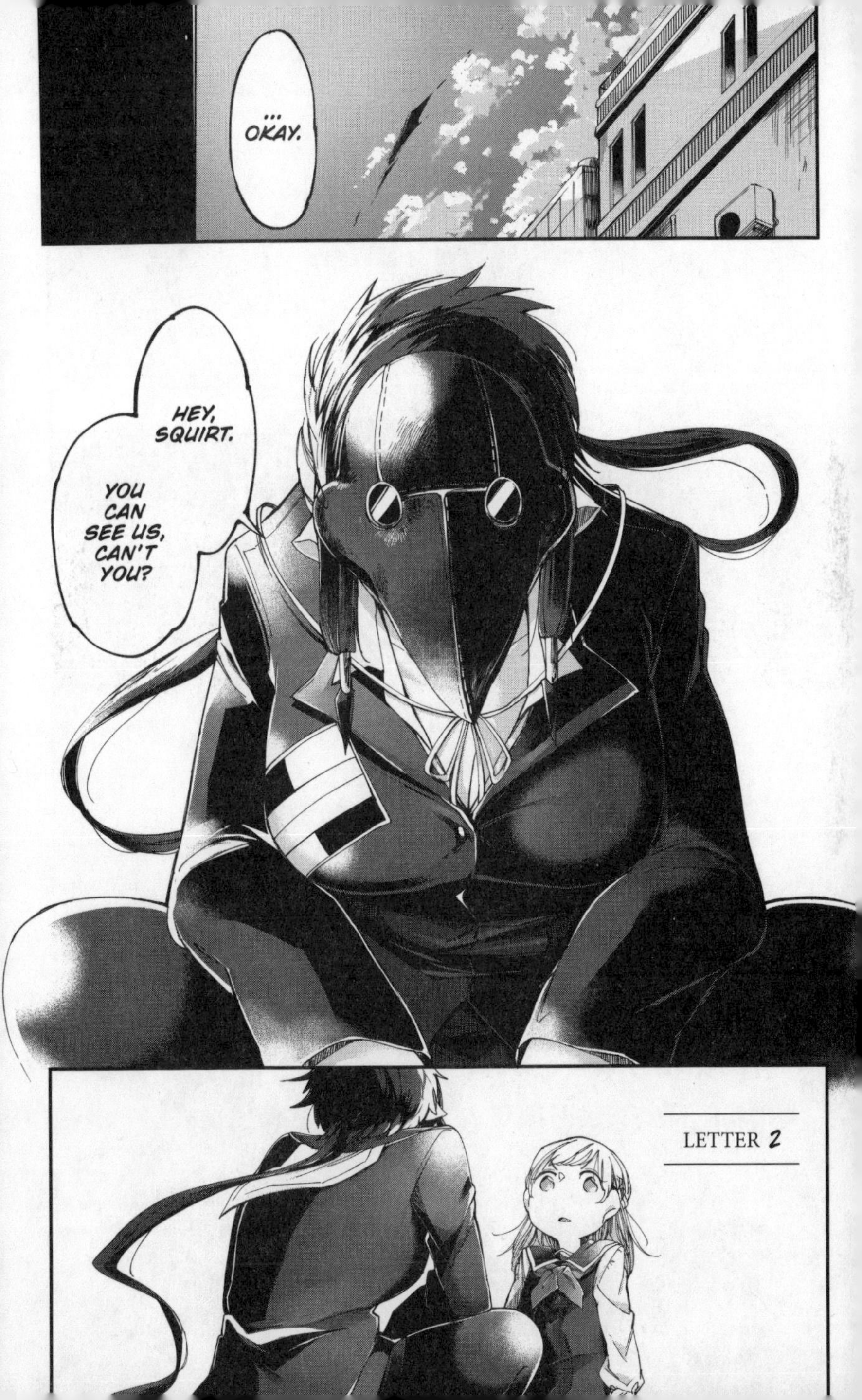
...OKAY.
HEY, SQUIRT.
YOU CAN SEE US, CAN'T YOU?
LETTER 2

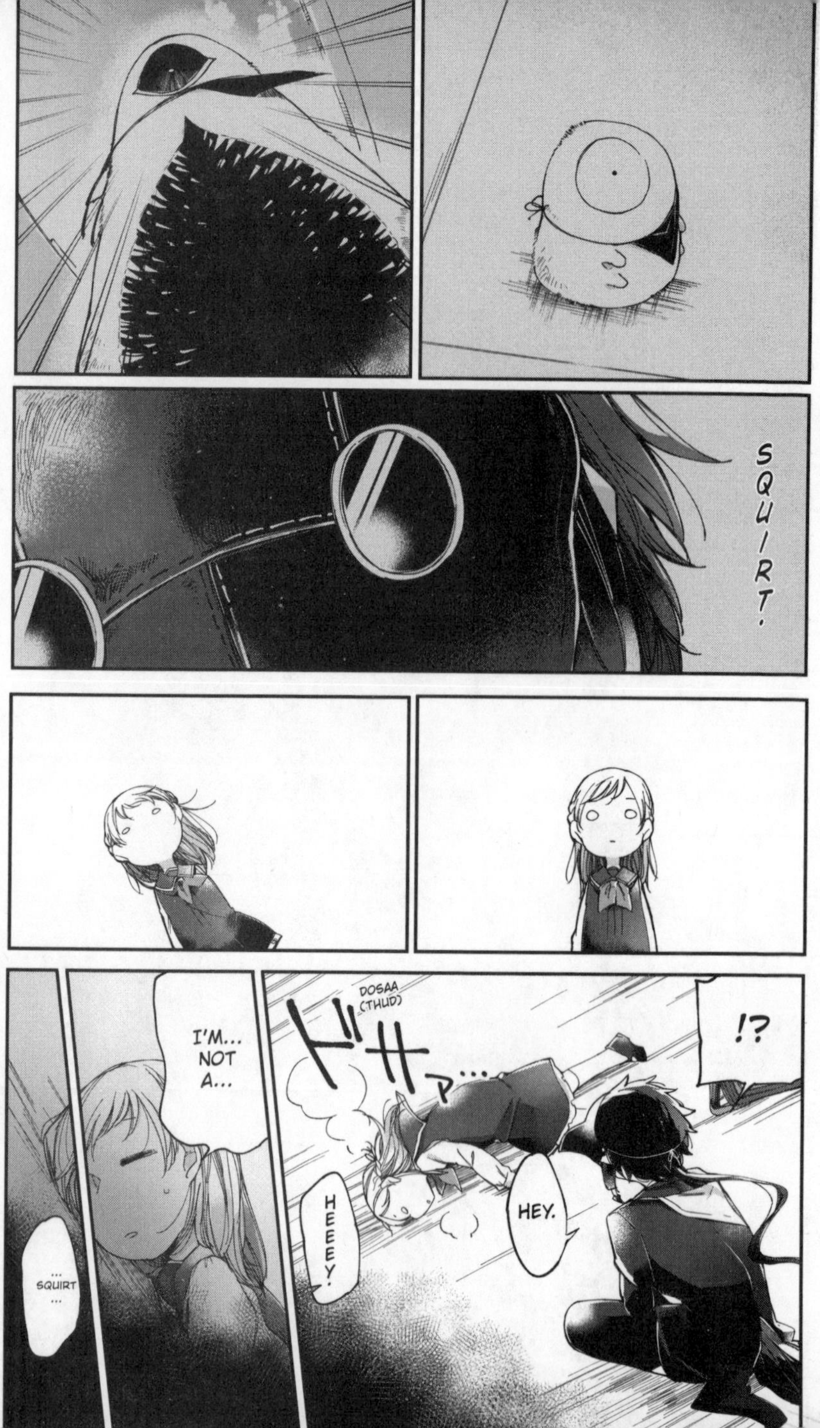
SQUIRT!
!?
DOSAA (THUD)
HEY.
HEEEY!
I'M... NOT A...
...SQUIRT...

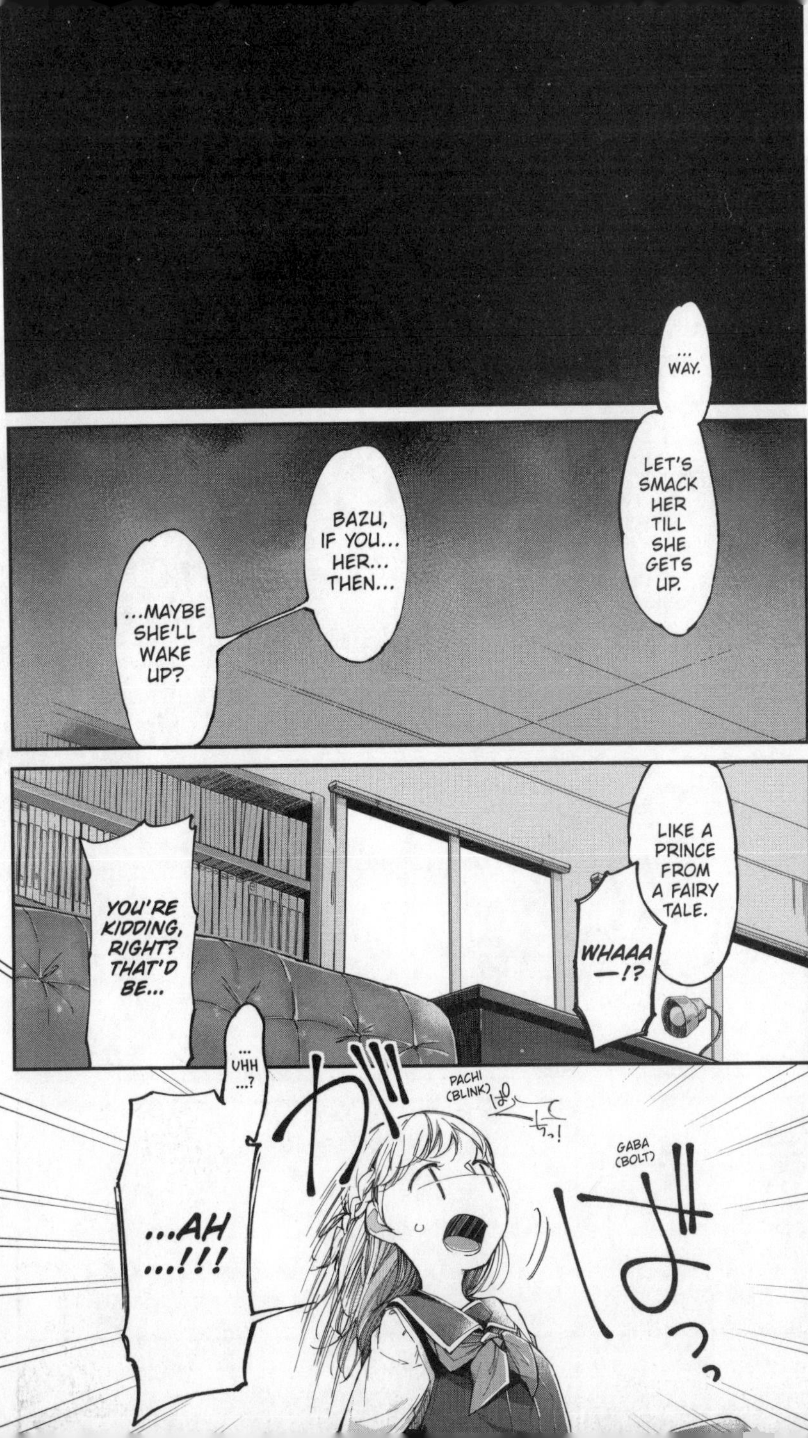

... WAY.
LET'S SMACK HER TILL SHE GETS UP.
BAZU, IF YOU... HER... THEN...
...MAYBE SHE'LL WAKE UP?
LIKE A PRINCE FROM A FAIRY TALE.
WHAAA—!?
YOU'RE KIDDING, RIGHT? THAT'D BE...
PACHI (BLINK)
GABA (BOLT)
...UHH ...?
...AH ...!!!

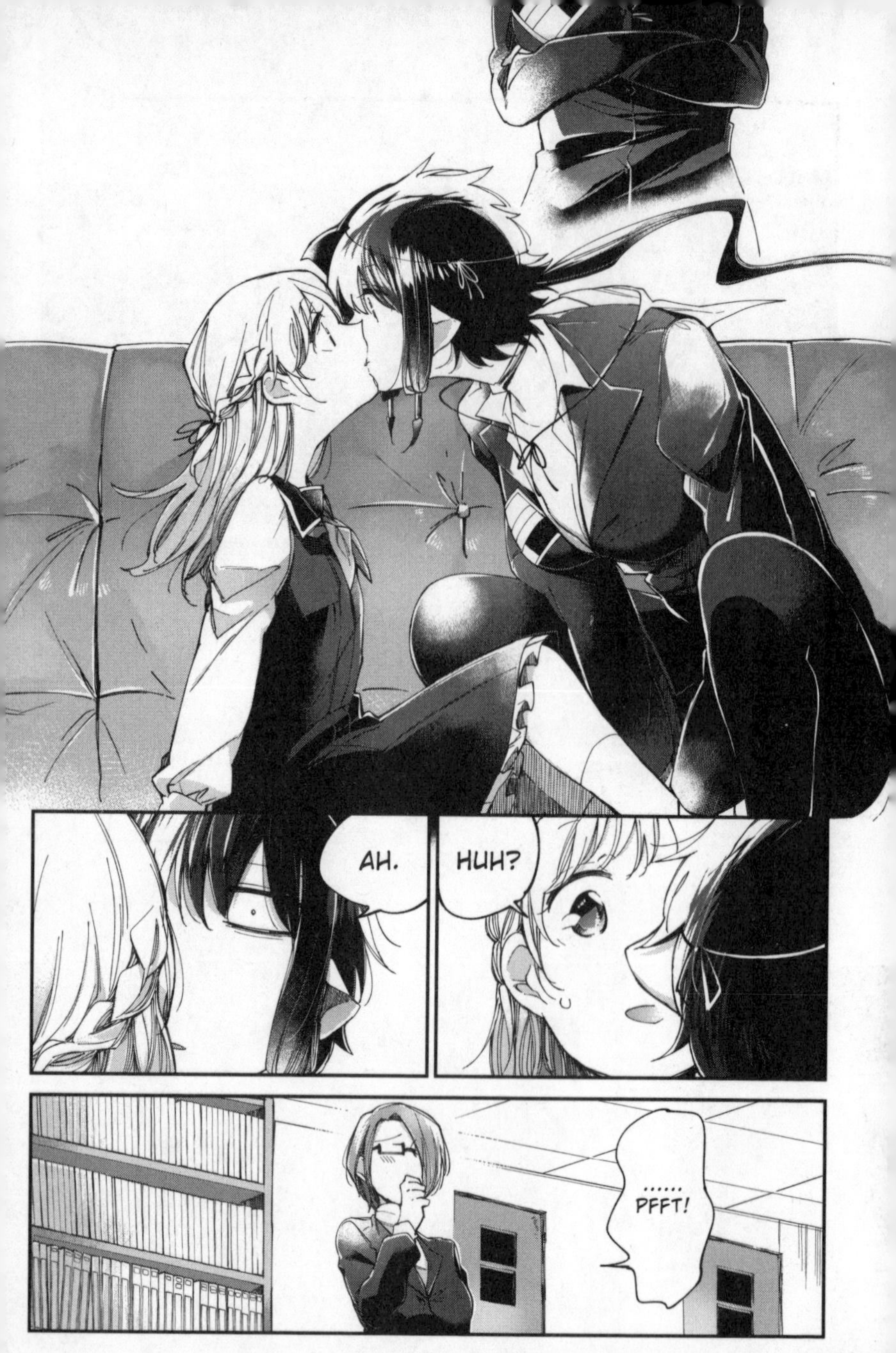
HUH?
AH.
......
PFFT!

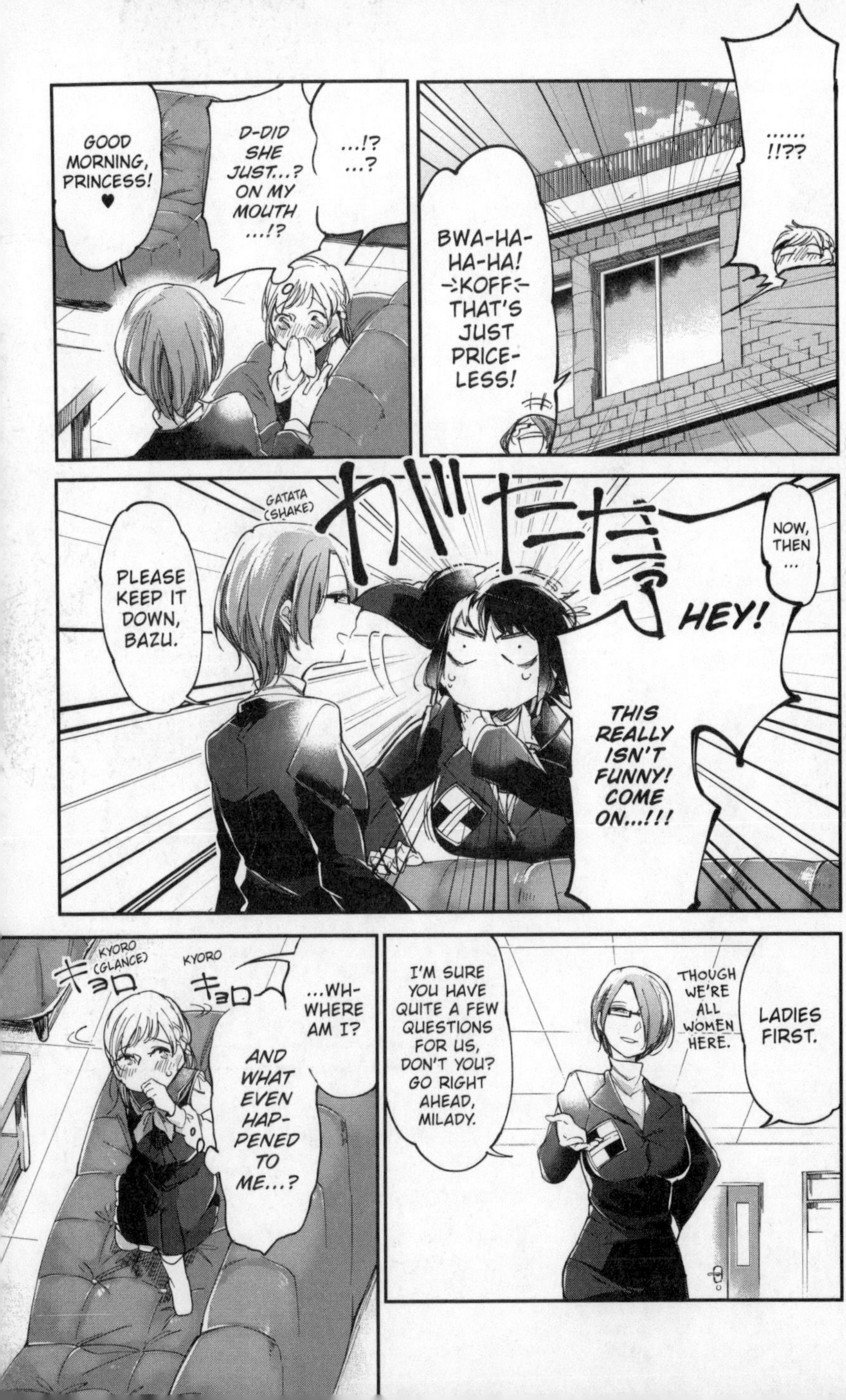
......!!??
BWA-HA-HA-HA! ⁃KOFF⁃ THAT'S JUST PRICELESS!
...!? ...?
D-DID SHE JUST...? ON MY MOUTH ...!?
GOOD MORNING, PRINCESS! ♥
NOW, THEN ...
ガタタ
GATATA (SHAKE)
HEY!
THIS REALLY ISN'T FUNNY! COME ON...!!!
PLEASE KEEP IT DOWN, BAZU.
LADIES FIRST.
THOUGH WE'RE ALL WOMEN HERE.
I'M SURE YOU HAVE QUITE A FEW QUESTIONS FOR US, DON'T YOU? GO RIGHT AHEAD, MILADY.
...WH-WHERE AM I?
AND WHAT EVEN HAPPENED TO ME...?
キョロ
KYORO
キョロ
KYORO (GLANCE)

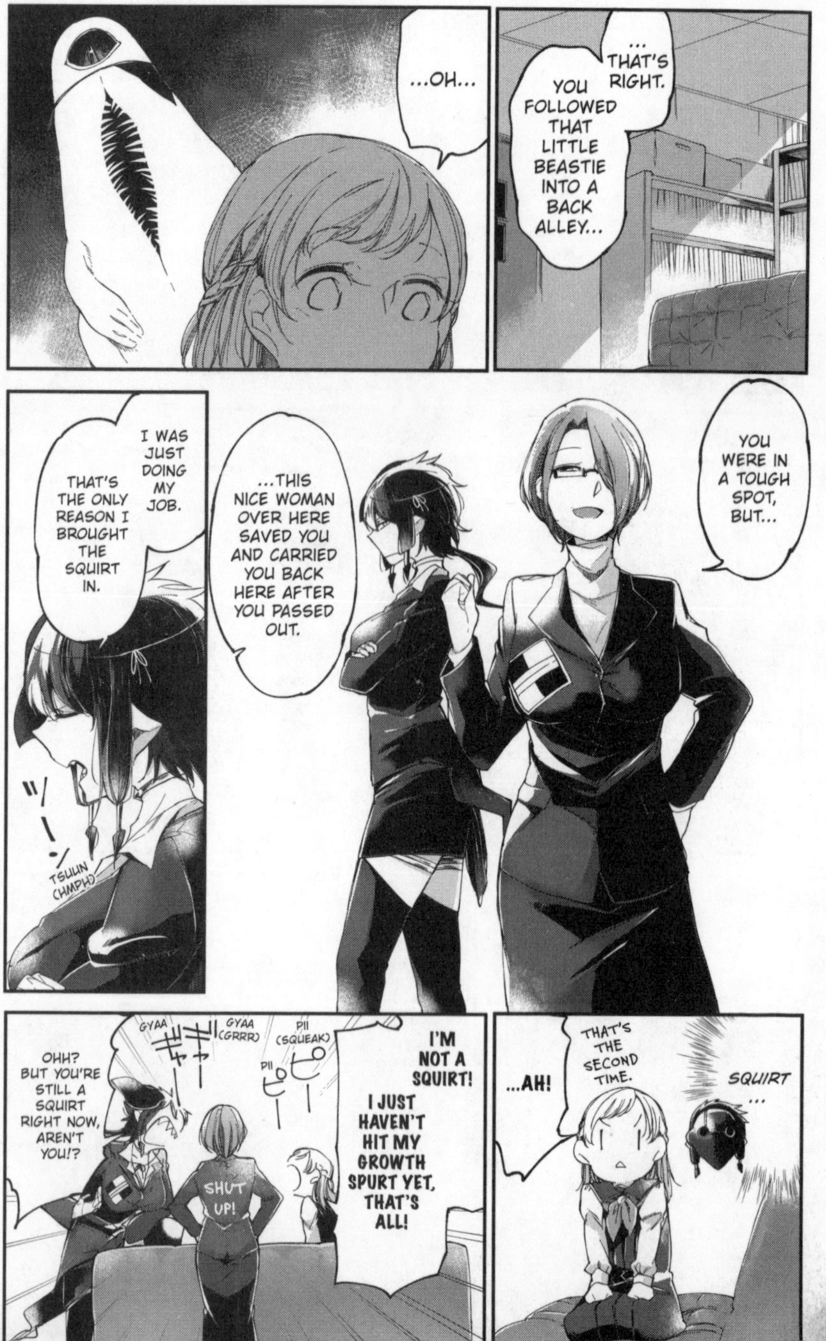

... THAT'S RIGHT.
YOU FOLLOWED THAT LITTLE BEASTIE INTO A BACK ALLEY...
...OH...
YOU WERE IN A TOUGH SPOT, BUT...
...THIS NICE WOMAN OVER HERE SAVED YOU AND CARRIED YOU BACK HERE AFTER YOU PASSED OUT.
I WAS JUST DOING MY JOB.
THAT'S THE ONLY REASON I BROUGHT THE SQUIRT IN.
TSUUN (HMPH)
SQUIRT...
THAT'S THE SECOND TIME.
...AH!
I'M NOT A SQUIRT!
I JUST HAVEN'T HIT MY GROWTH SPURT YET, THAT'S ALL!
PII (SQUEAK)
PII
GYAA (GRRR)
GYAA
OHH? BUT YOU'RE STILL A SQUIRT RIGHT NOW, AREN'T YOU!?
SHUT UP!

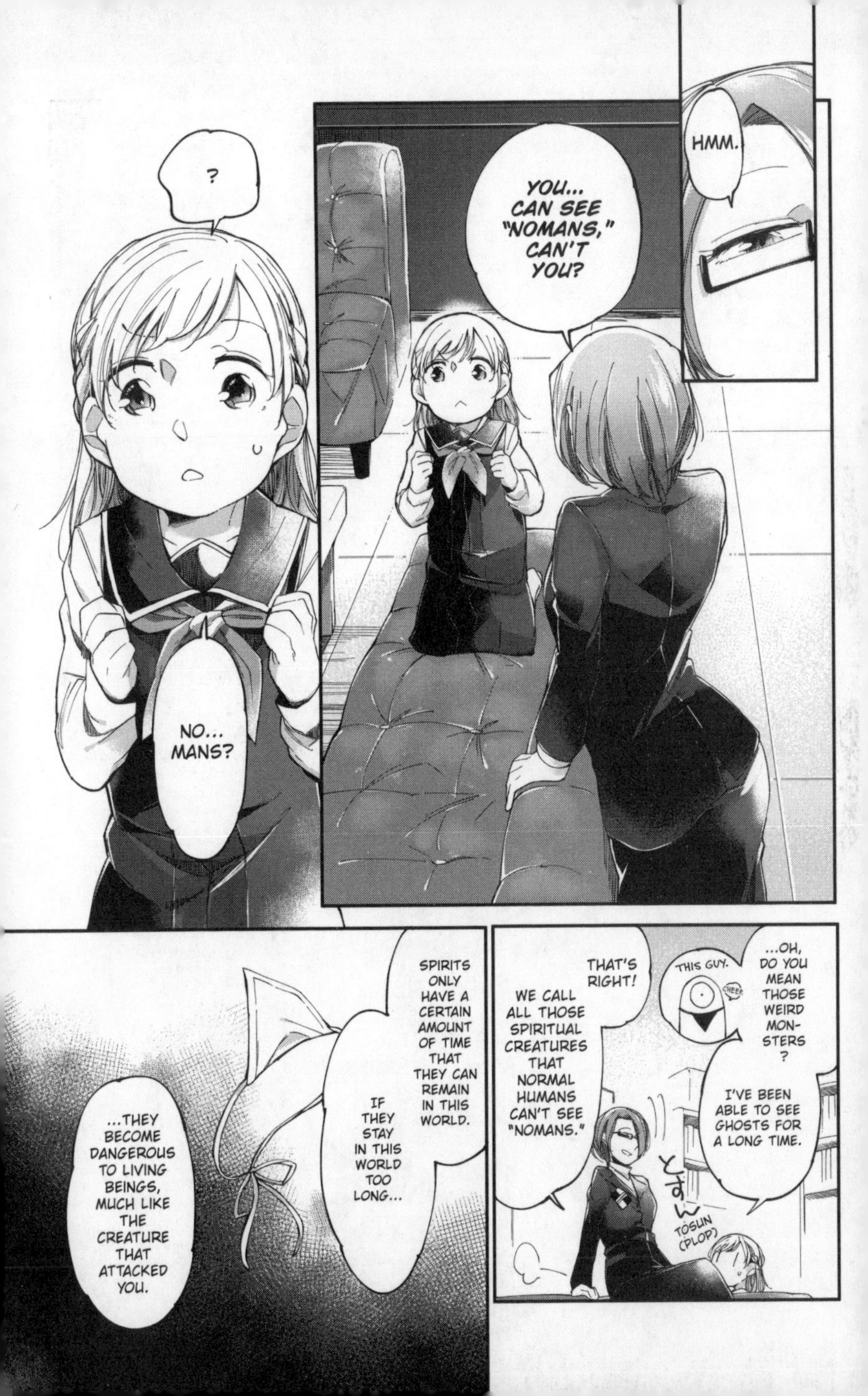
HMM.
YOU... CAN SEE "NOMANS," CAN'T YOU?
?
NO... MANS?
...OH, DO YOU MEAN THOSE WEIRD MON-STERS?
THIS GUY.
CHEEP
I'VE BEEN ABLE TO SEE GHOSTS FOR A LONG TIME.
THAT'S RIGHT!
WE CALL ALL THOSE SPIRITUAL CREATURES THAT NORMAL HUMANS CAN'T SEE "NOMANS."
とすん
TOSUN (PLOP)
SPIRITS ONLY HAVE A CERTAIN AMOUNT OF TIME THAT THEY CAN REMAIN IN THIS WORLD.
IF THEY STAY IN THIS WORLD TOO LONG...
...THEY BECOME DANGEROUS TO LIVING BEINGS, MUCH LIKE THE CREATURE THAT ATTACKED YOU.

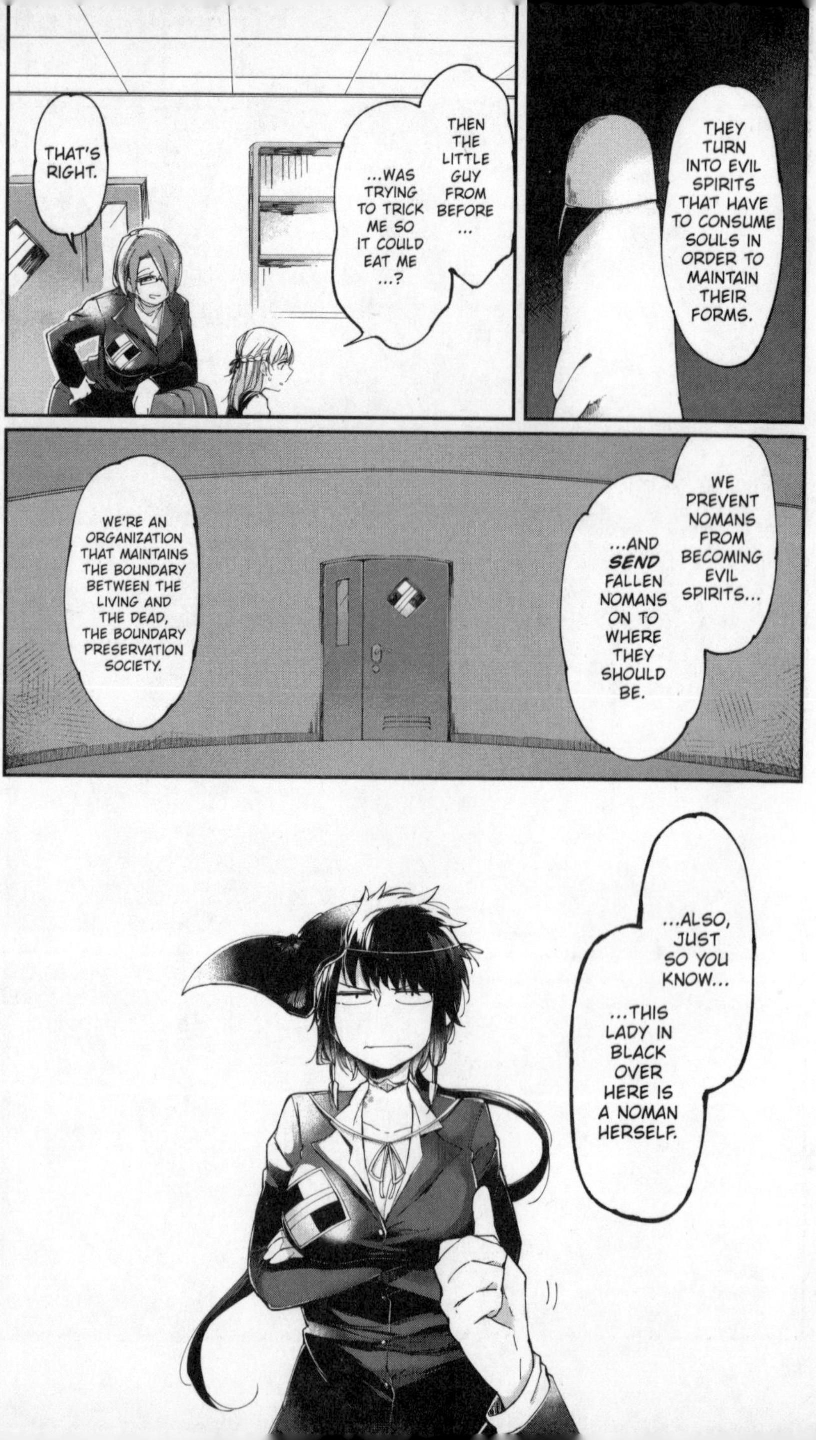
THEY TURN INTO EVIL SPIRITS THAT HAVE TO CONSUME SOULS IN ORDER TO MAINTAIN THEIR FORMS.
THEN THE LITTLE GUY FROM BEFORE ...
...WAS TRYING TO TRICK ME SO IT COULD EAT ME ...?
THAT'S RIGHT.
WE PREVENT NOMANS FROM BECOMING EVIL SPIRITS...
...AND **SEND** FALLEN NOMANS ON TO WHERE THEY SHOULD BE.
WE'RE AN ORGANIZATION THAT MAINTAINS THE BOUNDARY BETWEEN THE LIVING AND THE DEAD, THE BOUNDARY PRESERVATION SOCIETY.
...ALSO, JUST SO YOU KNOW...
...THIS LADY IN BLACK OVER HERE IS A NOMAN HERSELF.

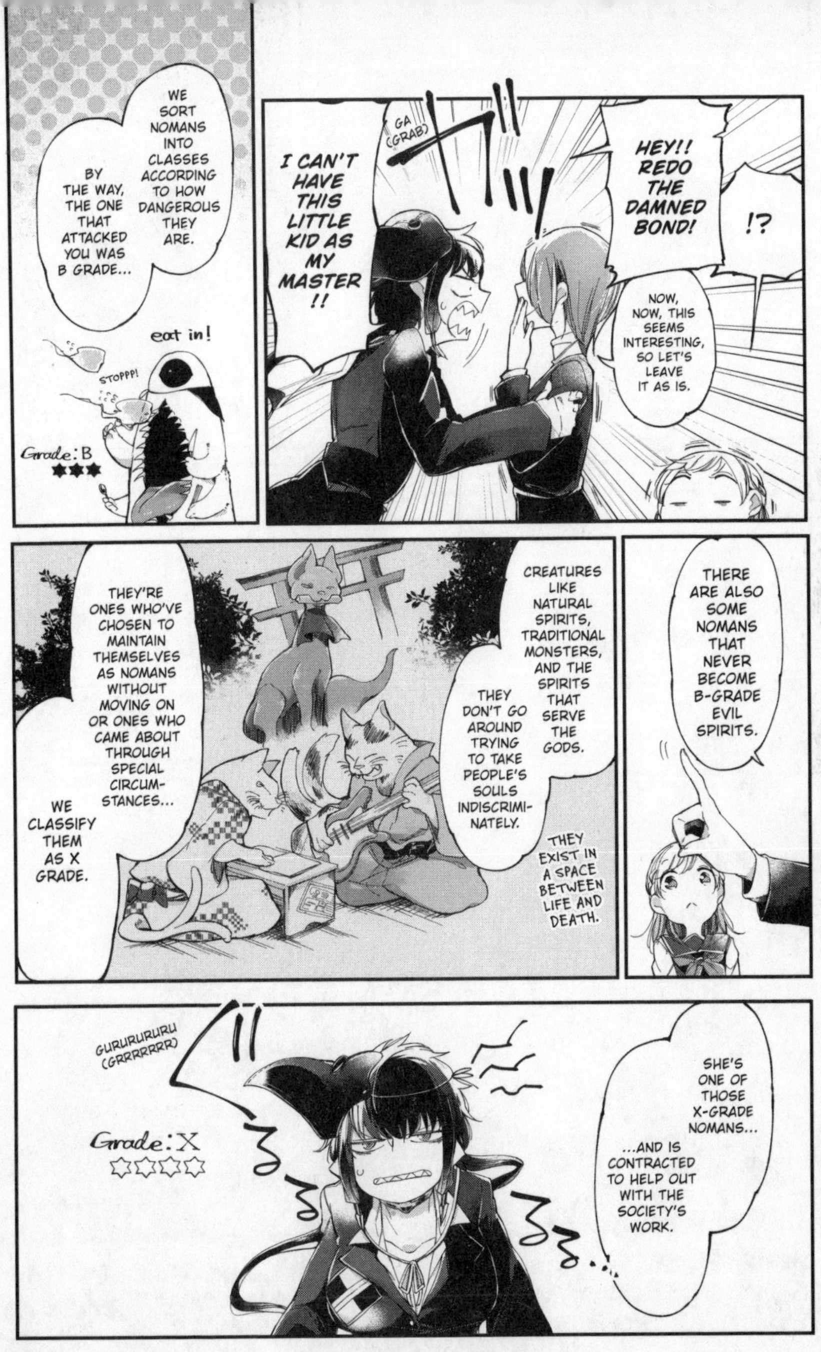
HEY!! REDO THE DAMNED BOND!
!?
GA (GRAB)
I CAN'T HAVE THIS LITTLE KID AS MY MASTER!!
NOW, NOW, THIS SEEMS INTERESTING, SO LET'S LEAVE IT AS IS.
WE SORT NOMANS INTO CLASSES ACCORDING TO HOW DANGEROUS THEY ARE.
BY THE WAY, THE ONE THAT ATTACKED YOU WAS B GRADE...
eat in!
STOPPP!
Grade: B
THERE ARE ALSO SOME NOMANS THAT NEVER BECOME B-GRADE EVIL SPIRITS.
CREATURES LIKE NATURAL SPIRITS, TRADITIONAL MONSTERS, AND THE SPIRITS THAT SERVE THE GODS.
THEY DON'T GO AROUND TRYING TO TAKE PEOPLE'S SOULS INDISCRIMINATELY.
THEY EXIST IN A SPACE BETWEEN LIFE AND DEATH.
THEY'RE ONES WHO'VE CHOSEN TO MAINTAIN THEMSELVES AS NOMANS WITHOUT MOVING ON OR ONES WHO CAME ABOUT THROUGH SPECIAL CIRCUMSTANCES...
WE CLASSIFY THEM AS X GRADE.
SHE'S ONE OF THOSE X-GRADE NOMANS...
...AND IS CONTRACTED TO HELP OUT WITH THE SOCIETY'S WORK.
GURURURURU (GRRRRRRR)
Grade: X

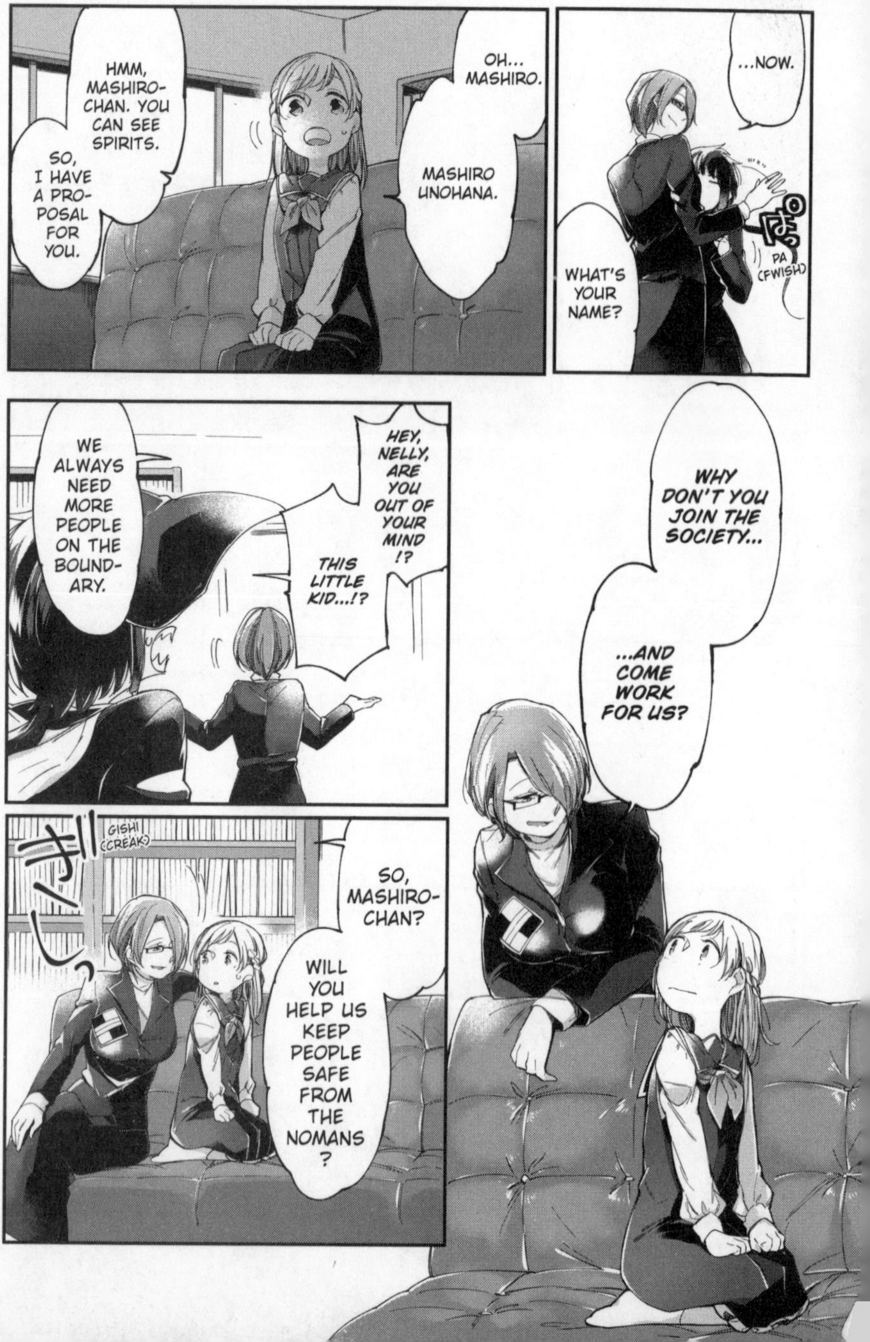
...NOW.
WHAT'S YOUR NAME?
ぱっ
PA (FWISH)
OH... MASHIRO.
MASHIRO UNOHANA.
HMM, MASHIRO-CHAN. YOU CAN SEE SPIRITS.
SO, I HAVE A PROPOSAL FOR YOU.
WHY DON'T YOU JOIN THE SOCIETY...
...AND COME WORK FOR US?
HEY, NELLY, ARE YOU OUT OF YOUR MIND!?
THIS LITTLE KID...!?
WE ALWAYS NEED MORE PEOPLE ON THE BOUNDARY.
SO, MASHIRO-CHAN?
WILL YOU HELP US KEEP PEOPLE SAFE FROM THE NOMANS?
ぎしっ
GISHI (CREAK)

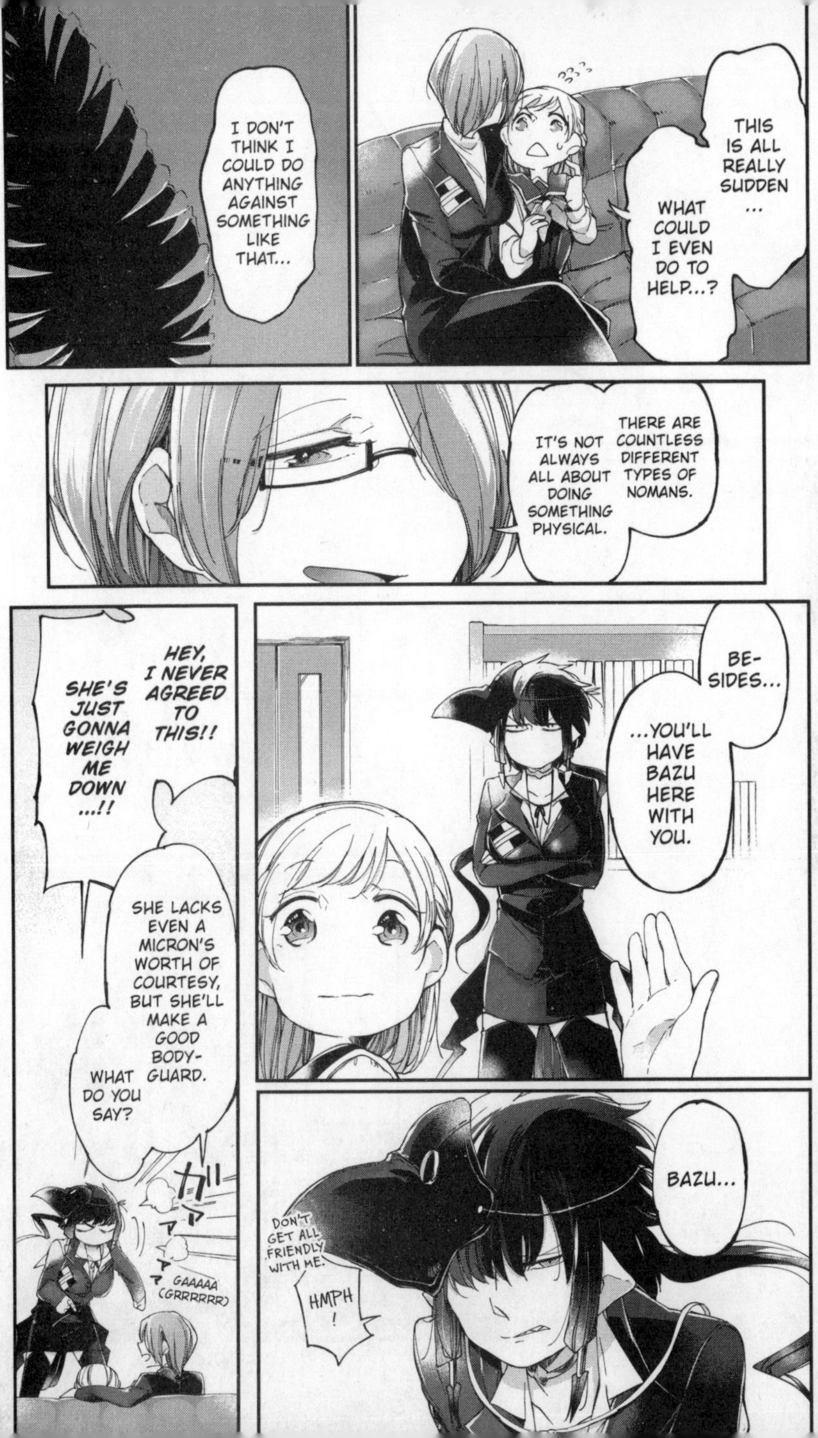
THIS IS ALL REALLY SUDDEN...
WHAT COULD I EVEN DO TO HELP...?
I DON'T THINK I COULD DO ANYTHING AGAINST SOMETHING LIKE THAT...
THERE ARE COUNTLESS DIFFERENT TYPES OF NOMANS.
IT'S NOT ALWAYS ALL ABOUT DOING SOMETHING PHYSICAL.
BE-SIDES...
...YOU'LL HAVE BAZU HERE WITH YOU.
BAZU...
DON'T GET ALL FRIENDLY WITH ME.
HMPH!
HEY, I NEVER AGREED TO THIS!!
SHE'S JUST GONNA WEIGH ME DOWN...!!
SHE LACKS EVEN A MICRON'S WORTH OF COURTESY, BUT SHE'LL MAKE A GOOD BODY-GUARD.
WHAT DO YOU SAY?
GAAAAA (GRRRRRR)

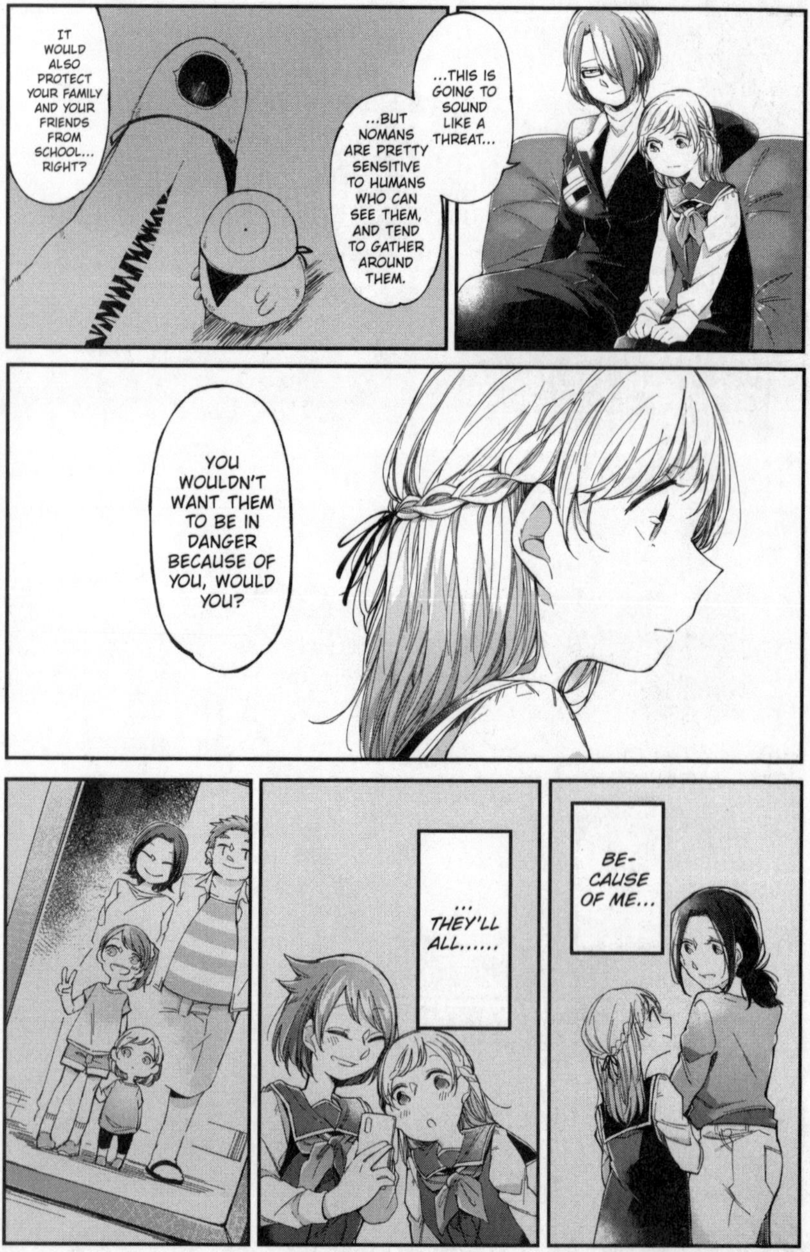
...THIS IS GOING TO SOUND LIKE A THREAT...
...BUT NOMANS ARE PRETTY SENSITIVE TO HUMANS WHO CAN SEE THEM, AND TEND TO GATHER AROUND THEM.
IT WOULD ALSO PROTECT YOUR FAMILY AND YOUR FRIENDS FROM SCHOOL... RIGHT?
YOU WOULDN'T WANT THEM TO BE IN DANGER BECAUSE OF YOU, WOULD YOU?
BE-CAUSE OF ME...
...THEY'LL ALL......

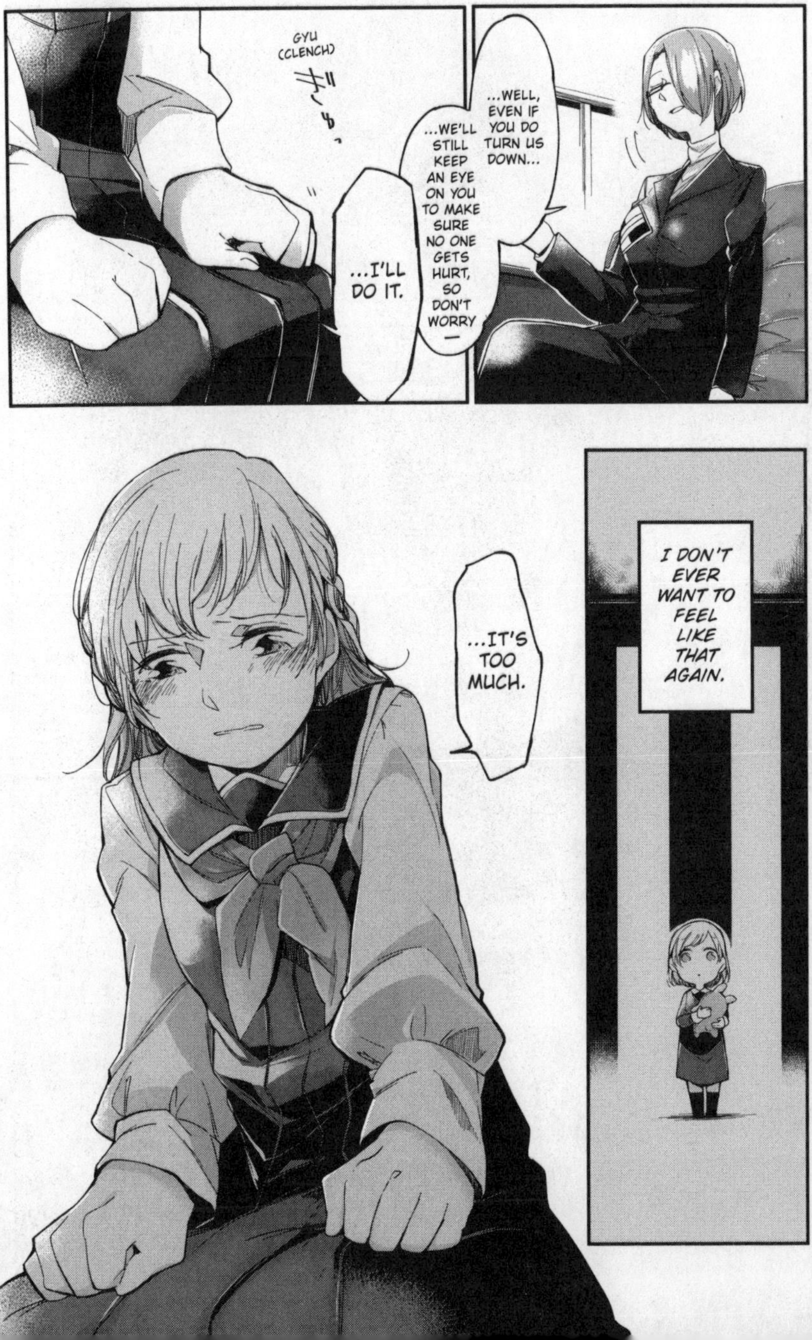

...WELL, EVEN IF YOU DO TURN US DOWN...
...WE'LL STILL KEEP AN EYE ON YOU TO MAKE SURE NO ONE GETS HURT, SO DON'T WORRY—
GYU (CLENCH)
...I'LL DO IT.
I DON'T EVER WANT TO FEEL LIKE THAT AGAIN.
...IT'S TOO MUCH.

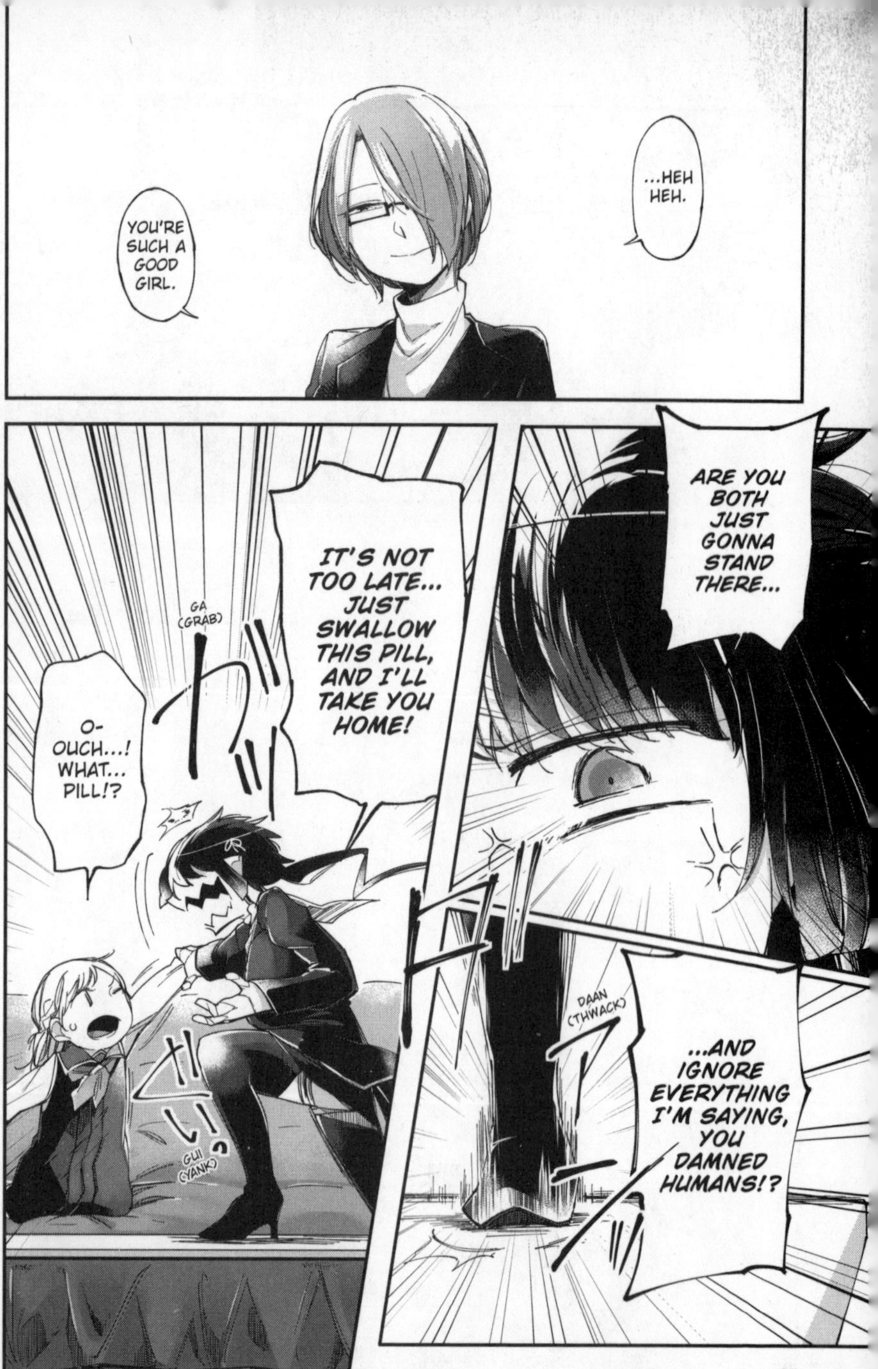
...HEH HEH.
YOU'RE SUCH A GOOD GIRL.
ARE YOU BOTH JUST GONNA STAND THERE...
DAAN (THWACK)
...AND IGNORE EVERYTHING I'M SAYING, YOU DAMNED HUMANS!?
IT'S NOT TOO LATE... JUST SWALLOW THIS PILL, AND I'LL TAKE YOU HOME!
GA (GRAB)
O-OUCH...! WHAT... PILL!?
GUI (YANK)

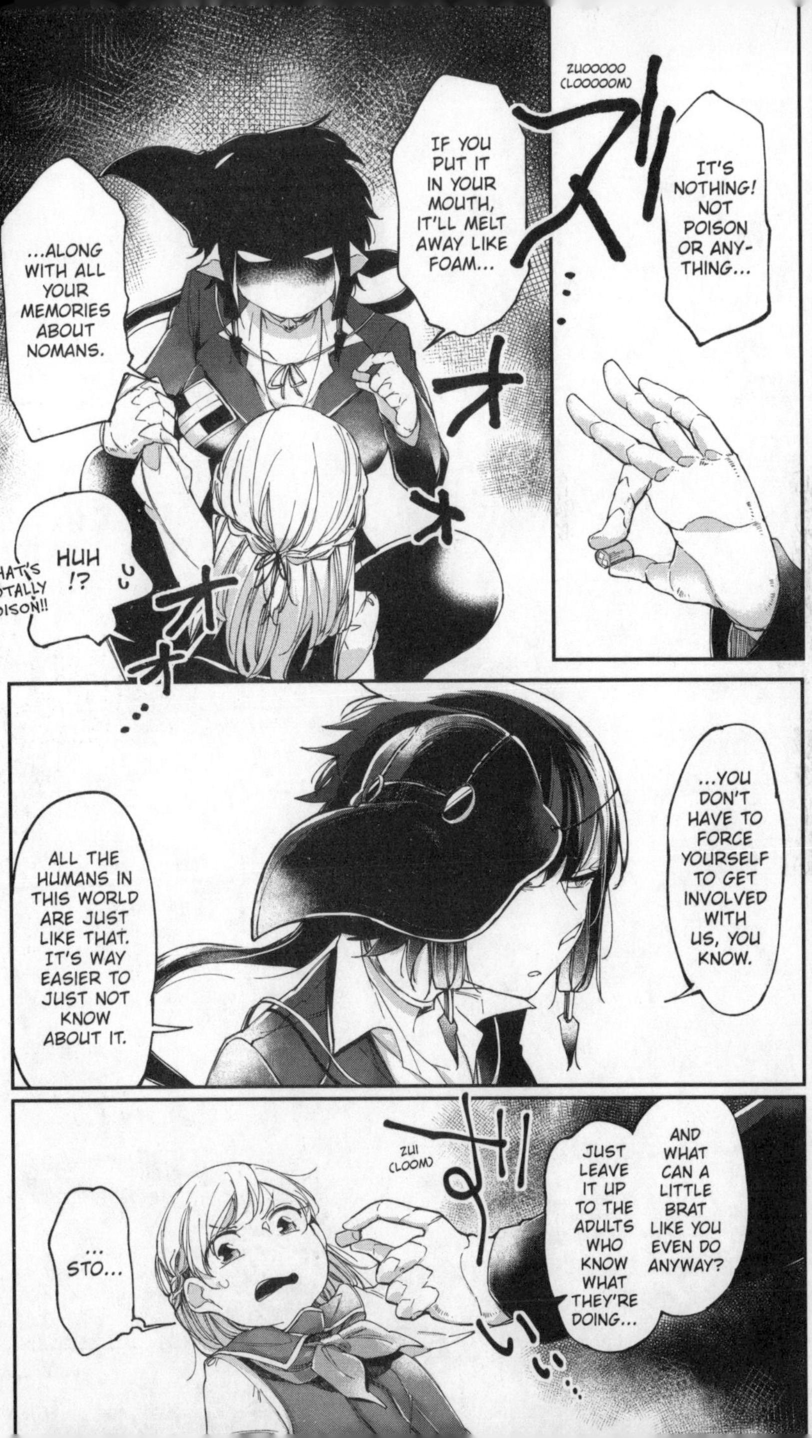
ZUOOOOO (LOOOOOM)
IT'S NOTHING! NOT POISON OR ANY-THING...
IF YOU PUT IT IN YOUR MOUTH, IT'LL MELT AWAY LIKE FOAM...
...ALONG WITH ALL YOUR MEMORIES ABOUT NOMANS.
HUH!?
THAT'S TOTALLY POISON!!
...YOU DON'T HAVE TO FORCE YOURSELF TO GET INVOLVED WITH US, YOU KNOW.
ALL THE HUMANS IN THIS WORLD ARE JUST LIKE THAT. IT'S WAY EASIER TO JUST NOT KNOW ABOUT IT.
AND WHAT CAN A LITTLE BRAT LIKE YOU EVEN DO ANYWAY?
JUST LEAVE IT UP TO THE ADULTS WHO KNOW WHAT THEY'RE DOING...
ZUI (LOOM)
... STO...

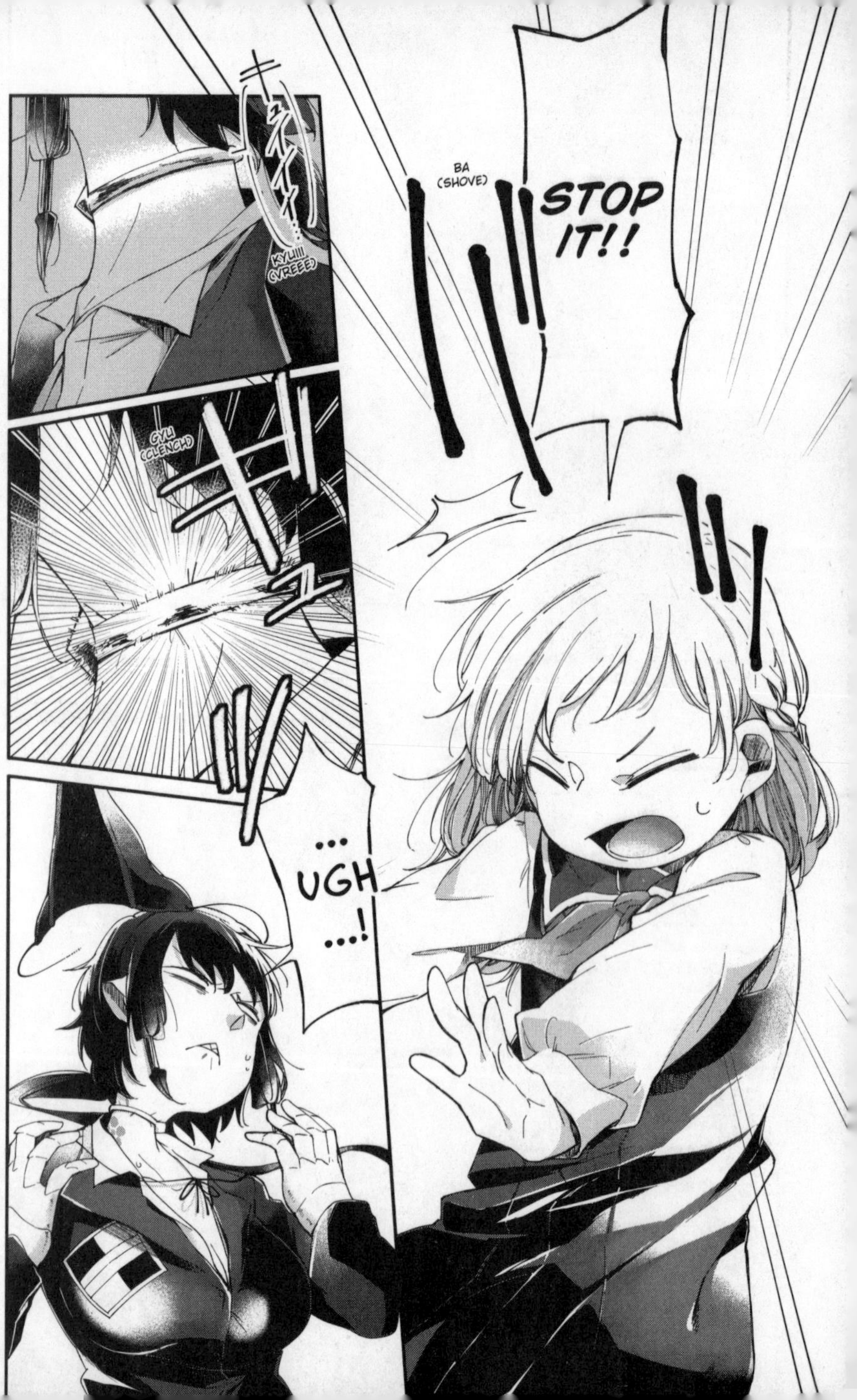
BA (SHOVE)
STOP IT!!
KYUIII (VREEE)
GYU (CLENCH)
... UGH ...!

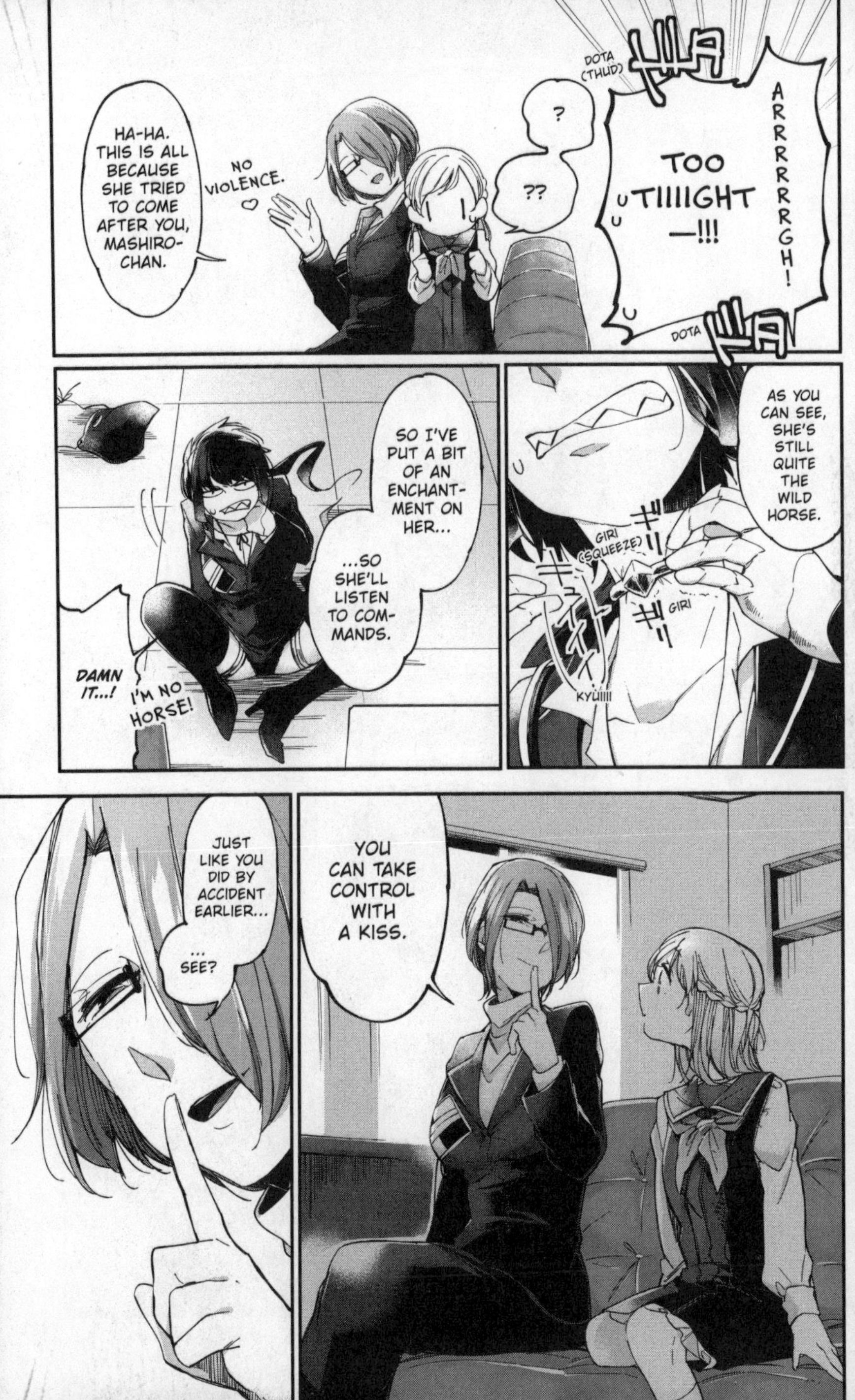
DOTA (THUD)
ARRRRRRGH!
TOO TIIIIIGHT—!!!
DOTA
?
??
NO VIOLENCE. ♡
HA-HA. THIS IS ALL BECAUSE SHE TRIED TO COME AFTER YOU, MASHIRO-CHAN.
AS YOU CAN SEE, SHE'S STILL QUITE THE WILD HORSE.
GIRI (SQUEEZE)
GIRI
KYUIIIII
SO I'VE PUT A BIT OF AN ENCHANTMENT ON HER...
...SO SHE'LL LISTEN TO COMMANDS.
I'M NO HORSE!
DAMN IT...!
YOU CAN TAKE CONTROL WITH A KISS.
JUST LIKE YOU DID BY ACCIDENT EARLIER...
...SEE?

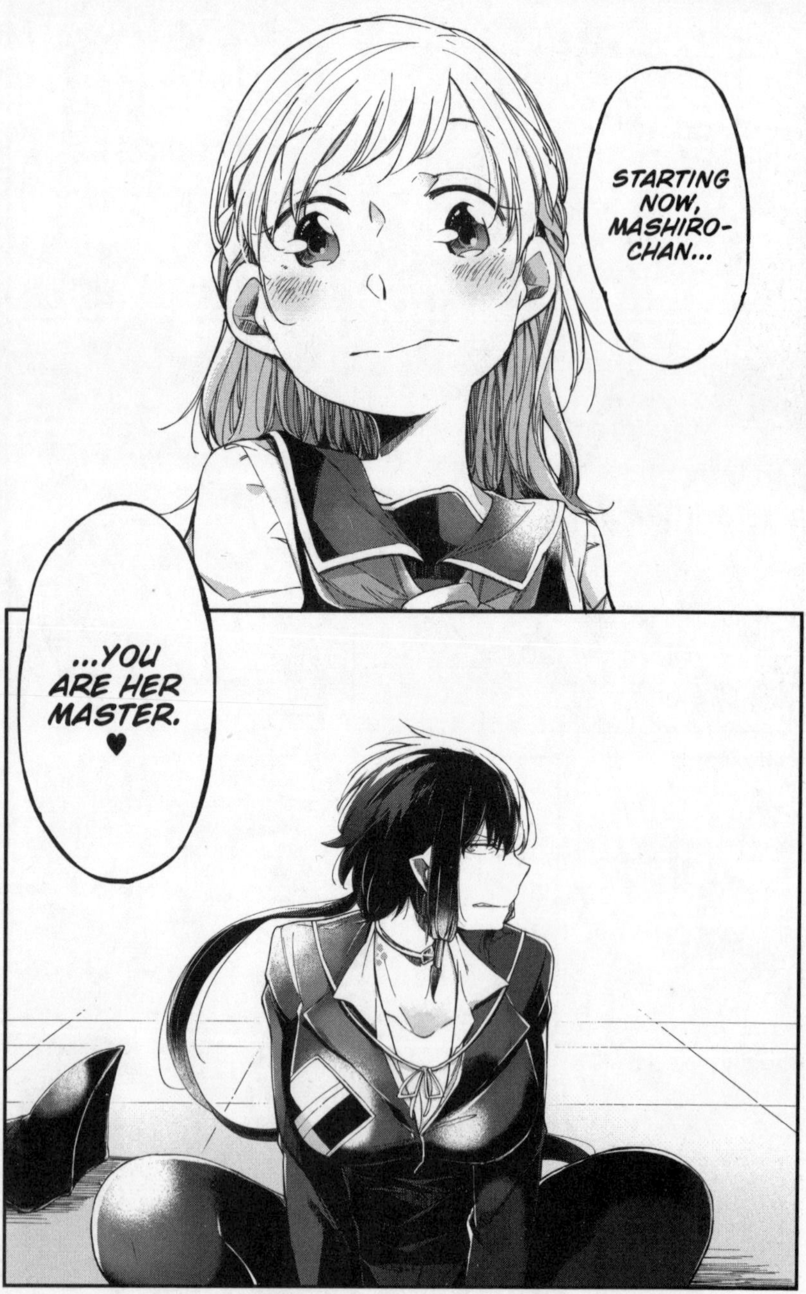
STARTING NOW, MASHIRO-CHAN...
...YOU ARE HER MASTER. ♥

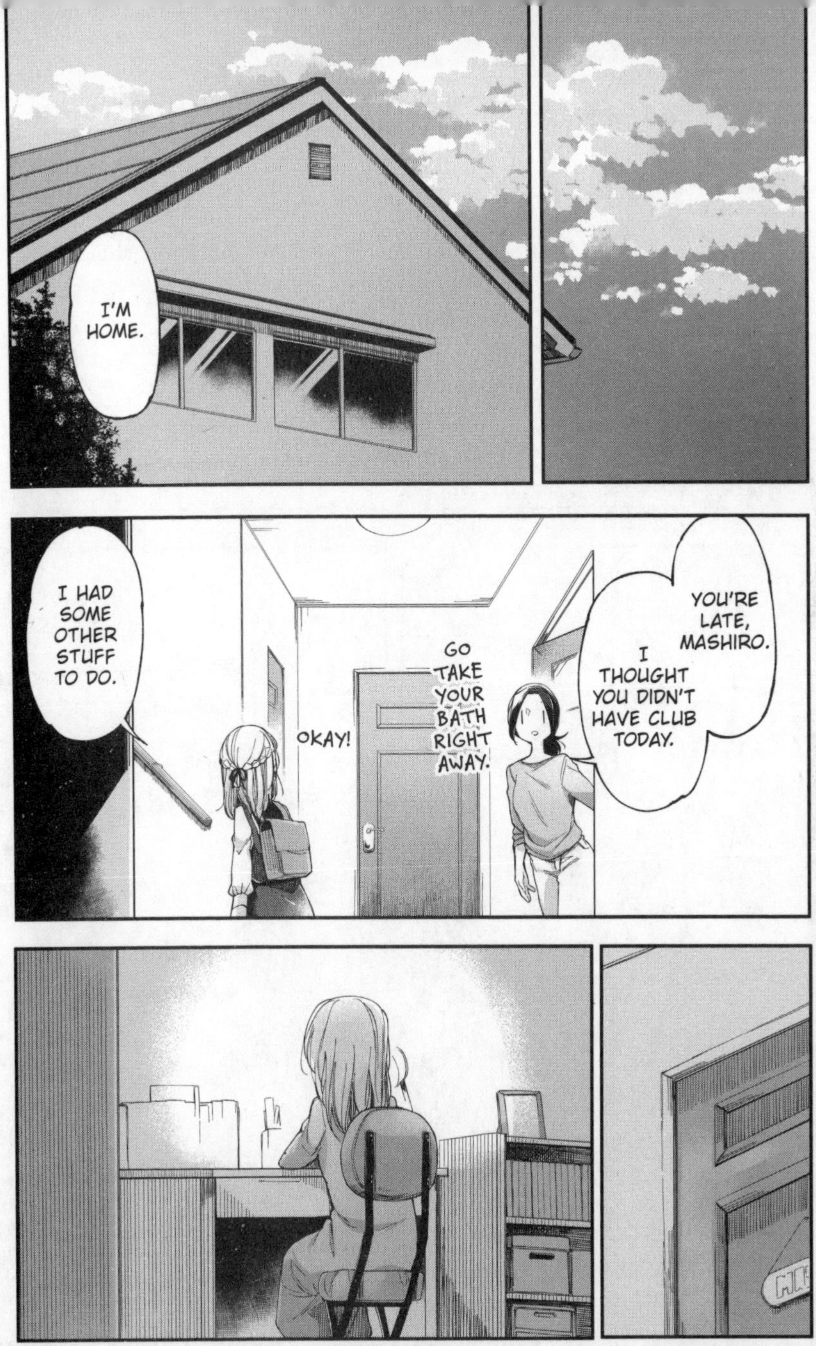
I'M HOME.
YOU'RE LATE, MASHIRO.
I THOUGHT YOU DIDN'T HAVE CLUB TODAY.
I HAD SOME OTHER STUFF TO DO.
GO TAKE YOUR BATH RIGHT AWAY.
OKAY!

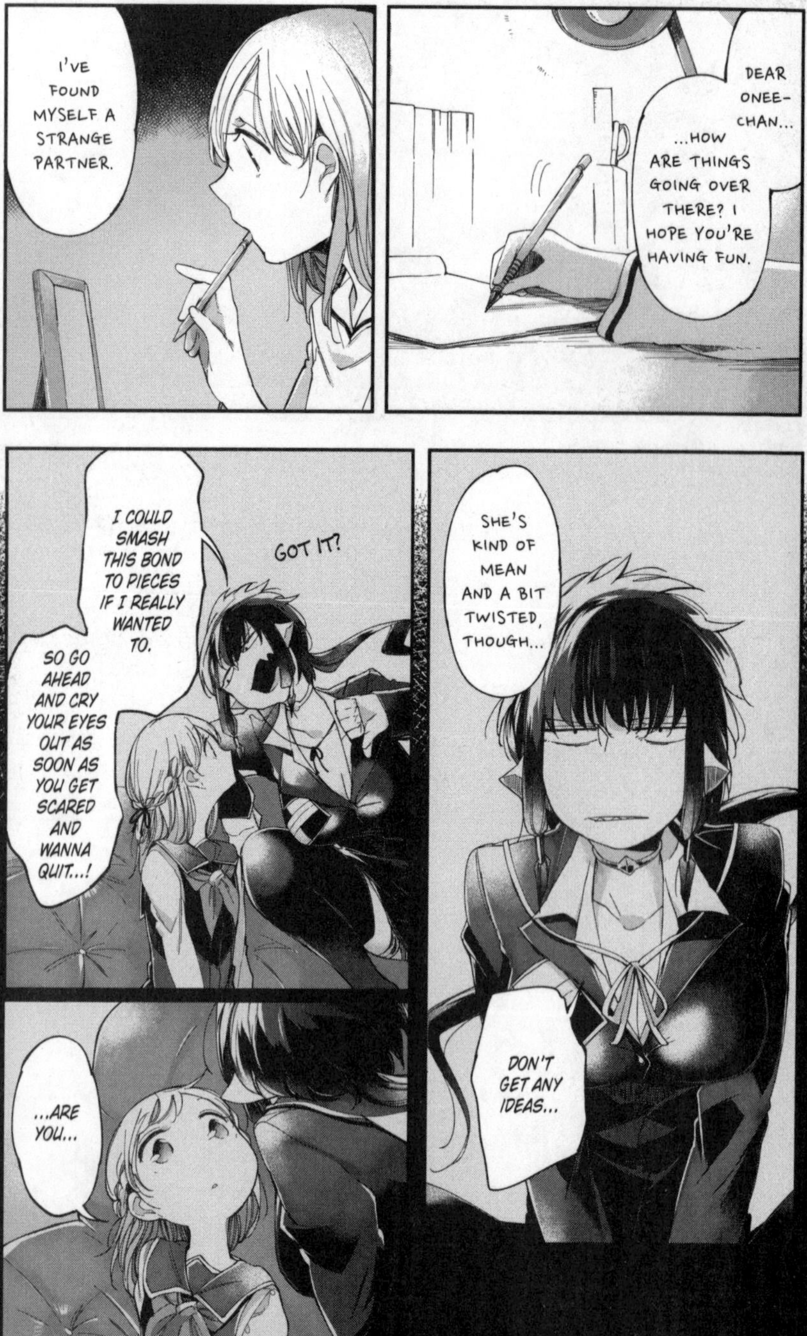
DEAR ONEE-CHAN...
...HOW ARE THINGS GOING OVER THERE? I HOPE YOU'RE HAVING FUN.
I'VE FOUND MYSELF A STRANGE PARTNER.
SHE'S KIND OF MEAN AND A BIT TWISTED, THOUGH...
DON'T GET ANY IDEAS...
I COULD SMASH THIS BOND TO PIECES IF I REALLY WANTED TO.
GOT IT?
SO GO AHEAD AND CRY YOUR EYES OUT AS SOON AS YOU GET SCARED AND WANNA QUIT...!
...ARE YOU...

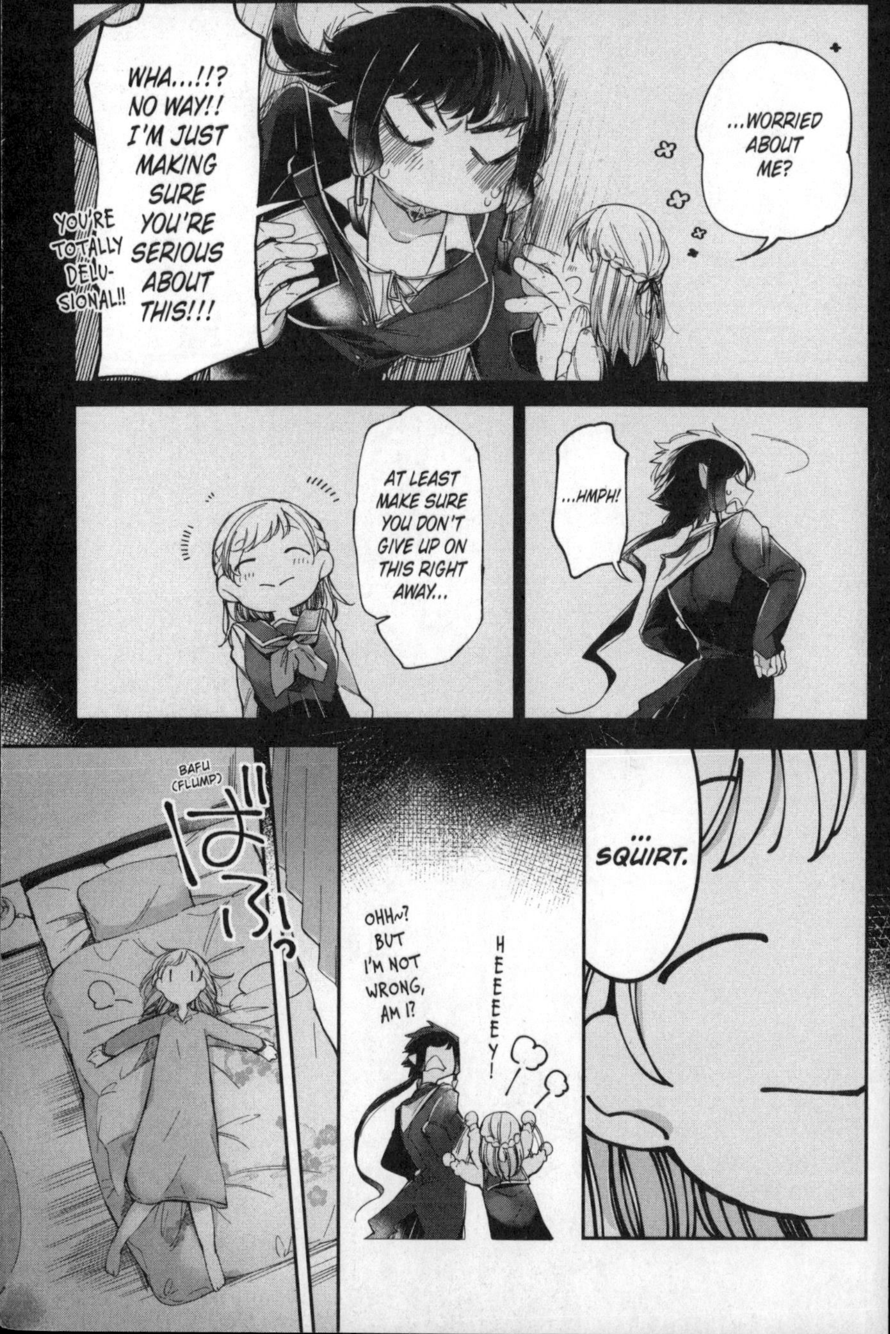
...WORRIED ABOUT ME?
WHA...!!? NO WAY!! I'M JUST MAKING SURE YOU'RE SERIOUS ABOUT THIS!!!
YOU'RE TOTALLY DELU-SIONAL!!
...HMPH!
AT LEAST MAKE SURE YOU DON'T GIVE UP ON THIS RIGHT AWAY...
... SQUIRT.
HEEEEEY!
OHH~? BUT I'M NOT WRONG, AM I?
BAFU (FLUMP)
ばふっ

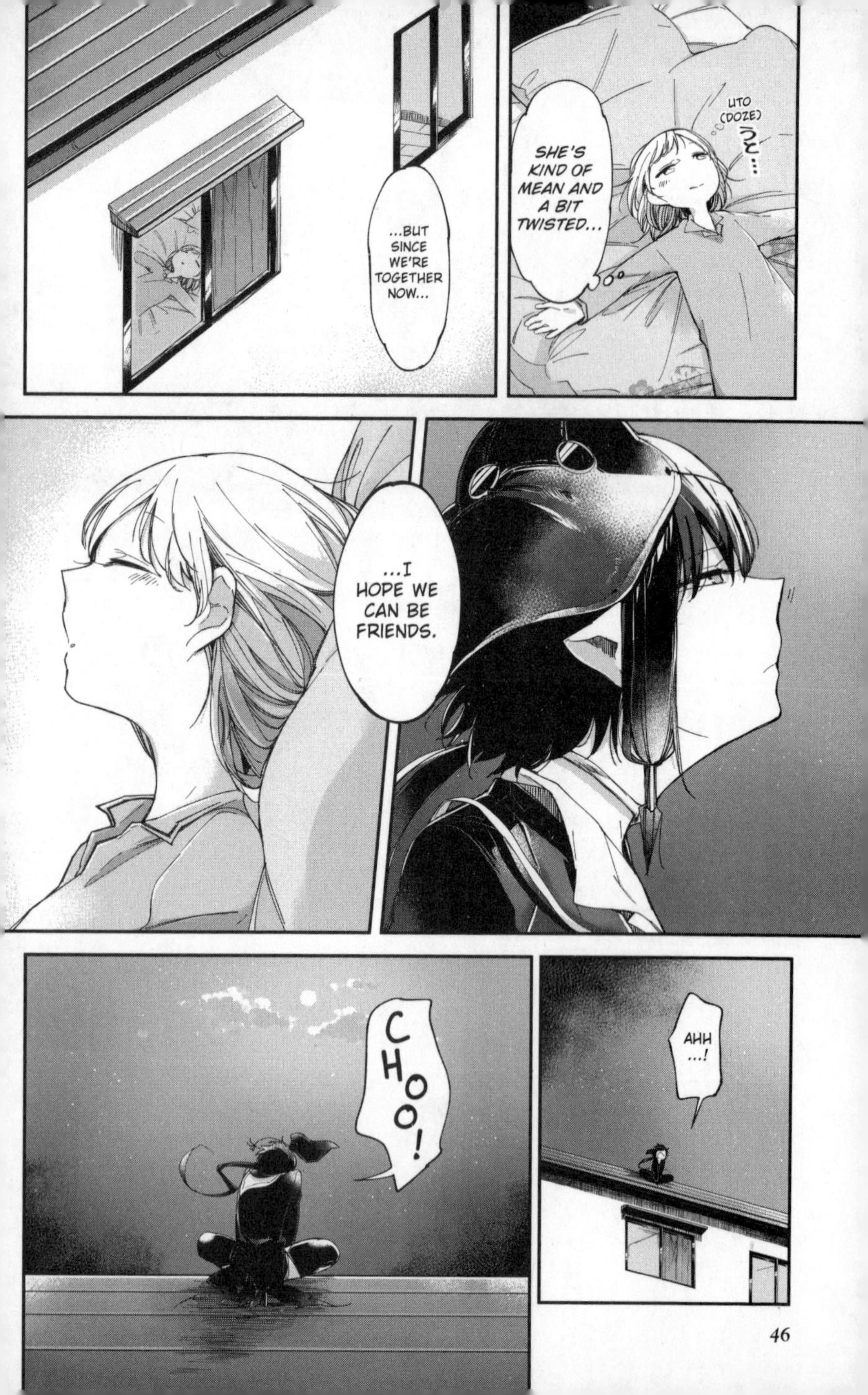
UTO (DOZE)
うと…
SHE'S KIND OF MEAN AND A BIT TWISTED...
...BUT SINCE WE'RE TOGETHER NOW...
...I HOPE WE CAN BE FRIENDS.
AHH ...!
CHOO!

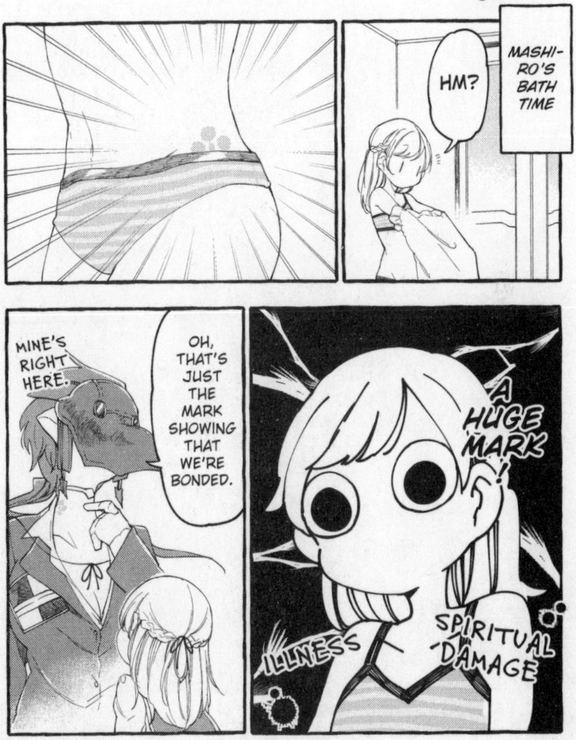
MASHIRO'S BATH TIME
HM?
A HUGE MARK!
SPIRITUAL DAMAGE
ILLNESS
OH, THAT'S JUST THE MARK SHOWING THAT WE'RE BONDED.
MINE'S RIGHT HERE.

Dear NOMAN

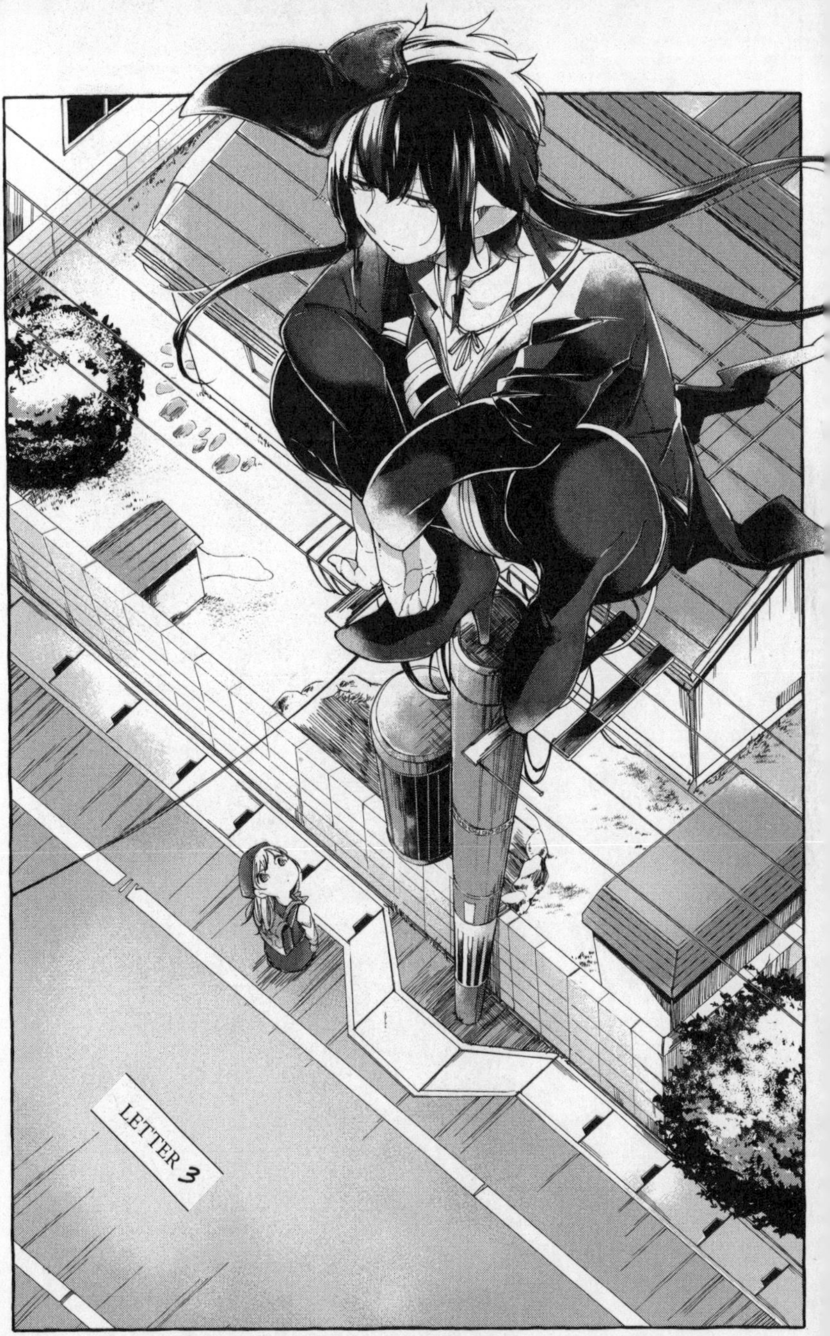
LETTER 3

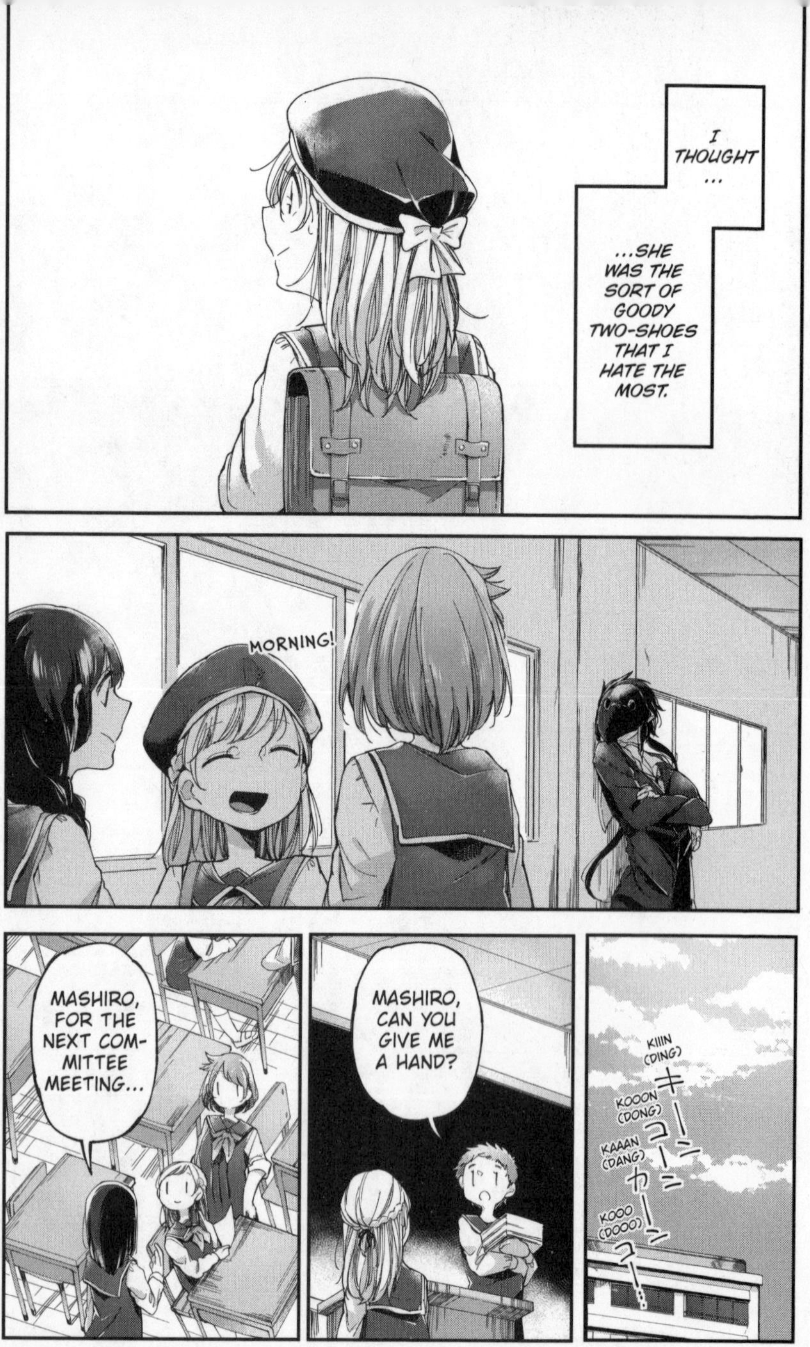
I THOUGHT ...
...SHE WAS THE SORT OF GOODY TWO-SHOES THAT I HATE THE MOST.
MORNING!
KIIIN (DING)
キーン
KOOON (DONG)
コーン
KAAAN (DANG)
カーン
KOOO (DOOO)
コー…
MASHIRO, CAN YOU GIVE ME A HAND?
MASHIRO, FOR THE NEXT COM-MITTEE MEETING...

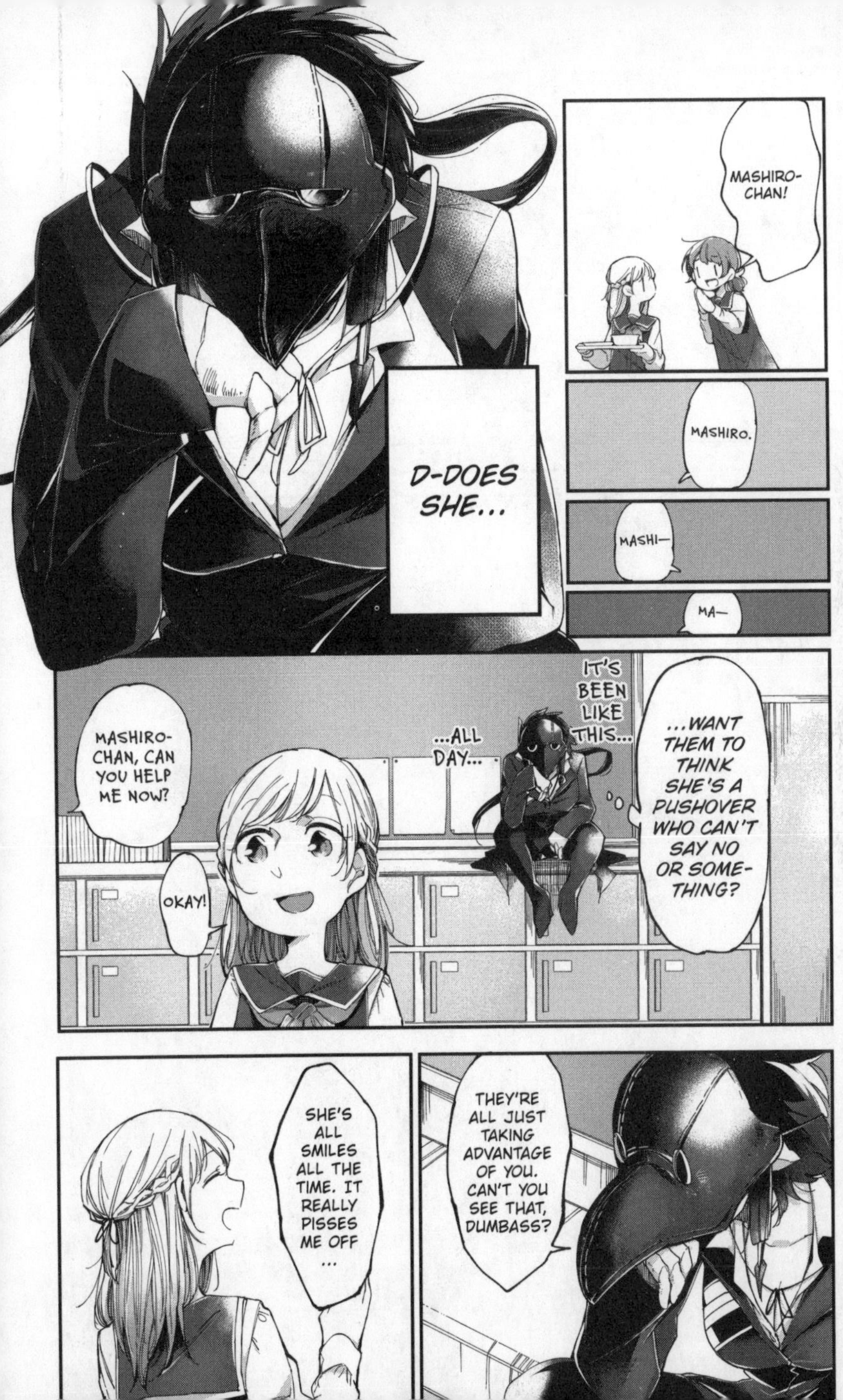
MASHIRO-CHAN!
MASHIRO.
MASHI—
MA—
D-DOES SHE...
...WANT THEM TO THINK SHE'S A PUSHOVER WHO CAN'T SAY NO OR SOME-THING?
IT'S BEEN LIKE THIS...
...ALL DAY...
MASHIRO-CHAN, CAN YOU HELP ME NOW?
OKAY!
THEY'RE ALL JUST TAKING ADVANTAGE OF YOU. CAN'T YOU SEE THAT, DUMBASS?
SHE'S ALL SMILES ALL THE TIME. IT REALLY PISSES ME OFF ...

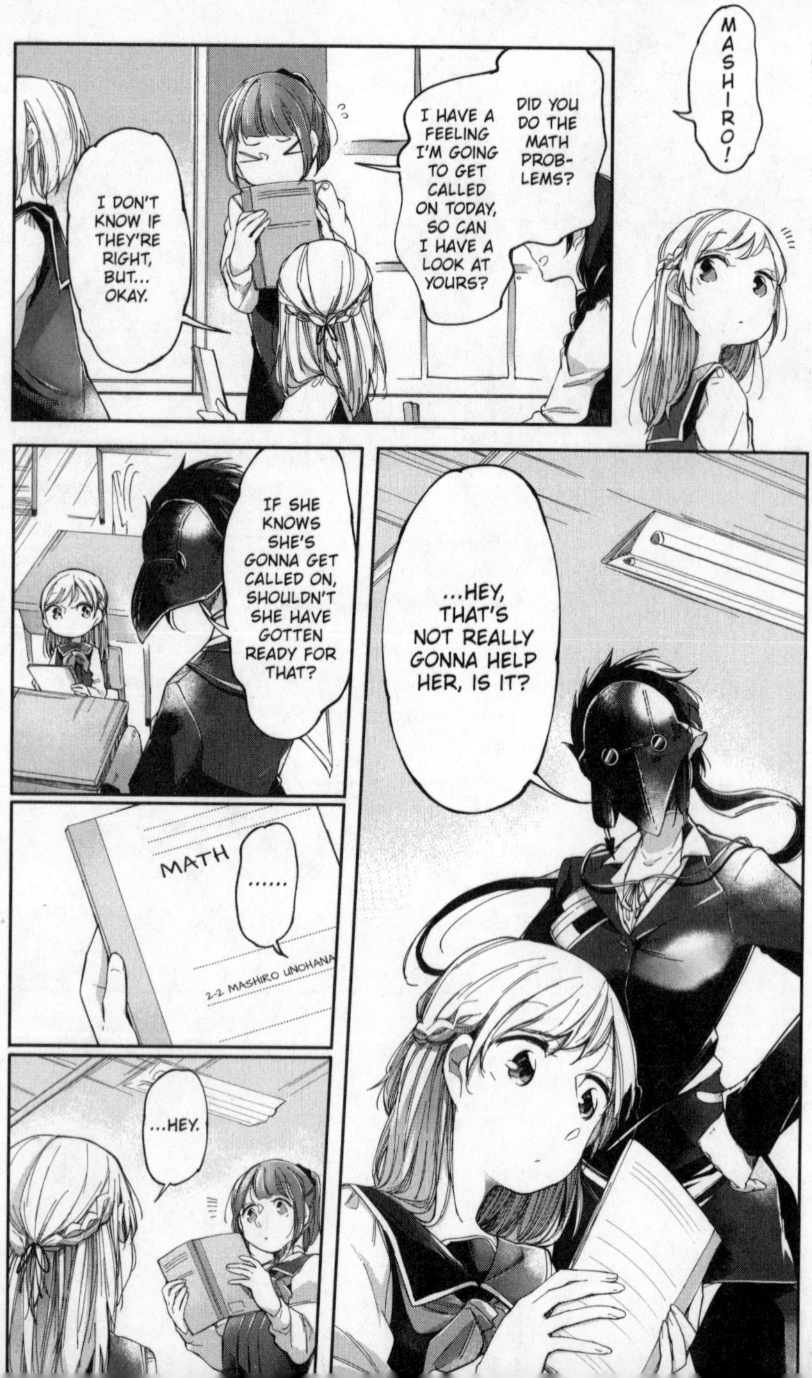
MASHIRO!
DID YOU DO THE MATH PROB-LEMS?
I HAVE A FEELING I'M GOING TO GET CALLED ON TODAY, SO CAN I HAVE A LOOK AT YOURS?
I DON'T KNOW IF THEY'RE RIGHT, BUT... OKAY.
...HEY, THAT'S NOT REALLY GONNA HELP HER, IS IT?
IF SHE KNOWS SHE'S GONNA GET CALLED ON, SHOULDN'T SHE HAVE GOTTEN READY FOR THAT?
MATH
......
2-2 MASHIRO UNOHANA
...HEY.

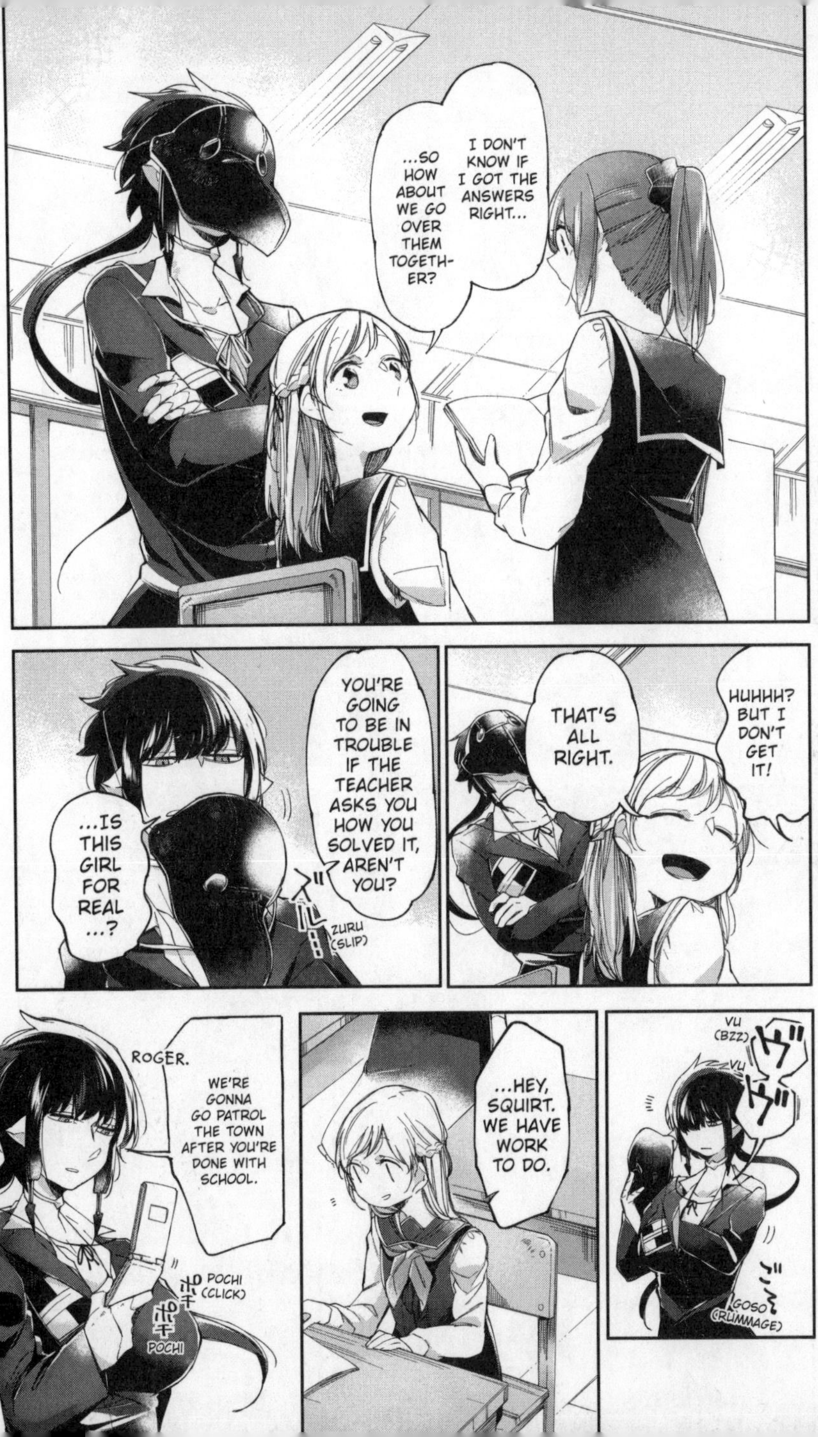
I DON'T KNOW IF I GOT THE ANSWERS RIGHT...
...SO HOW ABOUT WE GO OVER THEM TOGETH-ER?
HUHHH? BUT I DON'T GET IT!
THAT'S ALL RIGHT.
YOU'RE GOING TO BE IN TROUBLE IF THE TEACHER ASKS YOU HOW YOU SOLVED IT, AREN'T YOU?
ZURU (SLIP)
...IS THIS GIRL FOR REAL...?
VU (BZZ)
VU
GOSO (RUMMAGE)
...HEY, SQUIRT. WE HAVE WORK TO DO.
ROGER.
WE'RE GONNA GO PATROL THE TOWN AFTER YOU'RE DONE WITH SCHOOL.
POCHI (CLICK)
POCHI

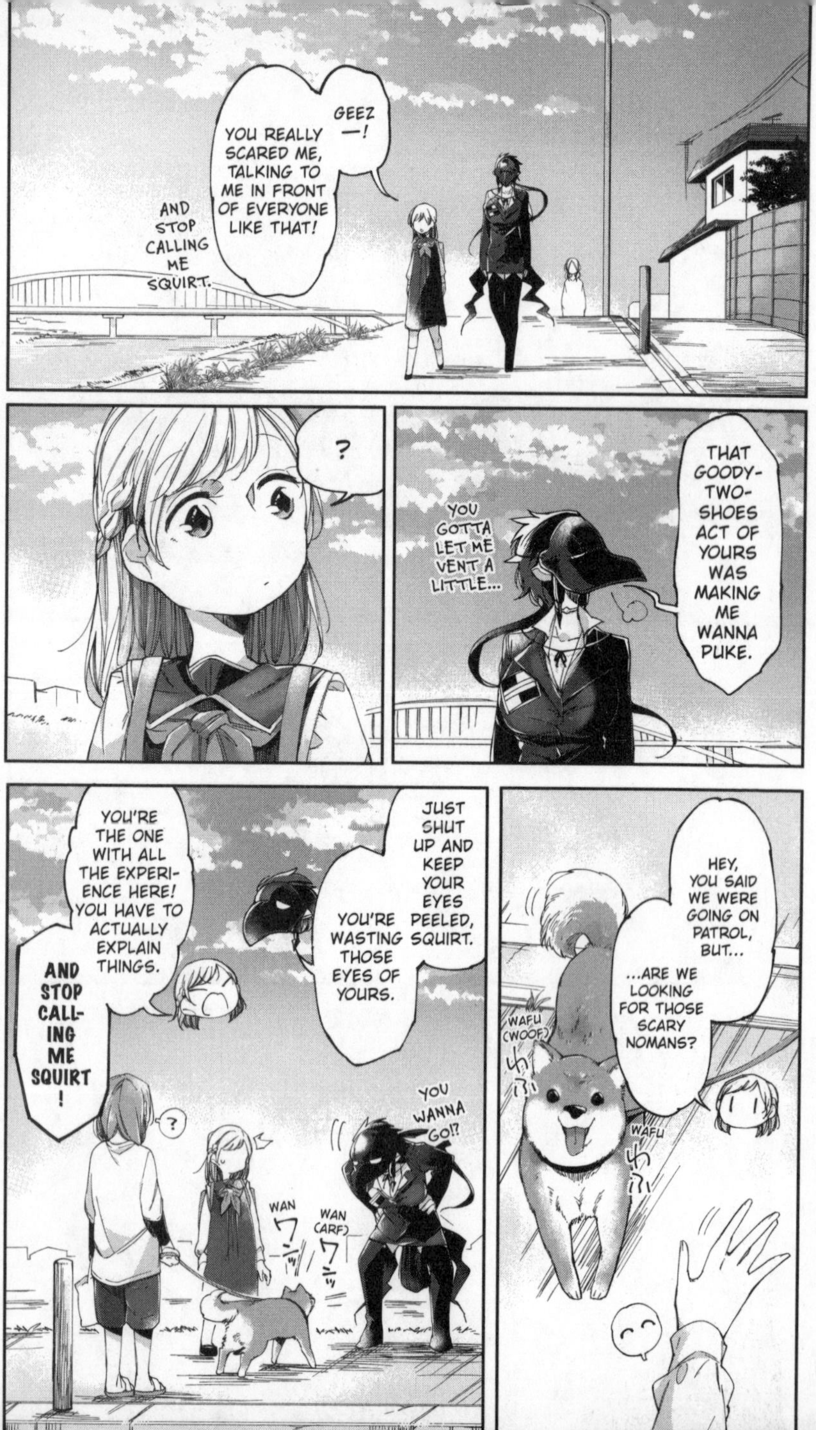
GEEZ—! YOU REALLY SCARED ME, TALKING TO ME IN FRONT OF EVERYONE LIKE THAT!
AND STOP CALLING ME SQUIRT.
THAT GOODY-TWO-SHOES ACT OF YOURS WAS MAKING ME WANNA PUKE.
YOU GOTTA LET ME VENT A LITTLE...
?
HEY, YOU SAID WE WERE GOING ON PATROL, BUT...
...ARE WE LOOKING FOR THOSE SCARY NOMANS?
WAFU (WOOF) わふ
WAFU わふ
JUST SHUT UP AND KEEP YOUR EYES PEELED, SQUIRT.
YOU'RE WASTING THOSE EYES OF YOURS.
YOU'RE THE ONE WITH ALL THE EXPERIENCE HERE! YOU HAVE TO ACTUALLY EXPLAIN THINGS.
AND STOP CALLING ME SQUIRT!
YOU WANNA GO!?
?
WAN (ARF) ワンッ
WAN ワンッ

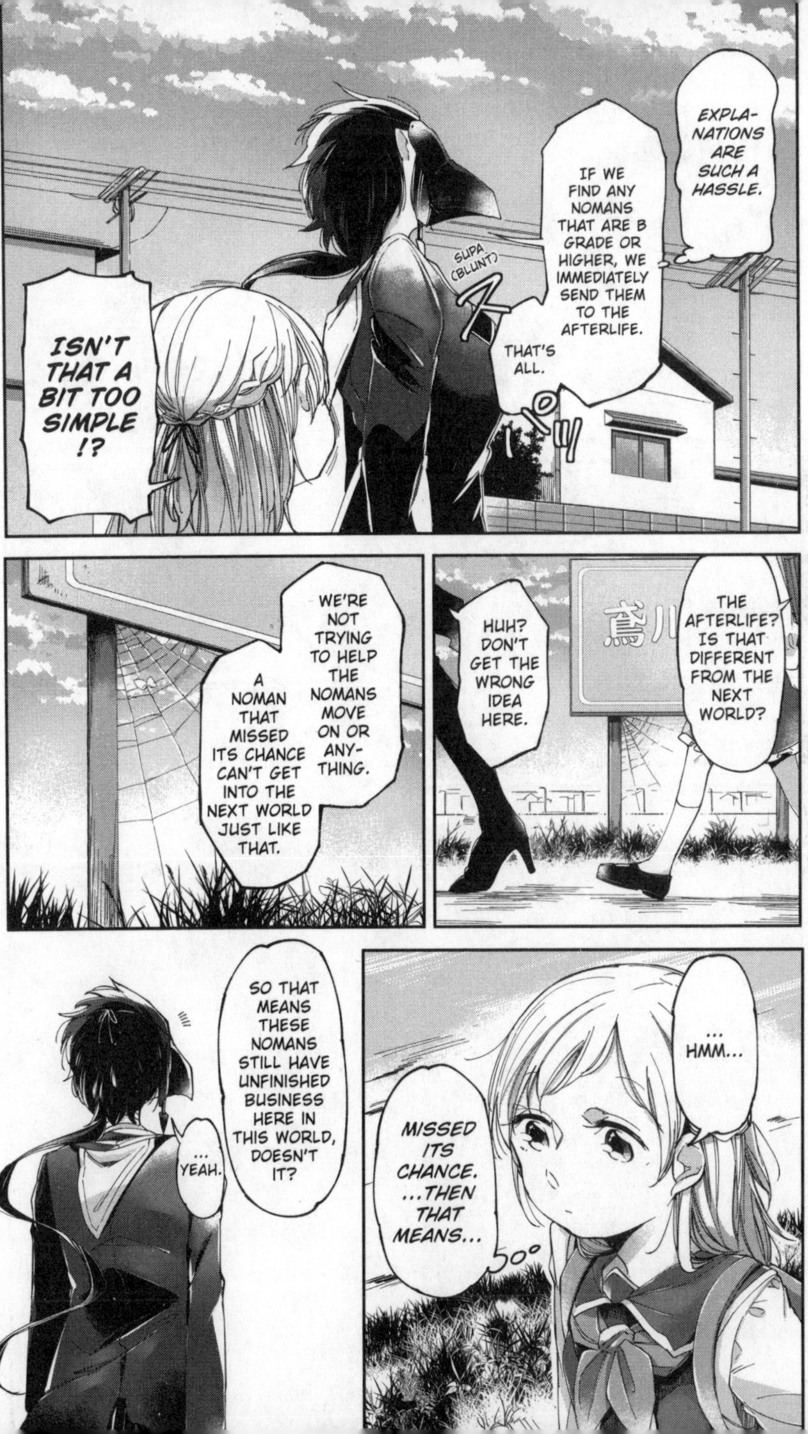
EXPLANATIONS ARE SUCH A HASSLE.
IF WE FIND ANY NOMANS THAT ARE B GRADE OR HIGHER, WE IMMEDIATELY SEND THEM TO THE AFTERLIFE.
SUPA (BLUNT)
THAT'S ALL.
ISN'T THAT A BIT TOO SIMPLE !?
THE AFTERLIFE? IS THAT DIFFERENT FROM THE NEXT WORLD?
HUH? DON'T GET THE WRONG IDEA HERE.
WE'RE NOT TRYING TO HELP THE NOMANS MOVE ON OR ANYTHING.
A NOMAN THAT MISSED ITS CHANCE CAN'T GET INTO THE NEXT WORLD JUST LIKE THAT.
... HMM...
MISSED ITS CHANCE. ...THEN THAT MEANS...
SO THAT MEANS THESE NOMANS STILL HAVE UNFINISHED BUSINESS HERE IN THIS WORLD, DOESN'T IT?
... YEAH.

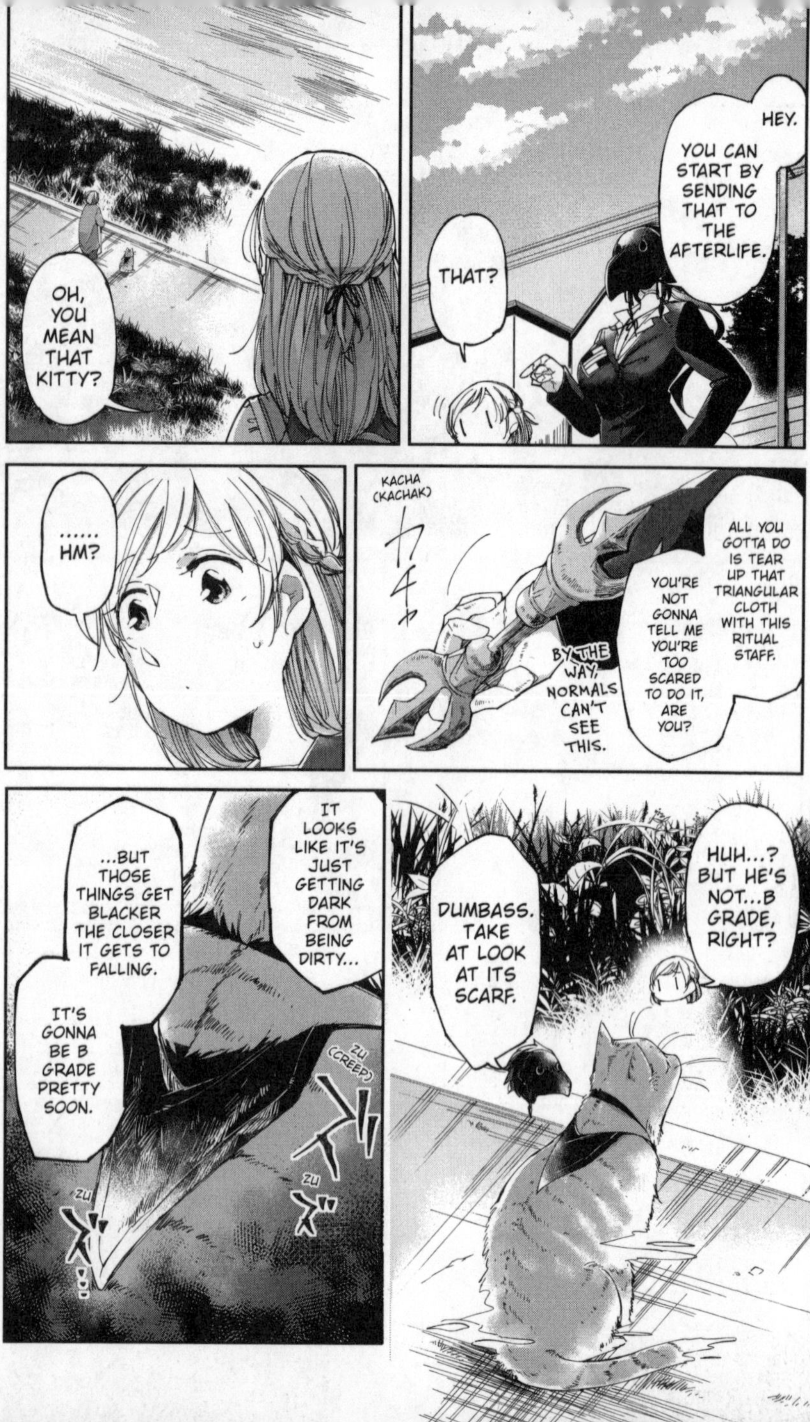
HEY.
YOU CAN START BY SENDING THAT TO THE AFTERLIFE.
THAT?
OH, YOU MEAN THAT KITTY?
ALL YOU GOTTA DO IS TEAR UP THAT TRIANGULAR CLOTH WITH THIS RITUAL STAFF.
YOU'RE NOT GONNA TELL ME YOU'RE TOO SCARED TO DO IT, ARE YOU?
KACHA (KACHAK)
BY THE WAY, NORMALS CAN'T SEE THIS.
......HM?
HUH...? BUT HE'S NOT...B GRADE, RIGHT?
DUMBASS. TAKE AT LOOK AT ITS SCARF.
IT LOOKS LIKE IT'S JUST GETTING DARK FROM BEING DIRTY...
...BUT THOSE THINGS GET BLACKER THE CLOSER IT GETS TO FALLING.
ZU (CREEP)
IT'S GONNA BE B GRADE PRETTY SOON.
ZU
ZU

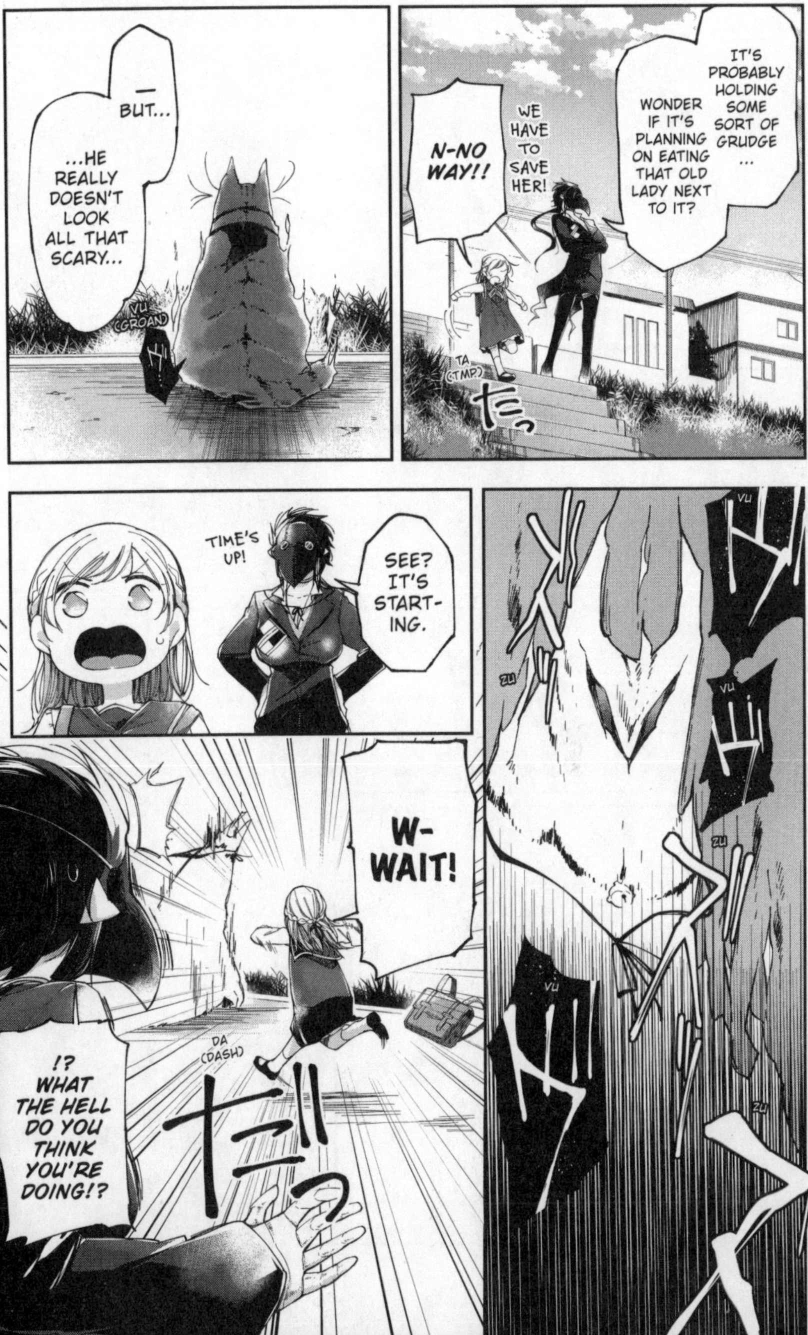
IT'S PROBABLY HOLDING SOME SORT OF GRUDGE...
WONDER IF IT'S PLANNING ON EATING THAT OLD LADY NEXT TO IT?
WE HAVE TO SAVE HER!
N-NO WAY!!
TA (TMP.)
— BUT...
...HE REALLY DOESN'T LOOK ALL THAT SCARY...
VU (GROAN)
VU
ZU
VU
ZU
VU
ZU
SEE? IT'S START-ING.
TIME'S UP!
W-WAIT!
DA (DASH)
!? WHAT THE HELL DO YOU THINK YOU'RE DOING!?

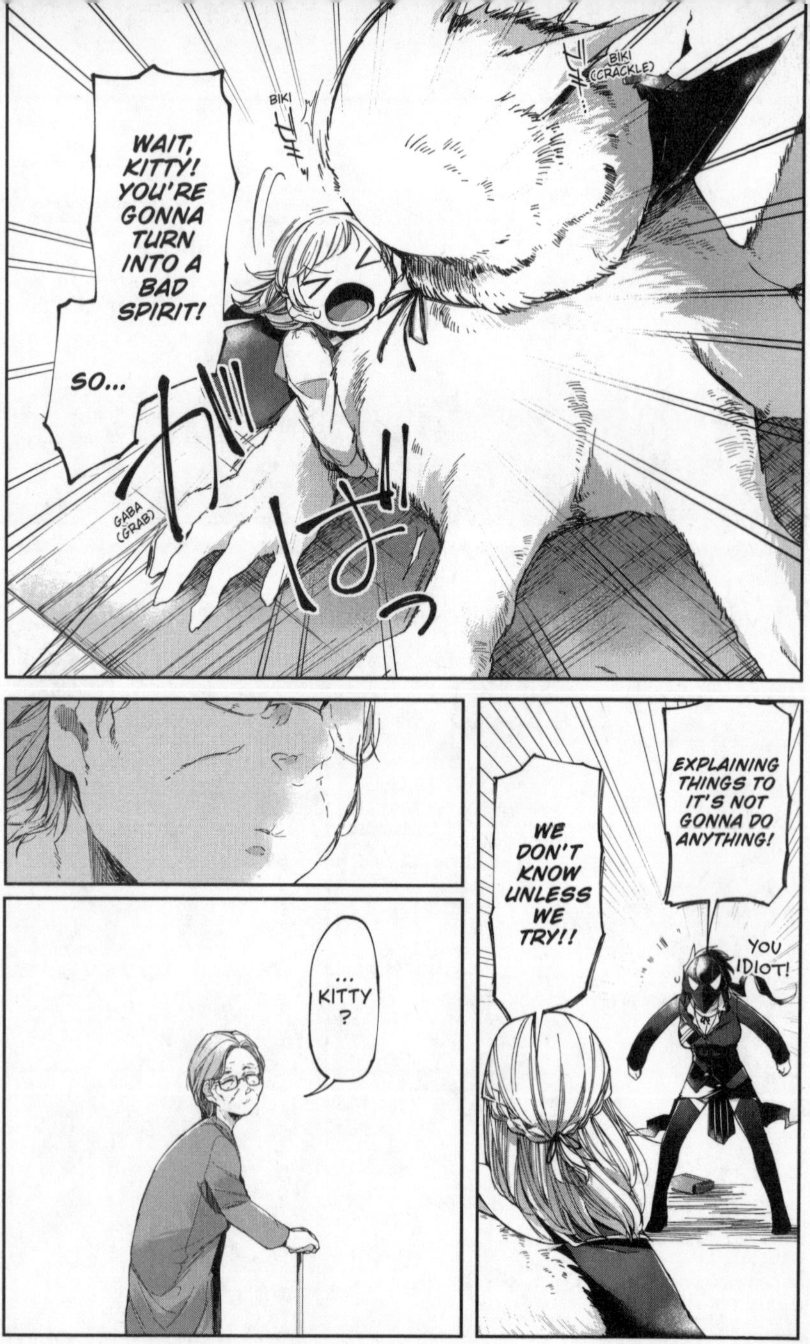
BIKI (CRACKLE)
BIKI
WAIT, KITTY! YOU'RE GONNA TURN INTO A BAD SPIRIT!
SO...
GABA (GRAB)
EXPLAINING THINGS TO IT'S NOT GONNA DO ANYTHING!
YOU IDIOT!
WE DON'T KNOW UNLESS WE TRY!!
... KITTY ?

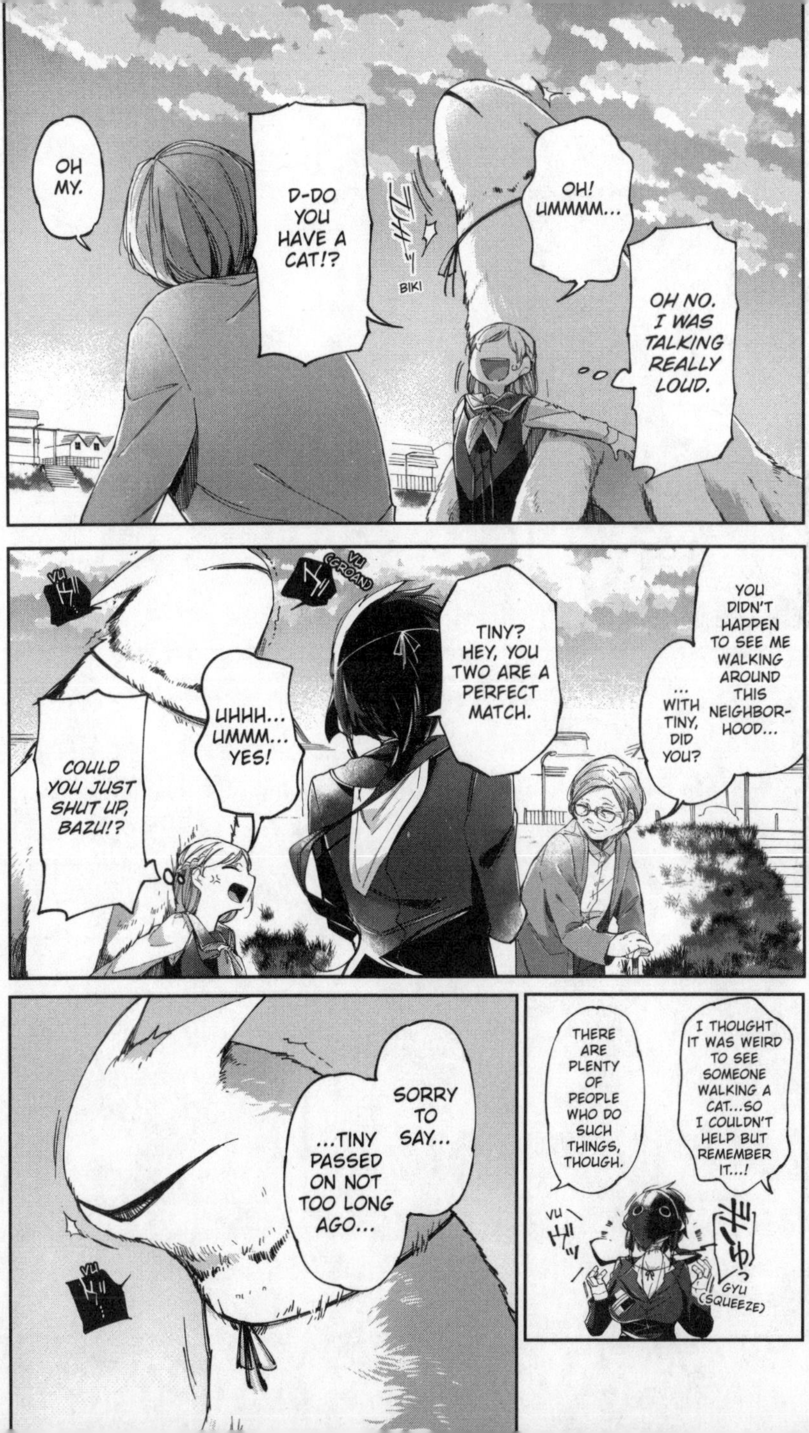
OH! UMMMM...
OH NO. I WAS TALKING REALLY LOUD.
BIKI
D-DO YOU HAVE A CAT!?
OH MY.
YOU DIDN'T HAPPEN TO SEE ME WALKING AROUND THIS NEIGHBORHOOD... ...WITH TINY, DID YOU?
TINY? HEY, YOU TWO ARE A PERFECT MATCH.
VU (GROAN)
UHHH... UMMM... YES!
VU
COULD YOU JUST SHUT UP, BAZU!?
I THOUGHT IT WAS WEIRD TO SEE SOMEONE WALKING A CAT...SO I COULDN'T HELP BUT REMEMBER IT...!
THERE ARE PLENTY OF PEOPLE WHO DO SUCH THINGS, THOUGH.
GYU (SQUEEZE)
VU
SORRY TO SAY...
...TINY PASSED ON NOT TOO LONG AGO...
VU

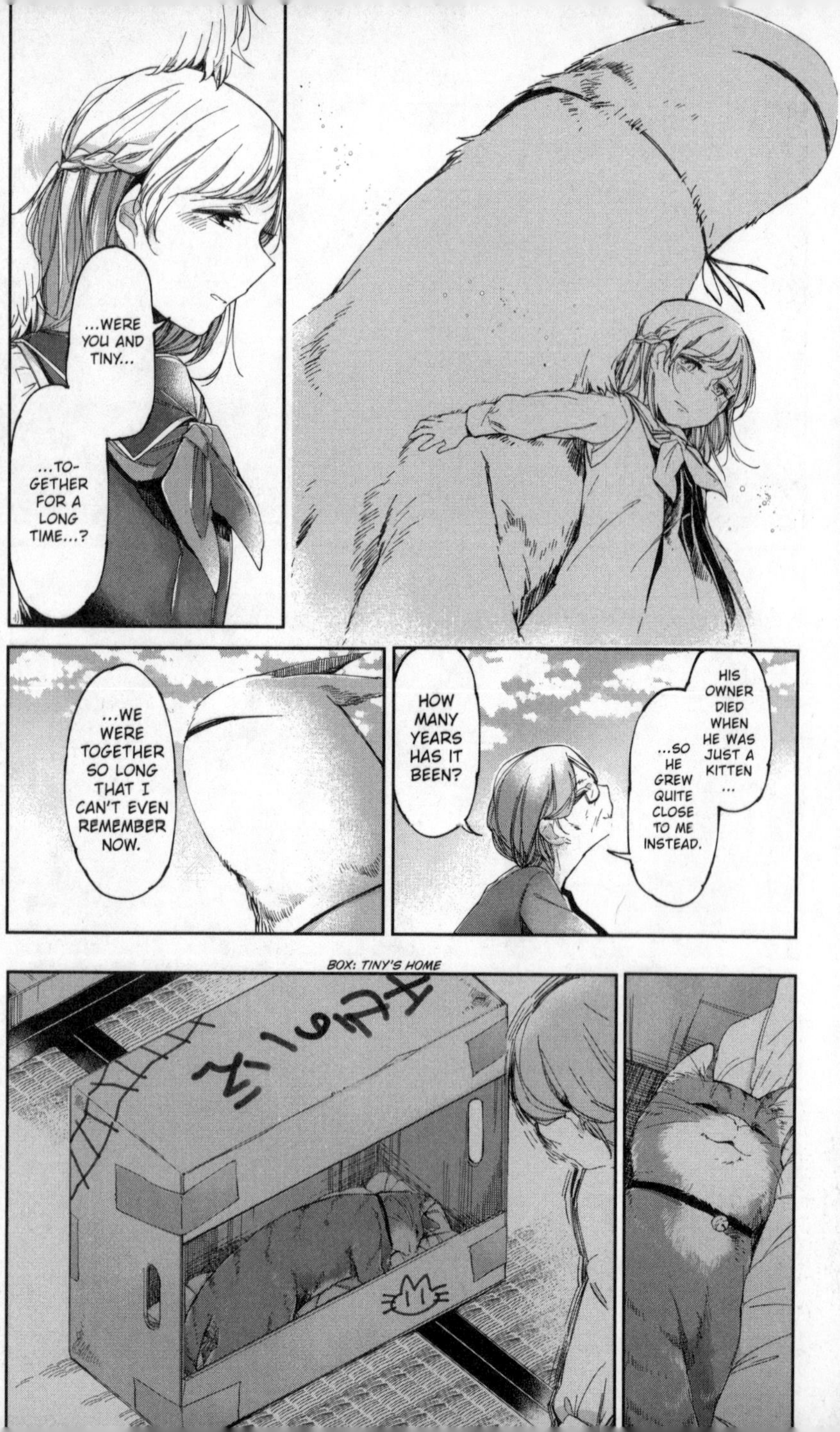
...WERE YOU AND TINY...
...TO-GETHER FOR A LONG TIME...?
HIS OWNER DIED WHEN HE WAS JUST A KITTEN ...
...SO HE GREW QUITE CLOSE TO ME INSTEAD.
HOW MANY YEARS HAS IT BEEN?
...WE WERE TOGETHER SO LONG THAT I CAN'T EVEN REMEMBER NOW.
BOX: TINY'S HOME

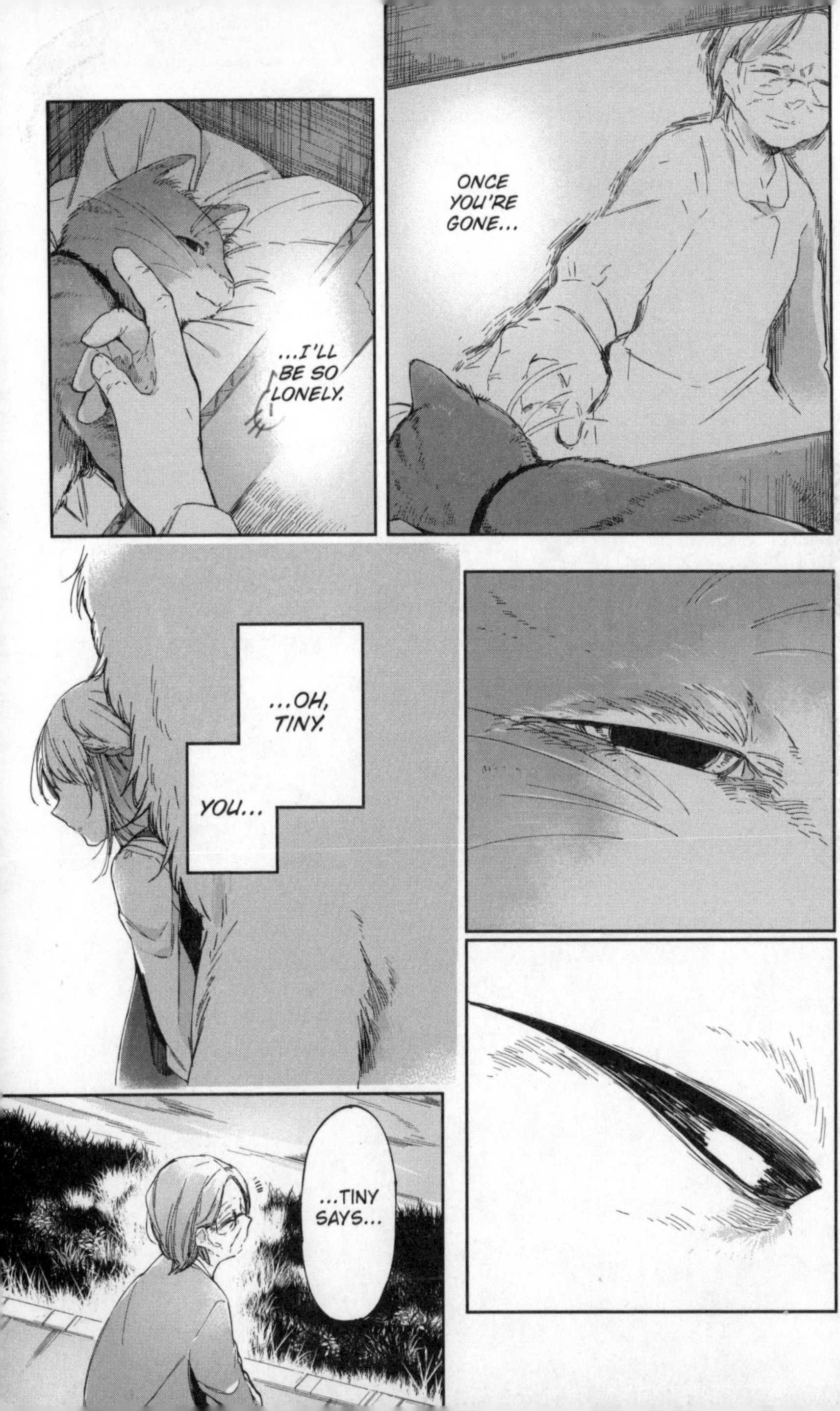
ONCE YOU'RE GONE...
...I'LL BE SO LONELY.
...OH, TINY.
YOU...
...TINY SAYS...

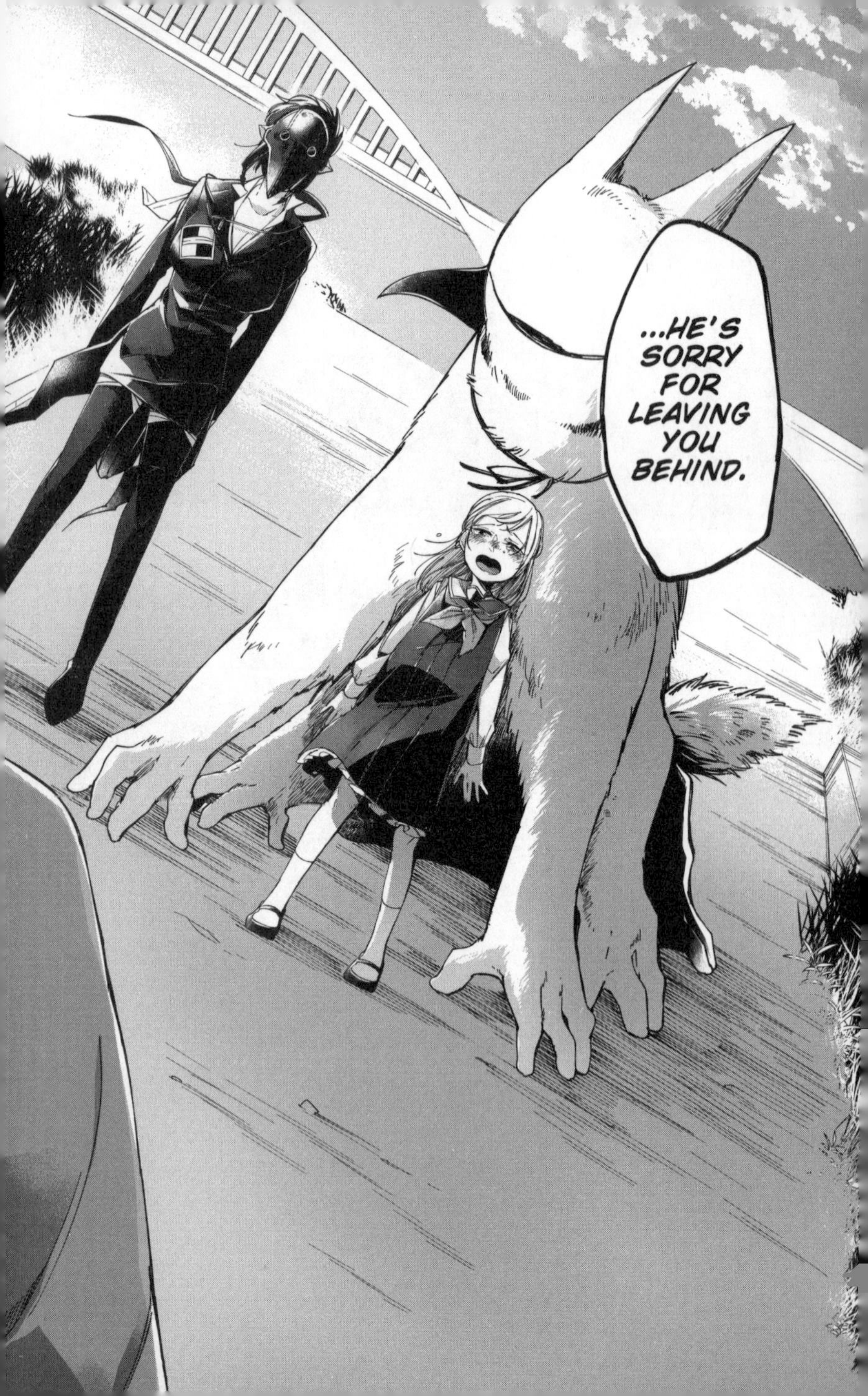
...HE'S SORRY FOR LEAVING YOU BEHIND.

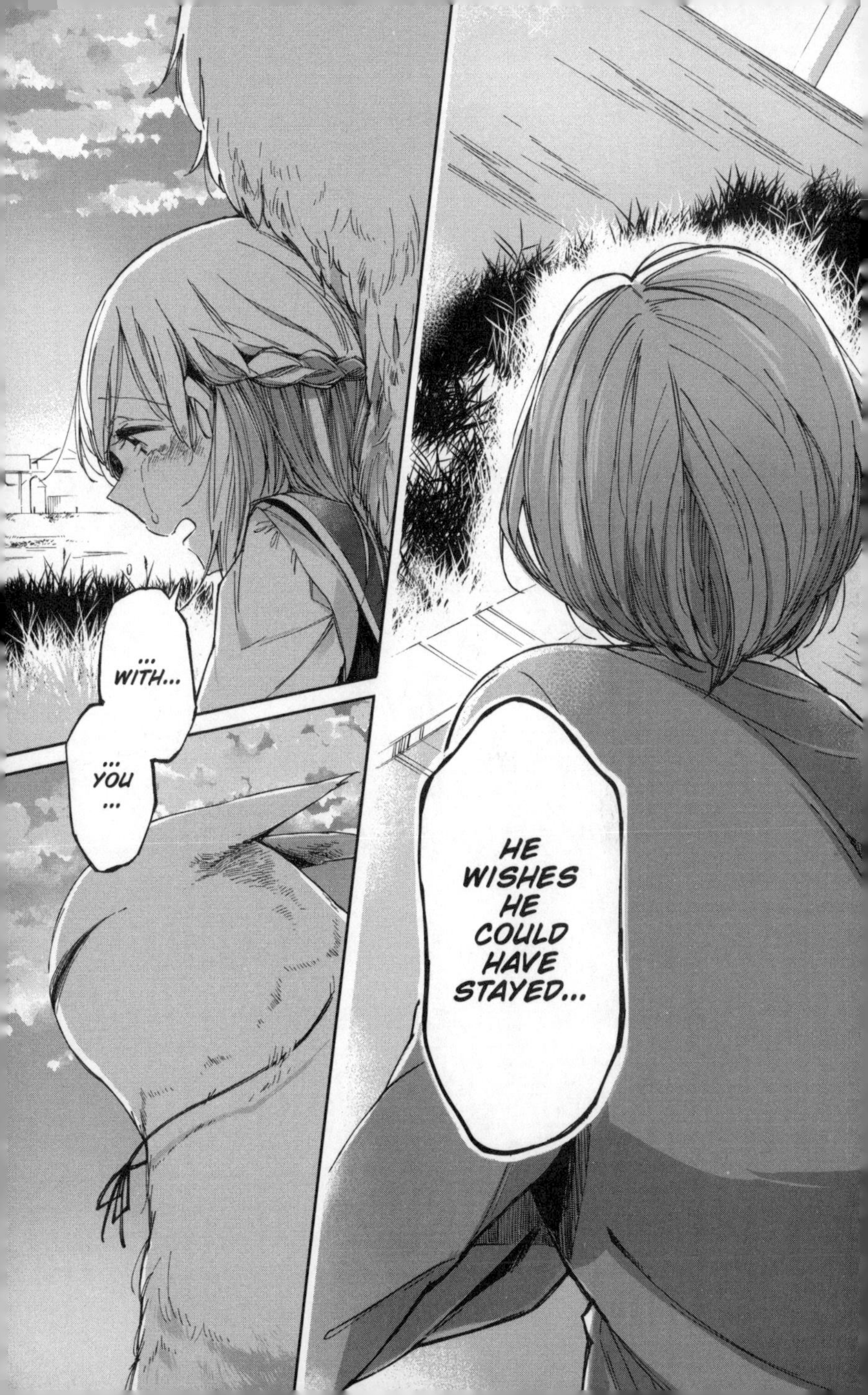
HE WISHES HE COULD HAVE STAYED...
...WITH...
...YOU...

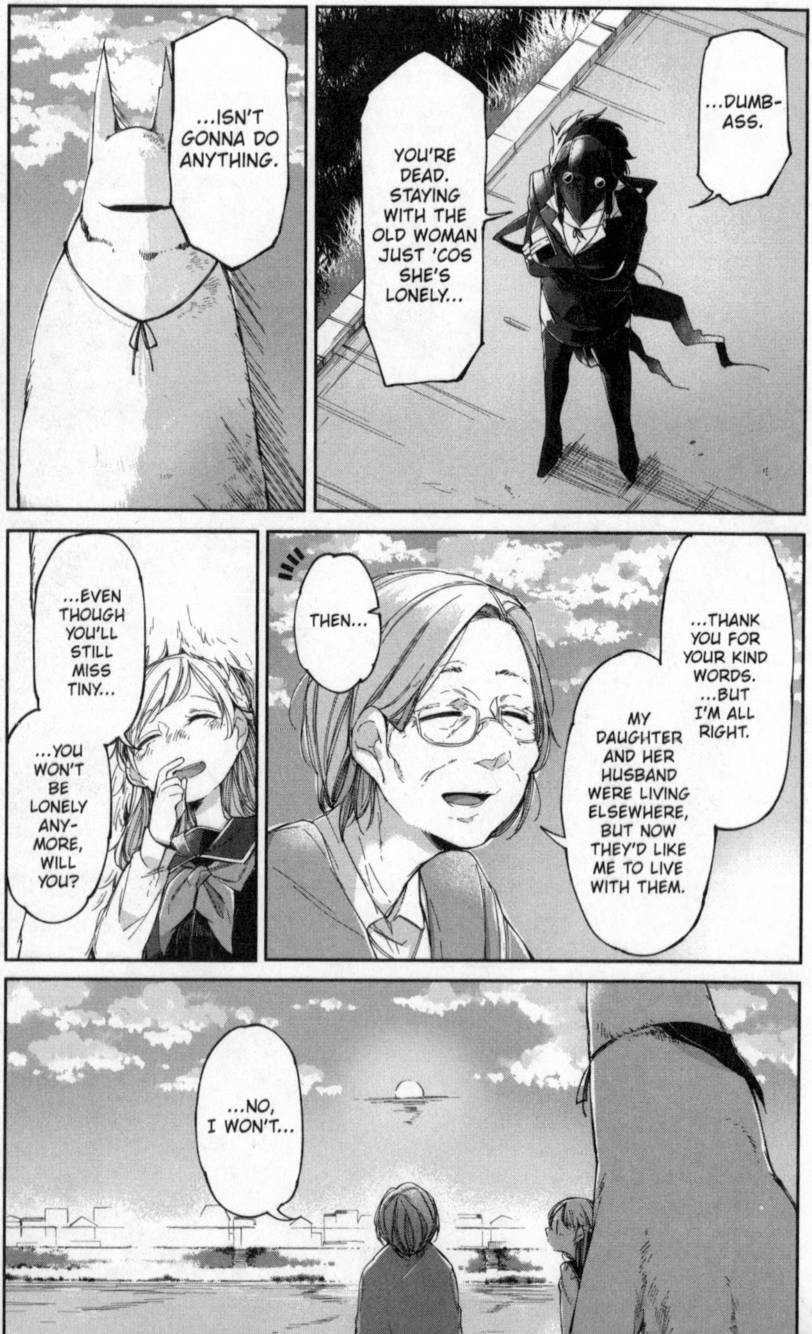
...DUMB-ASS.
YOU'RE DEAD. STAYING WITH THE OLD WOMAN JUST 'COS SHE'S LONELY...
...ISN'T GONNA DO ANYTHING.
...THANK YOU FOR YOUR KIND WORDS. ...BUT I'M ALL RIGHT.
MY DAUGHTER AND HER HUSBAND WERE LIVING ELSEWHERE, BUT NOW THEY'D LIKE ME TO LIVE WITH THEM.
THEN...
...EVEN THOUGH YOU'LL STILL MISS TINY...
...YOU WON'T BE LONELY ANY-MORE, WILL YOU?
...NO, I WON'T...

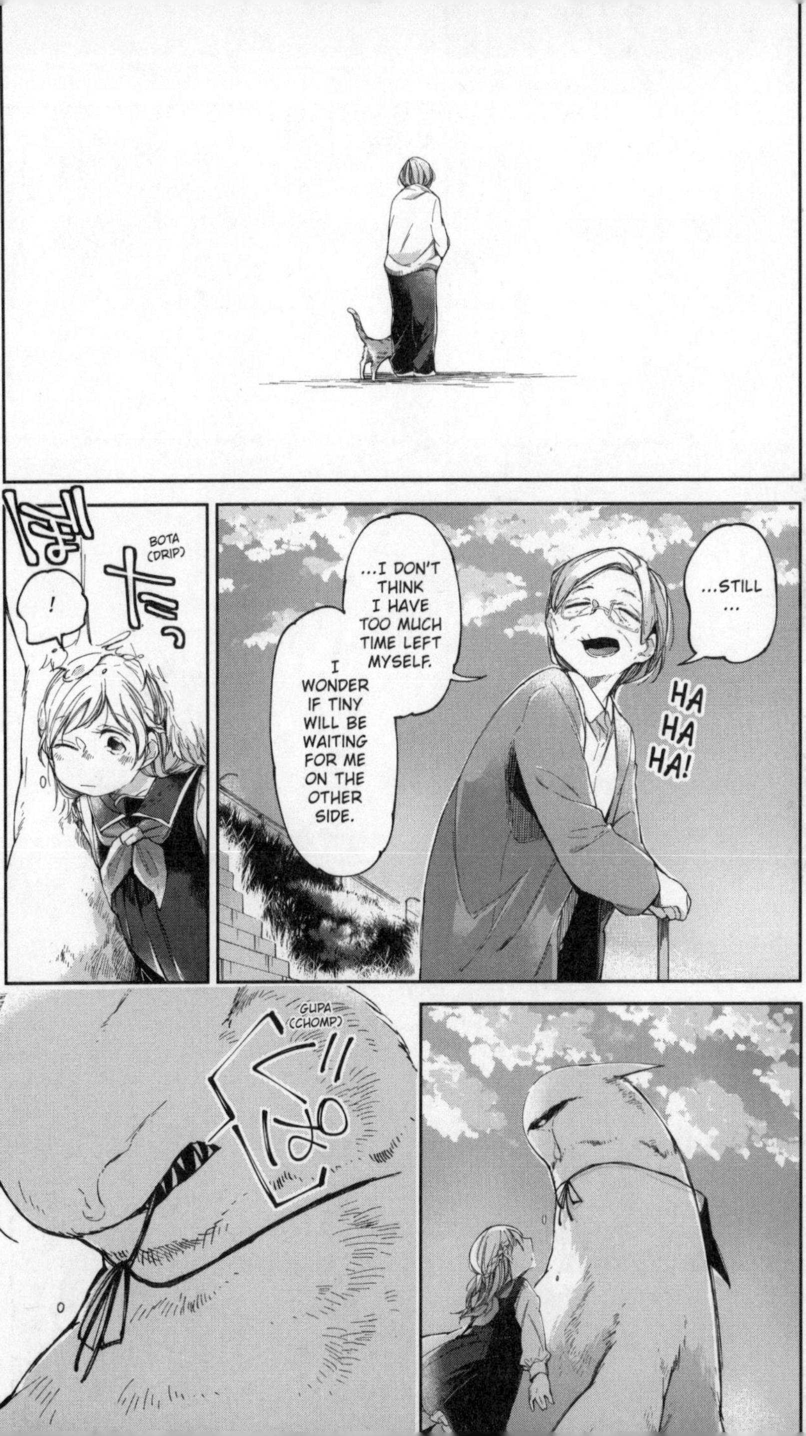
...STILL ...
HA HA HA!
...I DON'T THINK I HAVE TOO MUCH TIME LEFT MYSELF.
I WONDER IF TINY WILL BE WAITING FOR ME ON THE OTHER SIDE.
BOTA (DRIP)
ぼたっ
!
GUPA (CHOMP)
ぐぱ

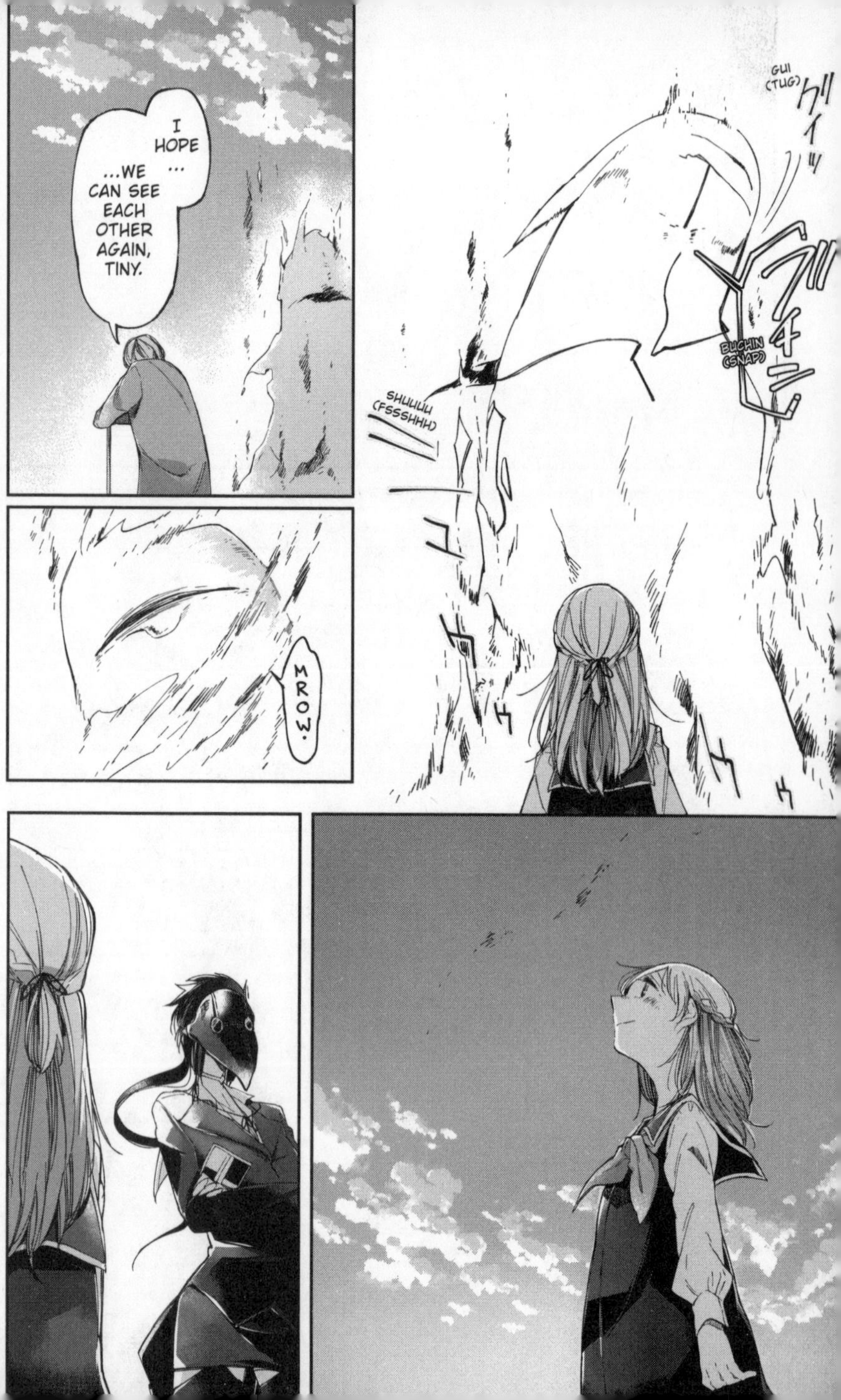
GUI (TUG)
BUCHIN (SNAP)
SHUUUU (FSSSHHH)
I HOPE ... ...WE CAN SEE EACH OTHER AGAIN, TINY.
MROW.

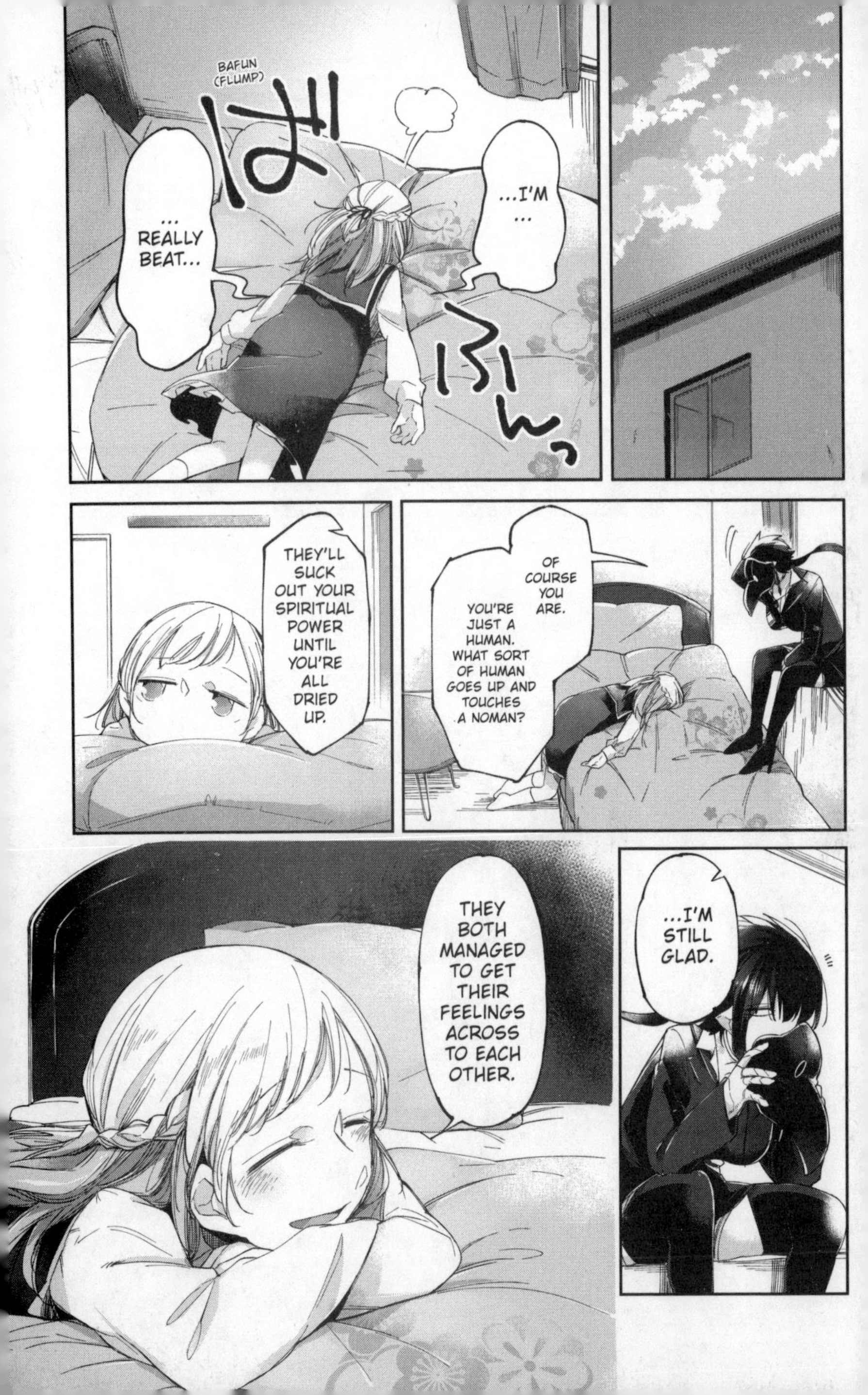
...I'M ...
BAFUN (FLUMP)
ばふんっ
... REALLY BEAT...
OF COURSE YOU ARE.
YOU'RE JUST A HUMAN. WHAT SORT OF HUMAN GOES UP AND TOUCHES A NOMAN?
THEY'LL SUCK OUT YOUR SPIRITUAL POWER UNTIL YOU'RE ALL DRIED UP.
...I'M STILL GLAD.
THEY BOTH MANAGED TO GET THEIR FEELINGS ACROSS TO EACH OTHER.

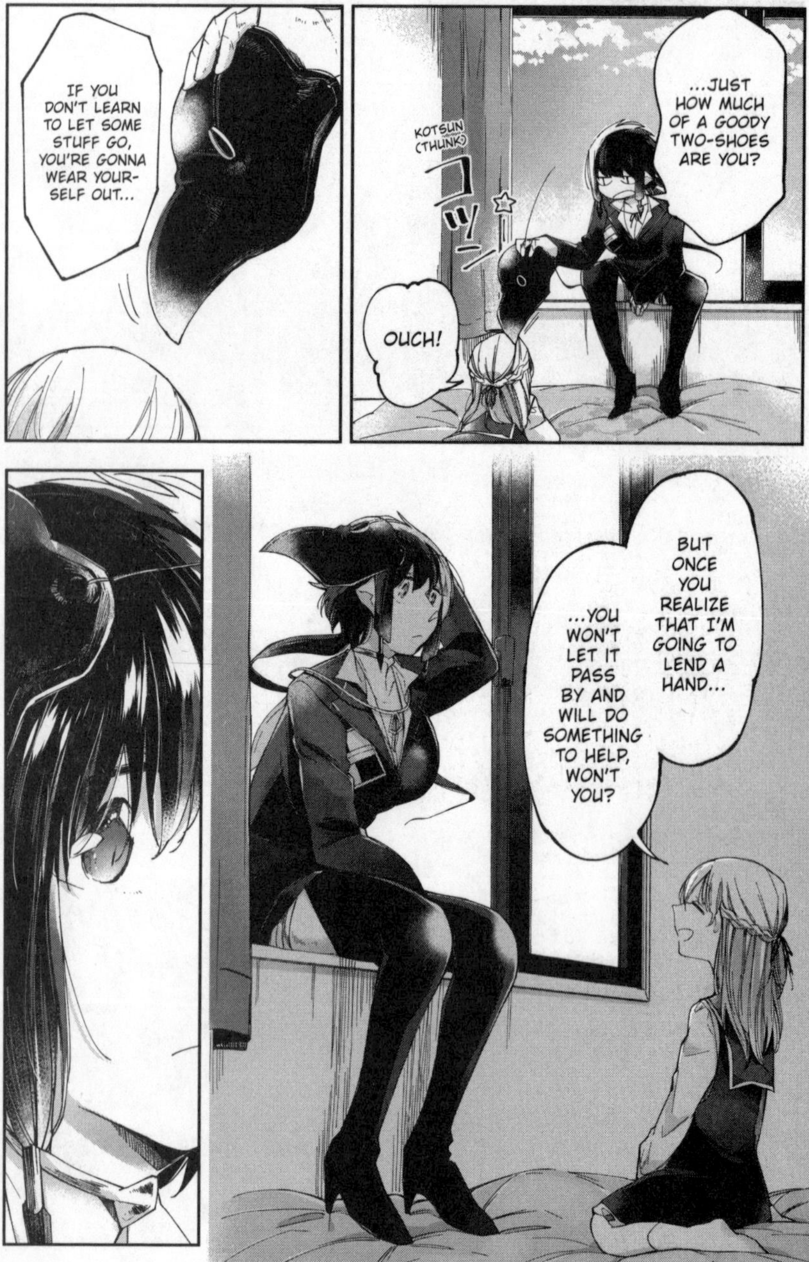
...JUST HOW MUCH OF A GOODY TWO-SHOES ARE YOU?
KOTSUN (THUNK)
コツーン
OUCH!
IF YOU DON'T LEARN TO LET SOME STUFF GO, YOU'RE GONNA WEAR YOURSELF OUT...
BUT ONCE YOU REALIZE THAT I'M GOING TO LEND A HAND...
...YOU WON'T LET IT PASS BY AND WILL DO SOMETHING TO HELP, WON'T YOU?

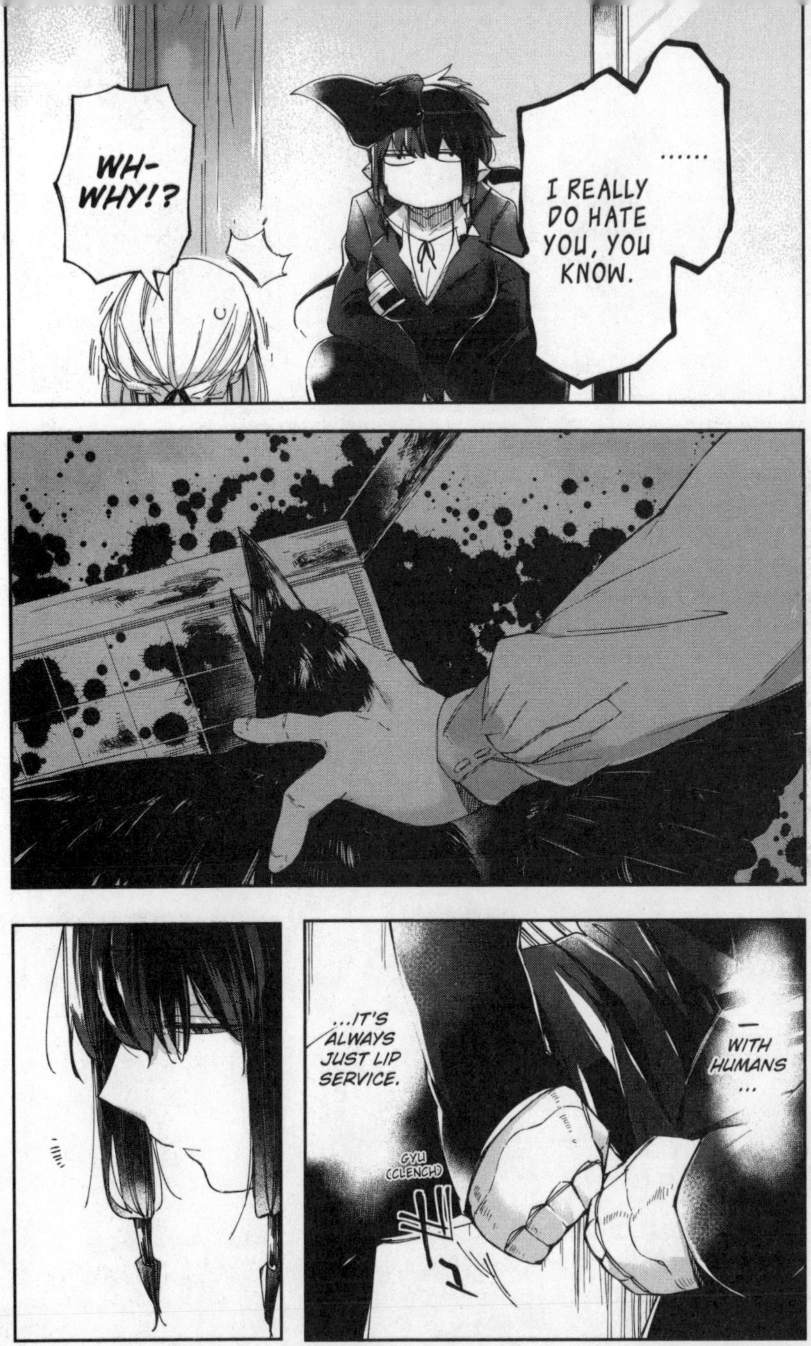
......
I REALLY DO HATE YOU, YOU KNOW.
WH- WHY!?
—WITH HUMANS...
...IT'S ALWAYS JUST LIP SERVICE.
GYU (CLENCH)

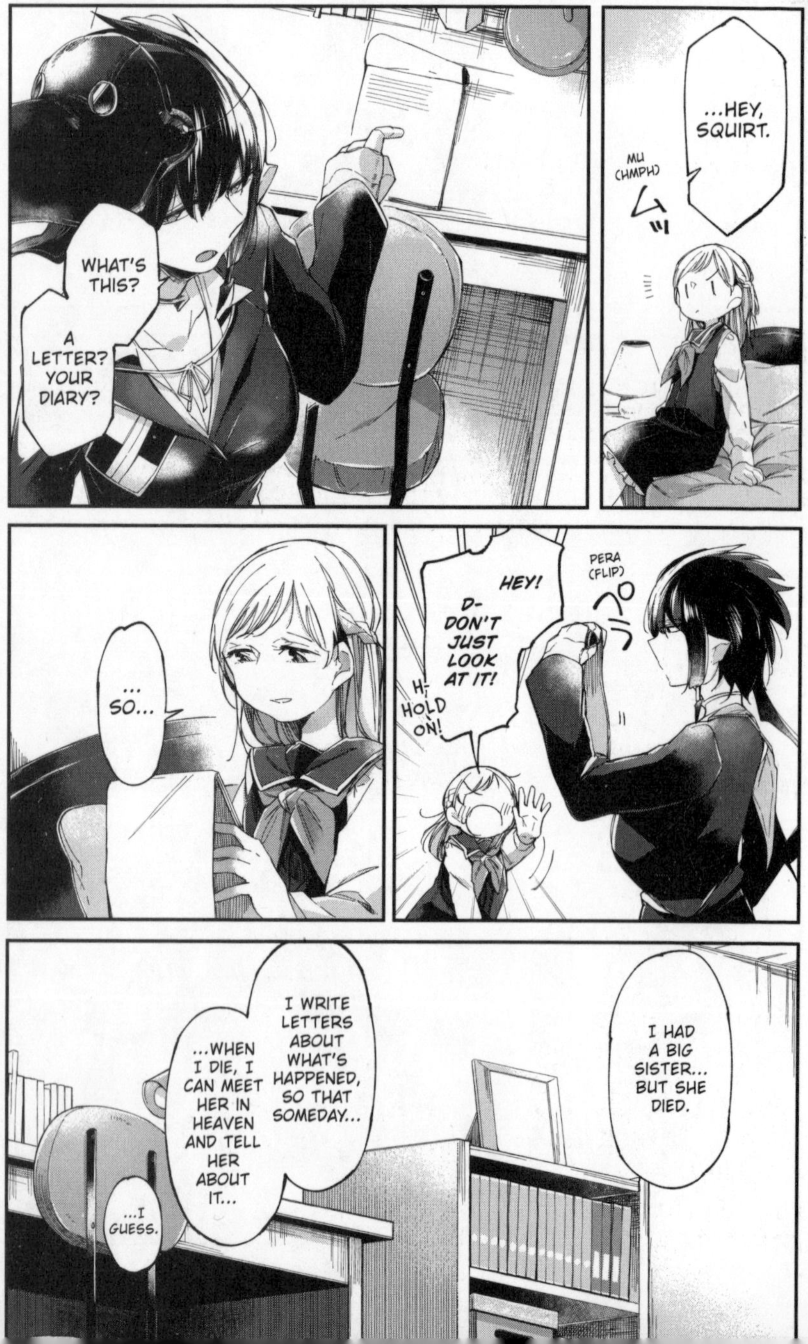
...HEY, SQUIRT.
MU (HMPH)
ムッ
WHAT'S THIS?
A LETTER? YOUR DIARY?
PERA (FLIP)
ペラ
HEY!
D-DON'T JUST LOOK AT IT!
H-HOLD ON!
... SO...
I HAD A BIG SISTER... BUT SHE DIED.
I WRITE LETTERS ABOUT WHAT'S HAPPENED, SO THAT SOMEDAY...
...WHEN I DIE, I CAN MEET HER IN HEAVEN AND TELL HER ABOUT IT...
...I GUESS.

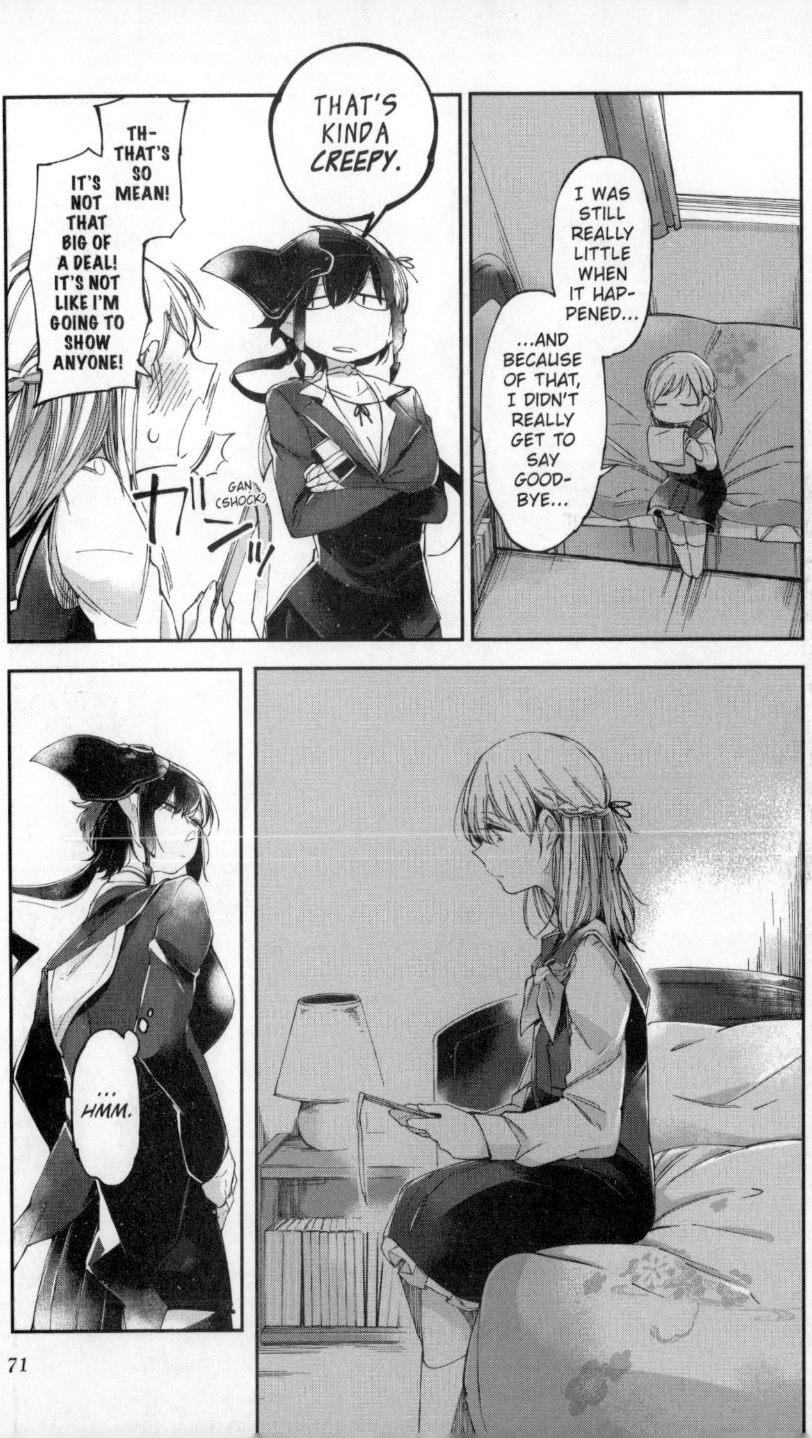
I WAS STILL REALLY LITTLE WHEN IT HAP-PENED...
...AND BECAUSE OF THAT, I DIDN'T REALLY GET TO SAY GOOD-BYE...
THAT'S KINDA CREEPY.
TH- THAT'S SO MEAN!
IT'S NOT THAT BIG OF A DEAL! IT'S NOT LIKE I'M GOING TO SHOW ANYONE!
GAN (SHOCK)
... HMM.

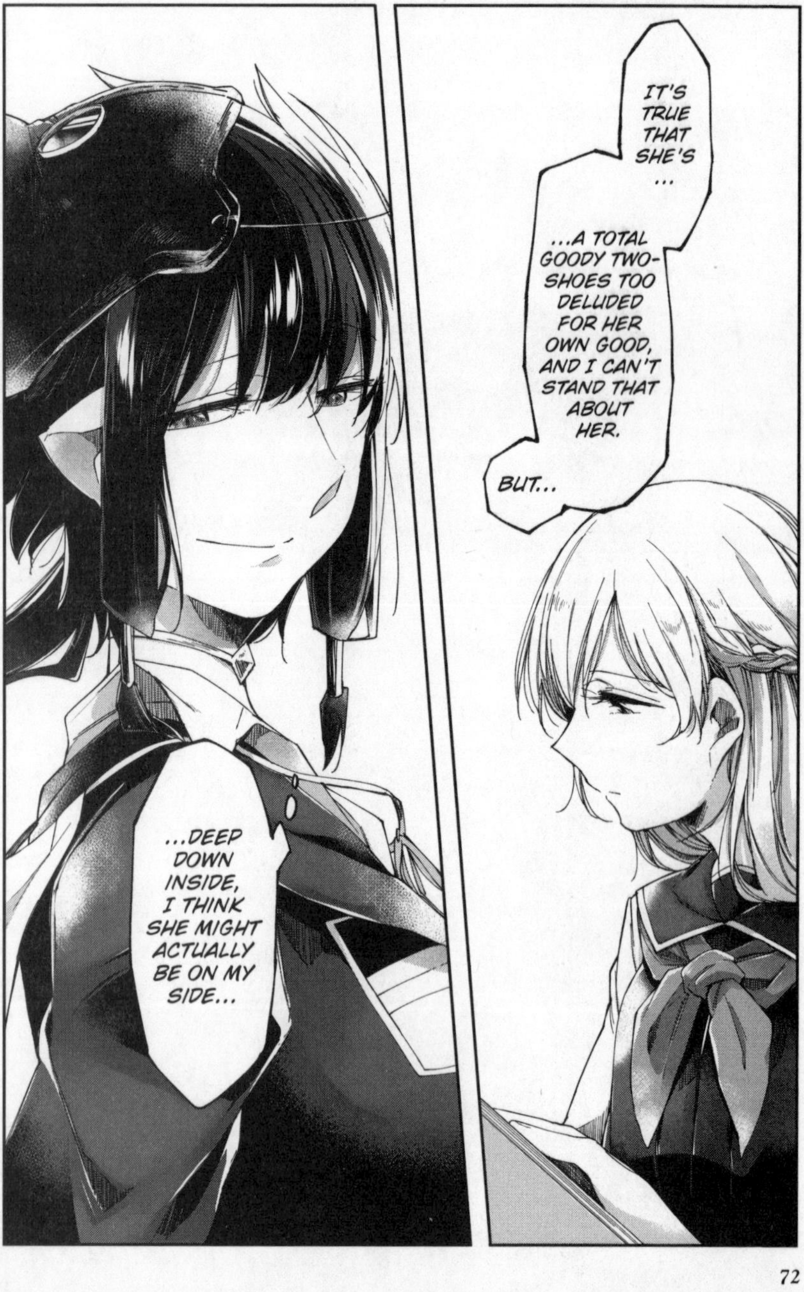
IT'S TRUE THAT SHE'S ...
...A TOTAL GOODY TWO-SHOES TOO DELUDED FOR HER OWN GOOD, AND I CAN'T STAND THAT ABOUT HER.
BUT...
...DEEP DOWN INSIDE, I THINK SHE MIGHT ACTUALLY BE ON MY SIDE...

HER FAVORITE

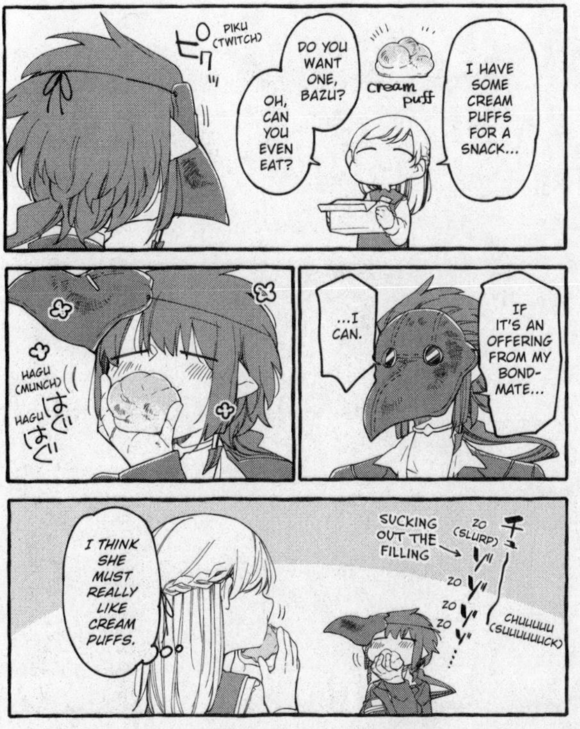
I HAVE SOME CREAM PUFFS FOR A SNACK...
cream puff
DO YOU WANT ONE, BAZU?
OH, CAN YOU EVEN EAT?
ピクッ
PIKU (TWITCH)
IF IT'S AN OFFERING FROM MY BOND-MATE...
...I CAN.
はぐはぐ
HAGU (MUNCH) HAGU
チュー
CHUUUUUU (SUUUUUUUCK)
ZO (SLURP) ZO ZO ZO
SUCKING OUT THE FILLING
I THINK SHE MUST REALLY LIKE CREAM PUFFS.

Dear NOMAN

LETTER 4

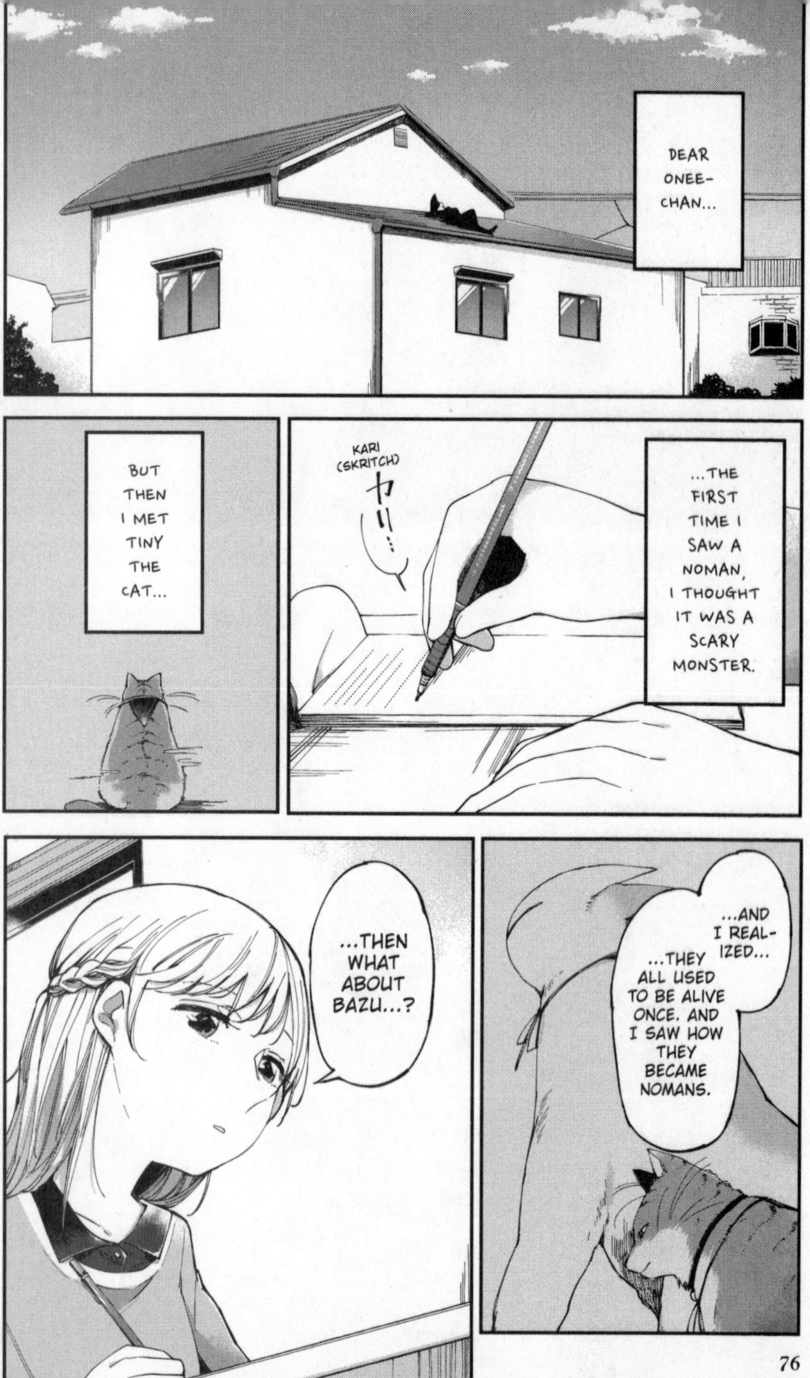
DEAR ONEE-CHAN...
...THE FIRST TIME I SAW A NOMAN, I THOUGHT IT WAS A SCARY MONSTER.
カリ…
KARI (SKRITCH)
BUT THEN I MET TINY THE CAT...
...AND I REAL-IZED...
...THEY ALL USED TO BE ALIVE ONCE. AND I SAW HOW THEY BECAME NOMANS.
...THEN WHAT ABOUT BAZU...?

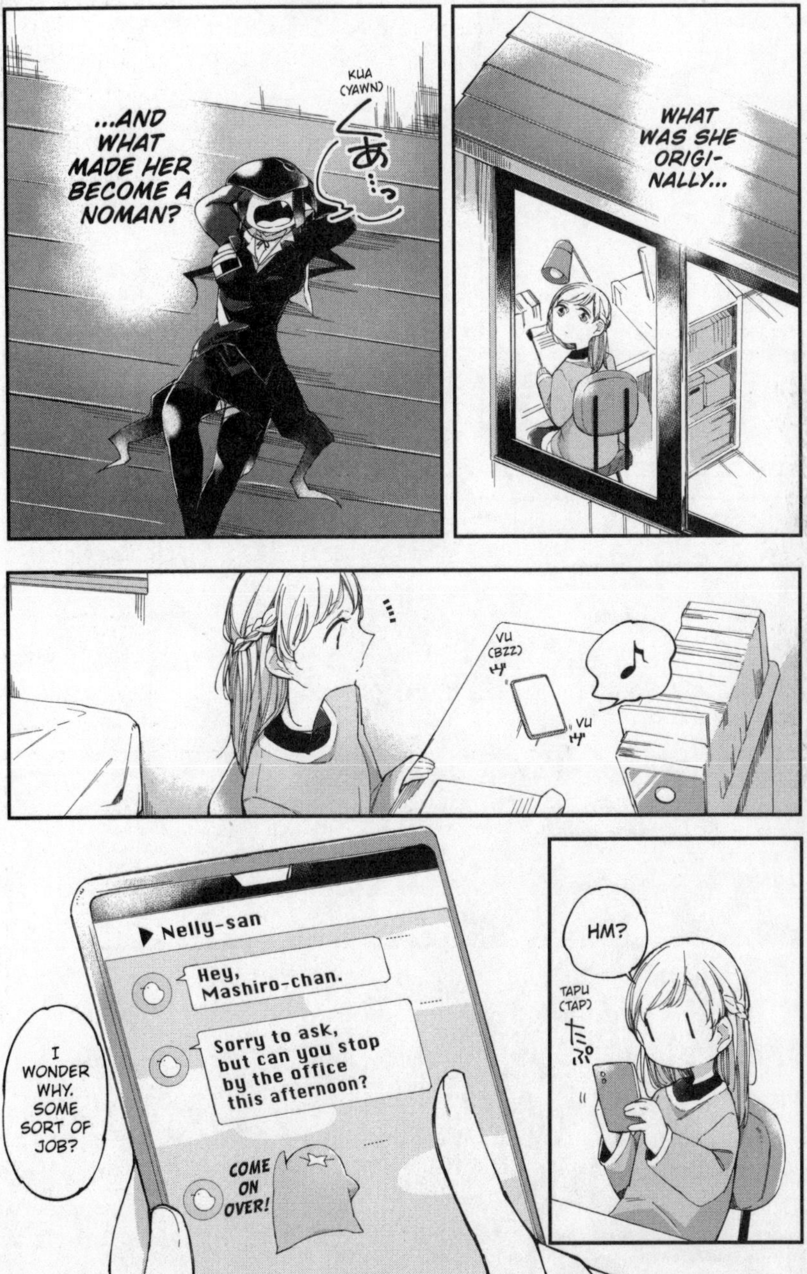
WHAT WAS SHE ORIGI-NALLY...
...AND WHAT MADE HER BECOME A NOMAN?
KUA (YAWN)
くあ…っ
♪
VU (BZZ)
ヴ
VU
ヴ
HM?
TAPU (TAP)
たぷ
▶ Nelly-san
Hey, Mashiro-chan.
Sorry to ask, but can you stop by the office this afternoon?
COME ON OVER!
I WONDER WHY. SOME SORT OF JOB?

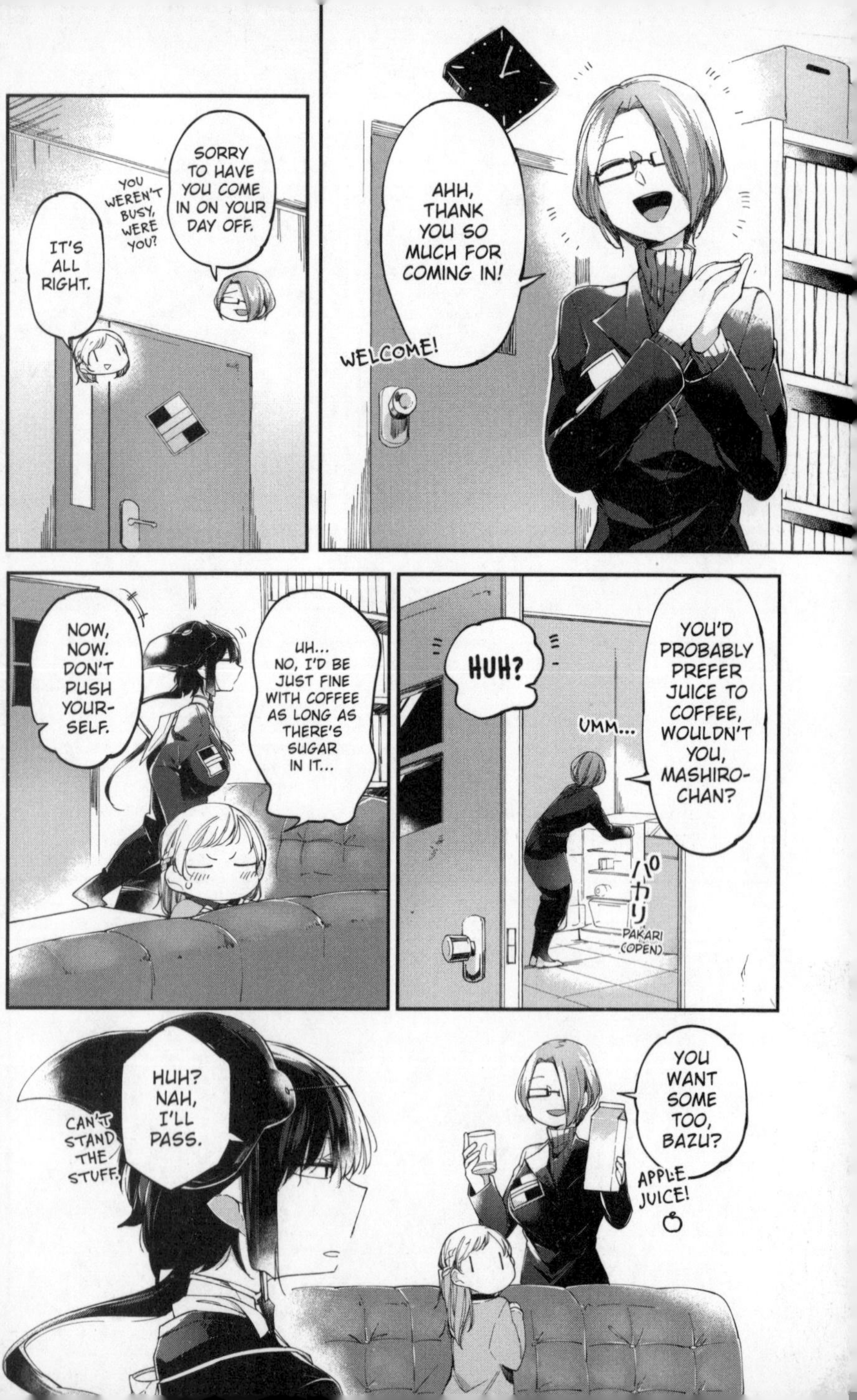
AHH, THANK YOU SO MUCH FOR COMING IN!
WELCOME!
SORRY TO HAVE YOU COME IN ON YOUR DAY OFF.
YOU WEREN'T BUSY, WERE YOU?
IT'S ALL RIGHT.
YOU'D PROBABLY PREFER JUICE TO COFFEE, WOULDN'T YOU, MASHIRO-CHAN?
HUH?
UMM...
パカリ
PAKARI (OPEN)
UH... NO, I'D BE JUST FINE WITH COFFEE AS LONG AS THERE'S SUGAR IN IT...
NOW, NOW. DON'T PUSH YOUR-SELF.
YOU WANT SOME TOO, BAZU?
APPLE JUICE!
HUH? NAH, I'LL PASS.
CAN'T STAND THE STUFF.

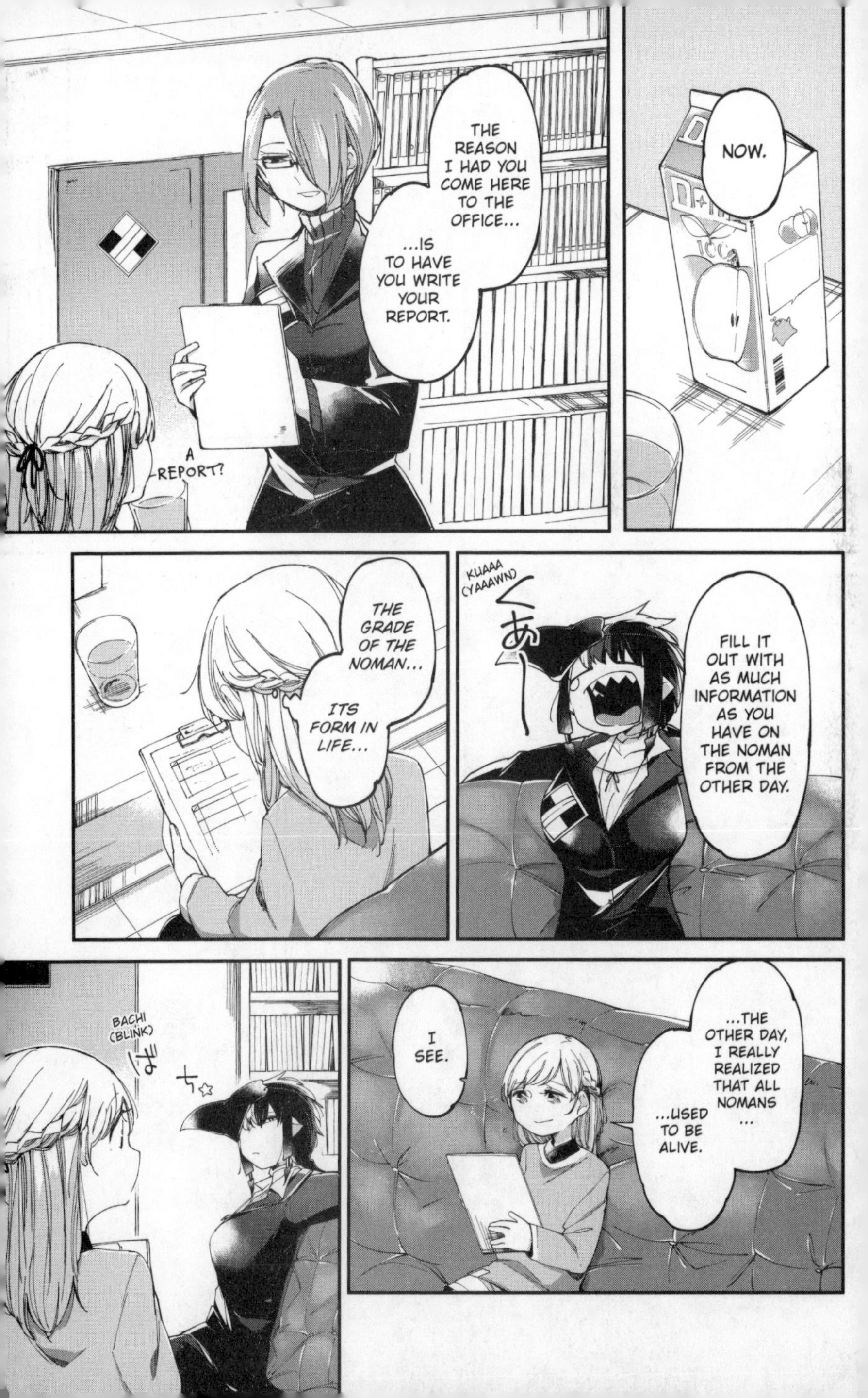
NOW.
THE REASON I HAD YOU COME HERE TO THE OFFICE...
...IS TO HAVE YOU WRITE YOUR REPORT.
A REPORT?
KUAAA (YAAAWN)
FILL IT OUT WITH AS MUCH INFORMATION AS YOU HAVE ON THE NOMAN FROM THE OTHER DAY.
THE GRADE OF THE NOMAN...
ITS FORM IN LIFE...
...THE OTHER DAY, I REALLY REALIZED THAT ALL NOMANS ...
...USED TO BE ALIVE.
I SEE.
BACHI (BLINK)

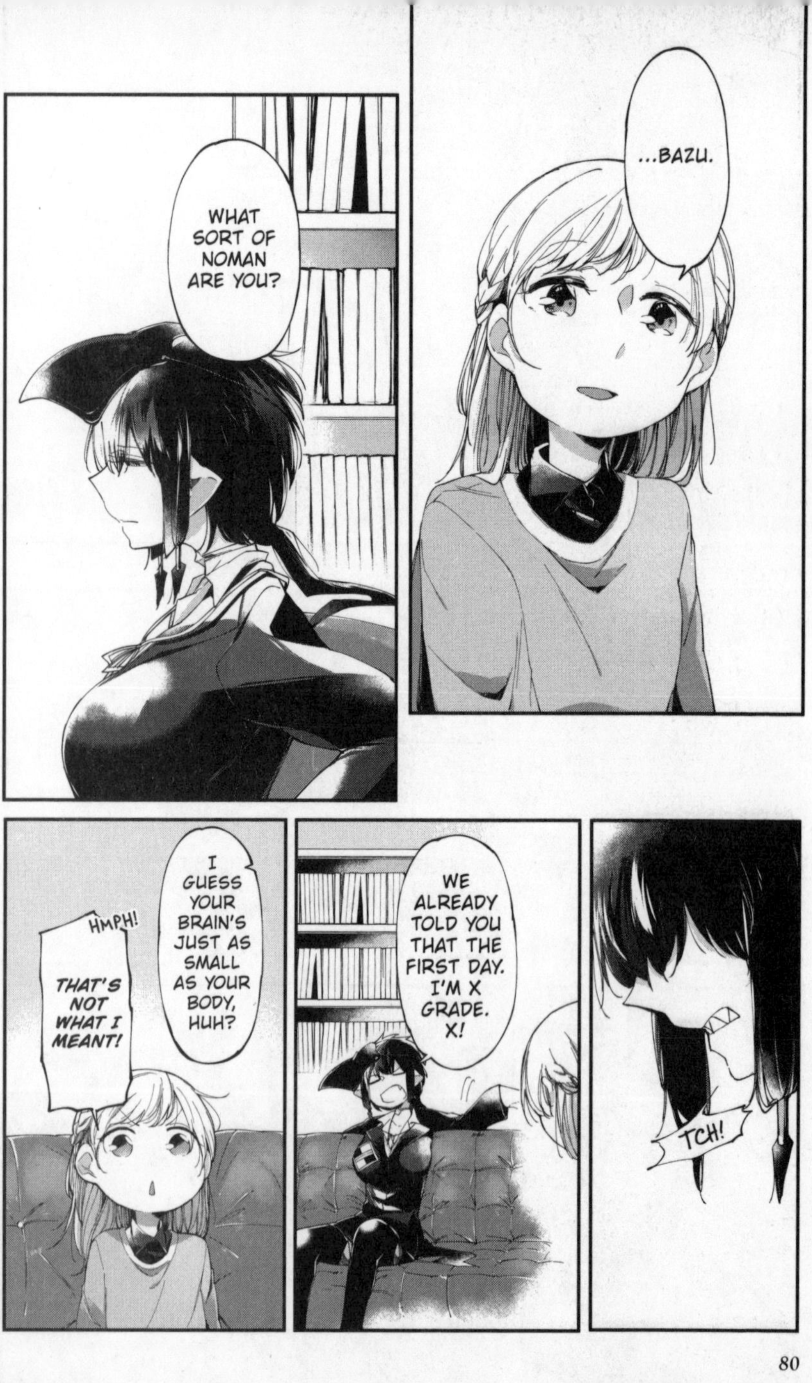
...BAZU.
WHAT SORT OF NOMAN ARE YOU?
TCH!
WE ALREADY TOLD YOU THAT THE FIRST DAY. I'M X GRADE. X!
I GUESS YOUR BRAIN'S JUST AS SMALL AS YOUR BODY, HUH?
HMPH!
THAT'S NOT WHAT I MEANT!

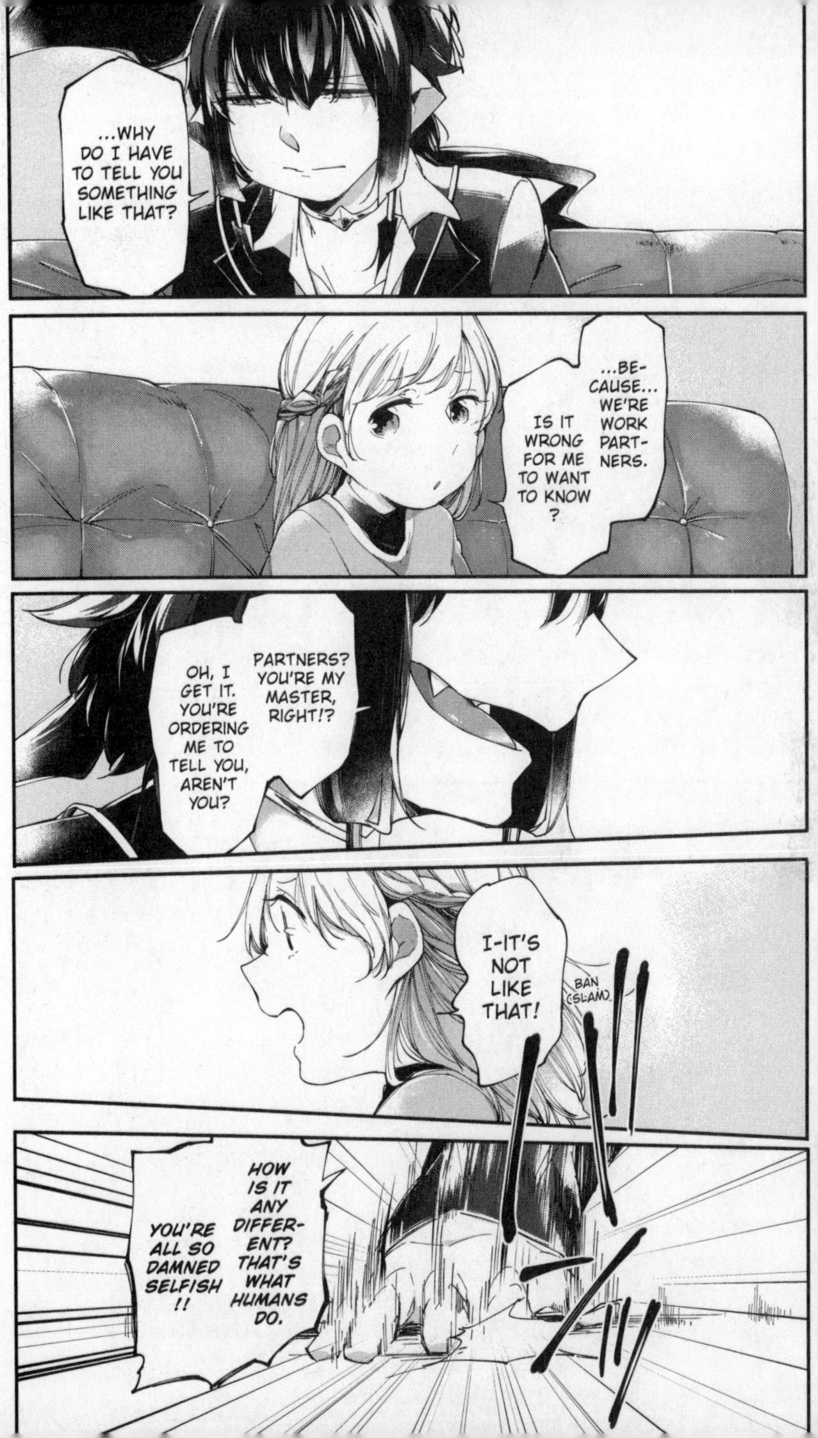
...WHY DO I HAVE TO TELL YOU SOMETHING LIKE THAT?
...BE-CAUSE... WE'RE WORK PART-NERS.
IS IT WRONG FOR ME TO WANT TO KNOW?
PARTNERS? YOU'RE MY MASTER, RIGHT!?
OH, I GET IT. YOU'RE ORDERING ME TO TELL YOU, AREN'T YOU?
I-IT'S NOT LIKE THAT!
BAN (SLAM)
HOW IS IT ANY DIFFER-ENT? THAT'S WHAT HUMANS DO.
YOU'RE ALL SO DAMNED SELFISH!!

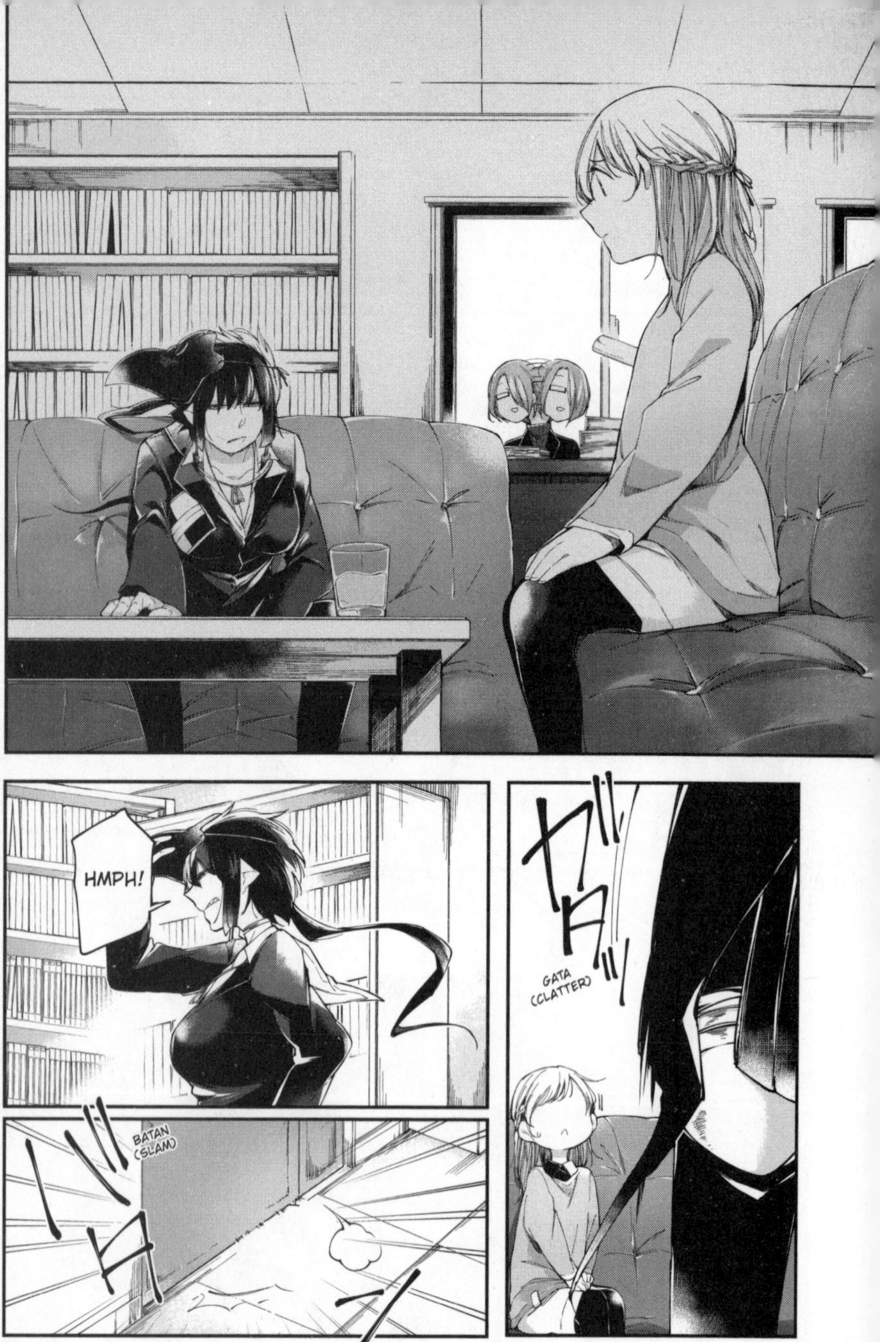
GATA (CLATTER)
HMPH!
BATAN (SLAM)

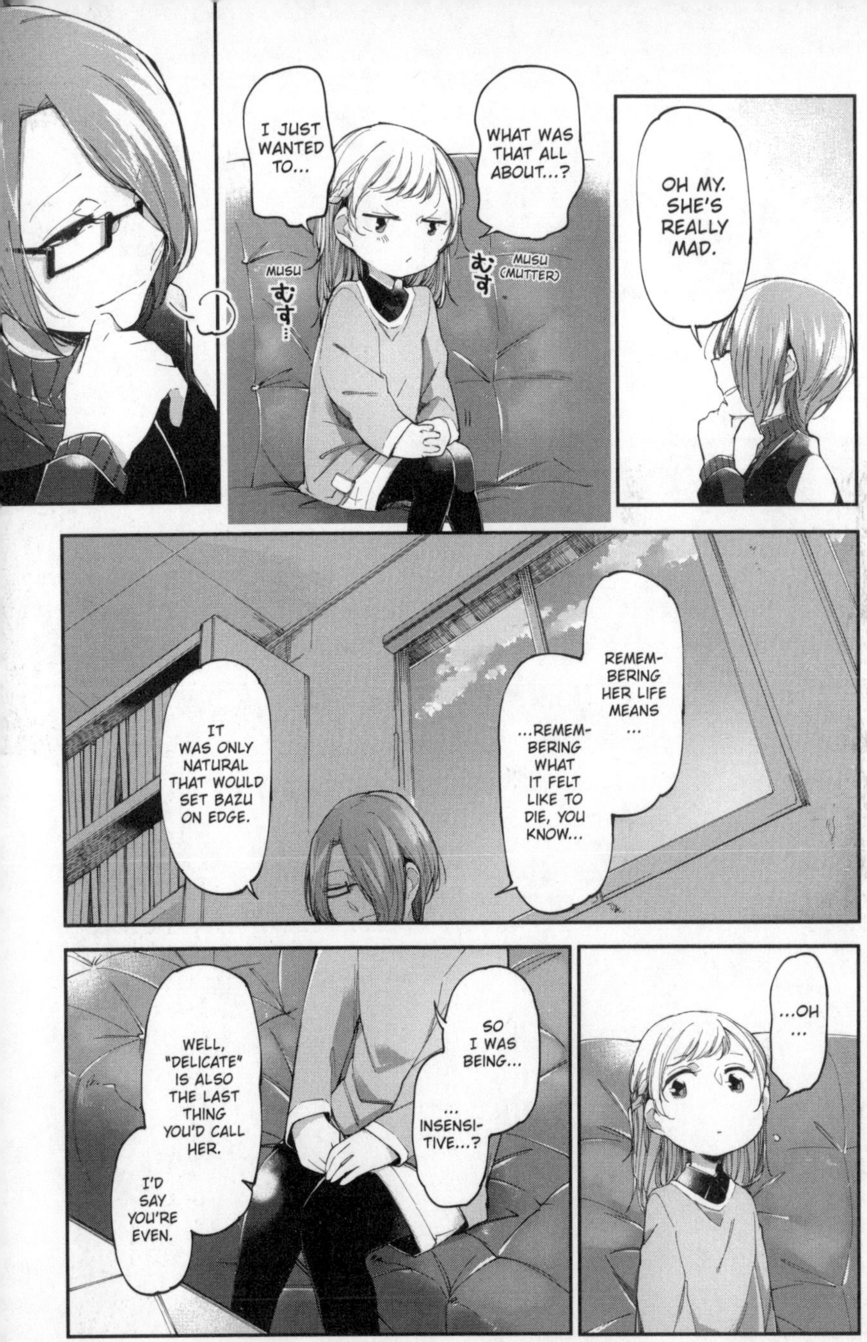
OH MY. SHE'S REALLY MAD.
WHAT WAS THAT ALL ABOUT...?
I JUST WANTED TO...
むす MUSU (MUTTER)
MUSU むす…
REMEMBERING HER LIFE MEANS...
...REMEMBERING WHAT IT FELT LIKE TO DIE, YOU KNOW...
IT WAS ONLY NATURAL THAT WOULD SET BAZU ON EDGE.
...OH...
SO I WAS BEING...
...INSENSITIVE...?
WELL, "DELICATE" IS ALSO THE LAST THING YOU'D CALL HER.
I'D SAY YOU'RE EVEN.

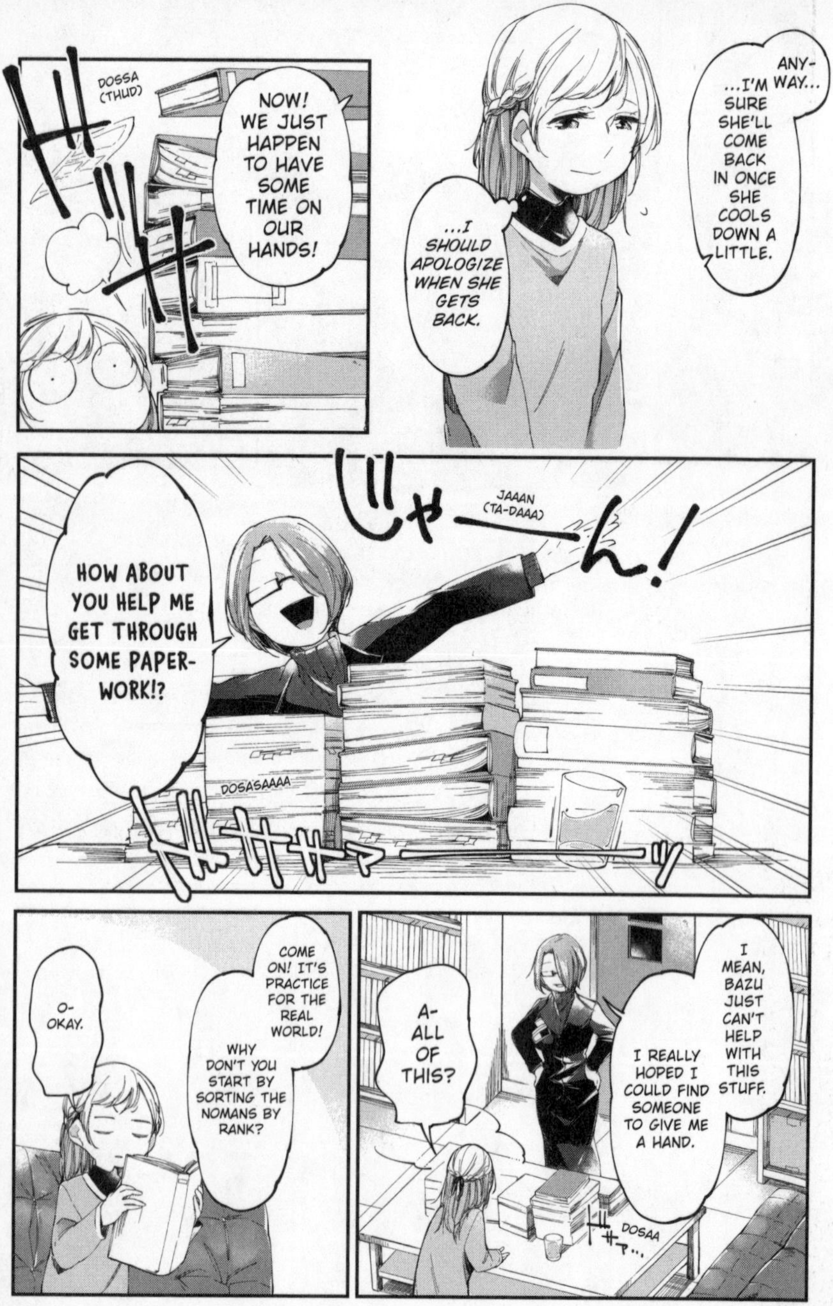
ANY-WAY... ...I'M SURE SHE'LL COME BACK IN ONCE SHE COOLS DOWN A LITTLE.
...I SHOULD APOLOGIZE WHEN SHE GETS BACK.
NOW! WE JUST HAPPEN TO HAVE SOME TIME ON OUR HANDS!
DOSSA (THUD)
JAAAN (TA-DAAA)
HOW ABOUT YOU HELP ME GET THROUGH SOME PAPER-WORK!?
DOSASAAAA
I MEAN, BAZU JUST CAN'T HELP WITH THIS STUFF.
I REALLY HOPED I COULD FIND SOMEONE TO GIVE ME A HAND.
A-ALL OF THIS?
DOSAA
COME ON! IT'S PRACTICE FOR THE REAL WORLD!
WHY DON'T YOU START BY SORTING THE NOMANS BY RANK?
O-OKAY.

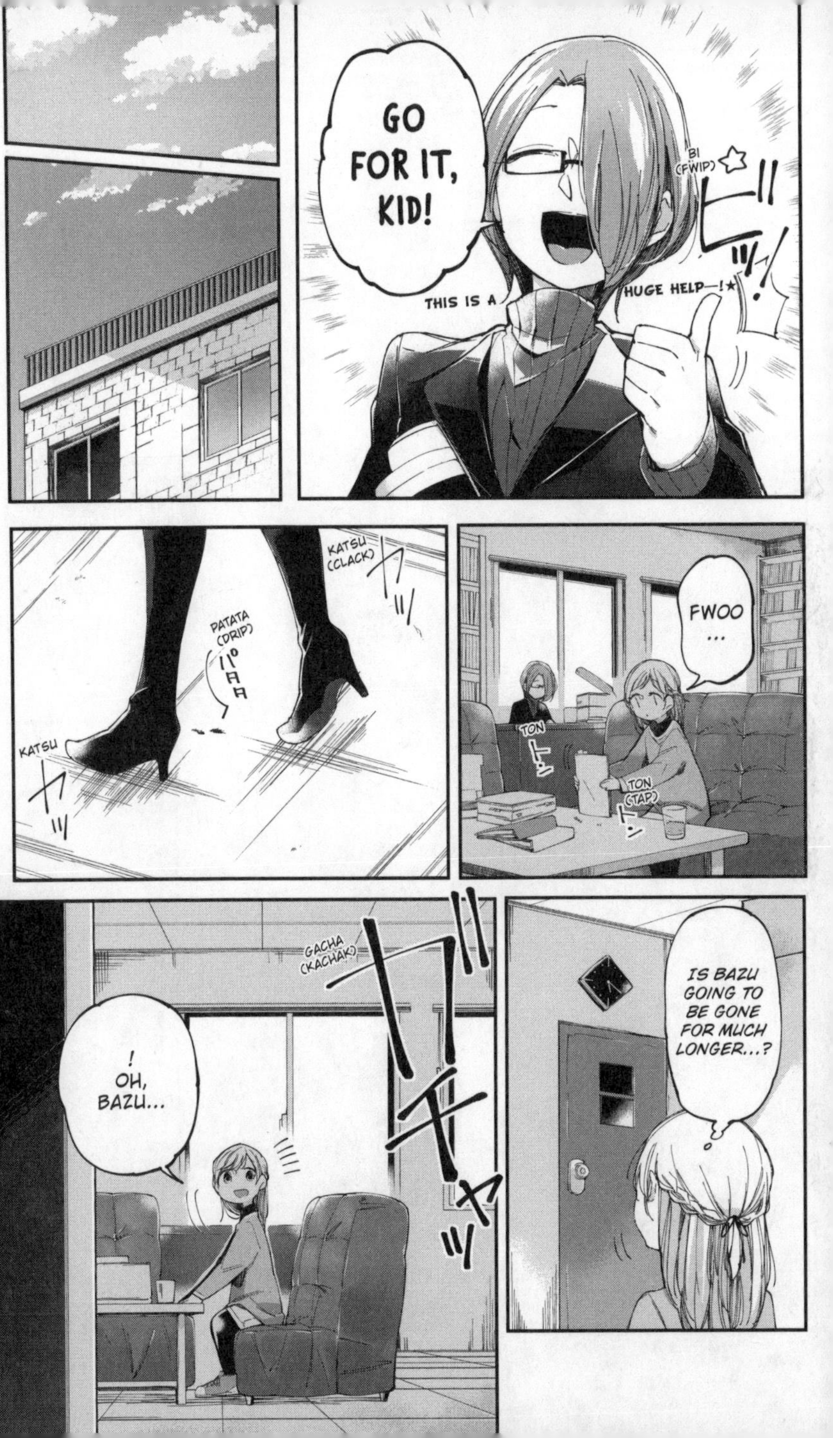
GO FOR IT, KID!
BI (FWIP)
THIS IS A HUGE HELP—!★
FWOO ...
TON
TON (TAP)
KATSU (CLACK)
PATATA (DRIP)
KATSU
IS BAZU GOING TO BE GONE FOR MUCH LONGER...?
GACHA (KACHAK)
! OH, BAZU...

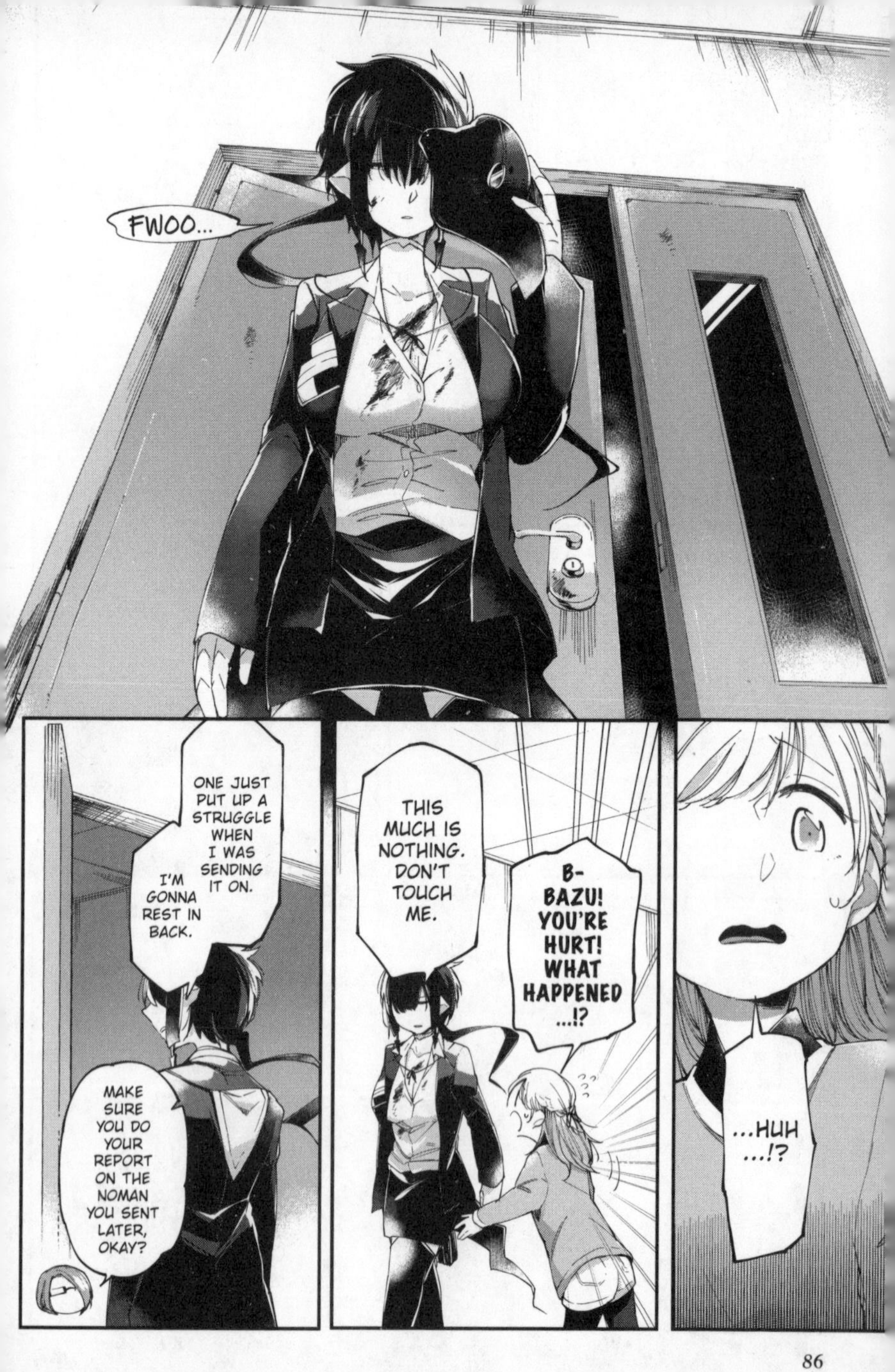
FWOO...
...HUH ...!?
B-BAZU! YOU'RE HURT! WHAT HAPPENED ...!?
THIS MUCH IS NOTHING. DON'T TOUCH ME.
ONE JUST PUT UP A STRUGGLE WHEN I WAS SENDING IT ON.
I'M GONNA REST IN BACK.
MAKE SURE YOU DO YOUR REPORT ON THE NOMAN YOU SENT LATER, OKAY?

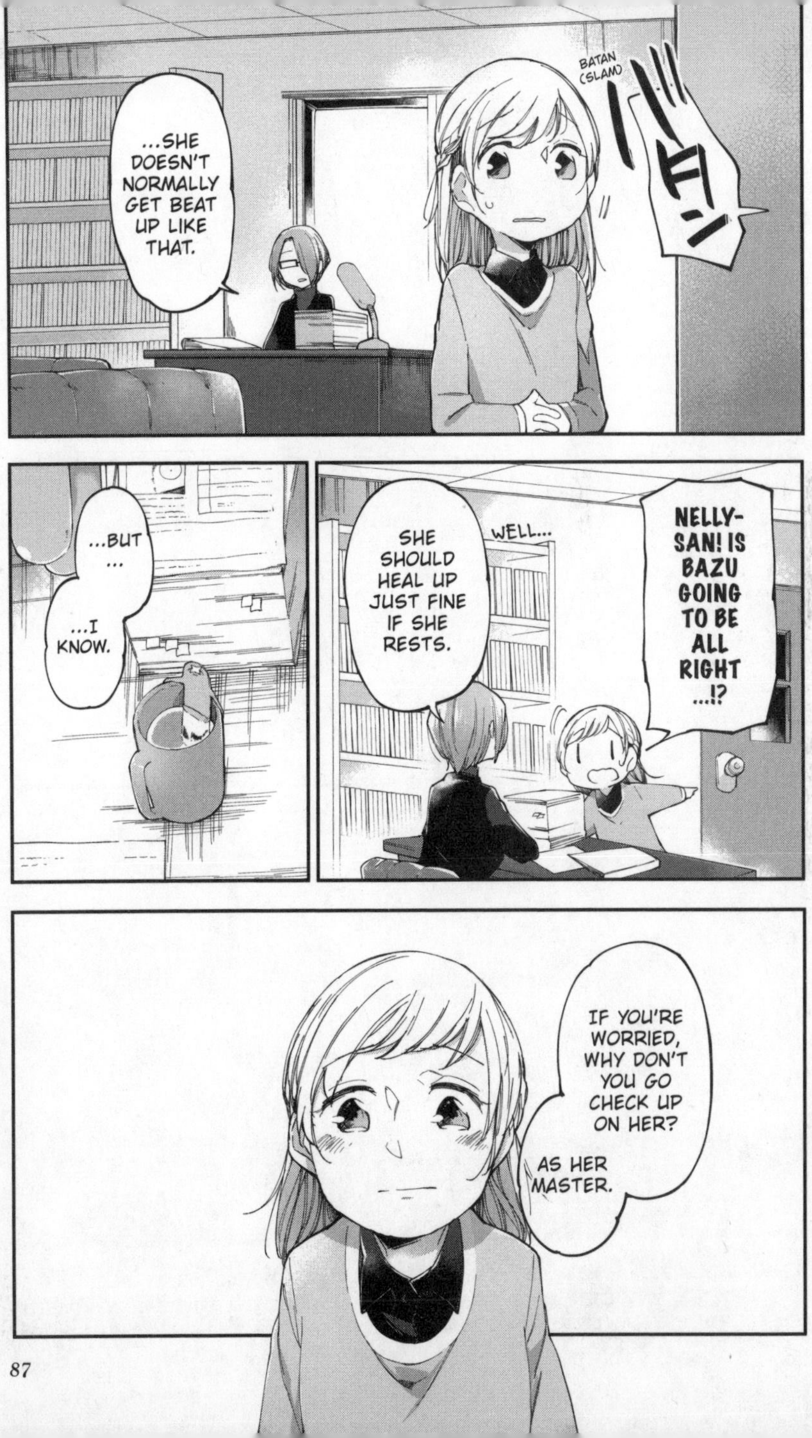
BATAN (SLAM)
バタン
...SHE DOESN'T NORMALLY GET BEAT UP LIKE THAT.
NELLY-SAN! IS BAZU GOING TO BE ALL RIGHT ...!?
WELL...
SHE SHOULD HEAL UP JUST FINE IF SHE RESTS.
...BUT ...
...I KNOW.
IF YOU'RE WORRIED, WHY DON'T YOU GO CHECK UP ON HER?
AS HER MASTER.

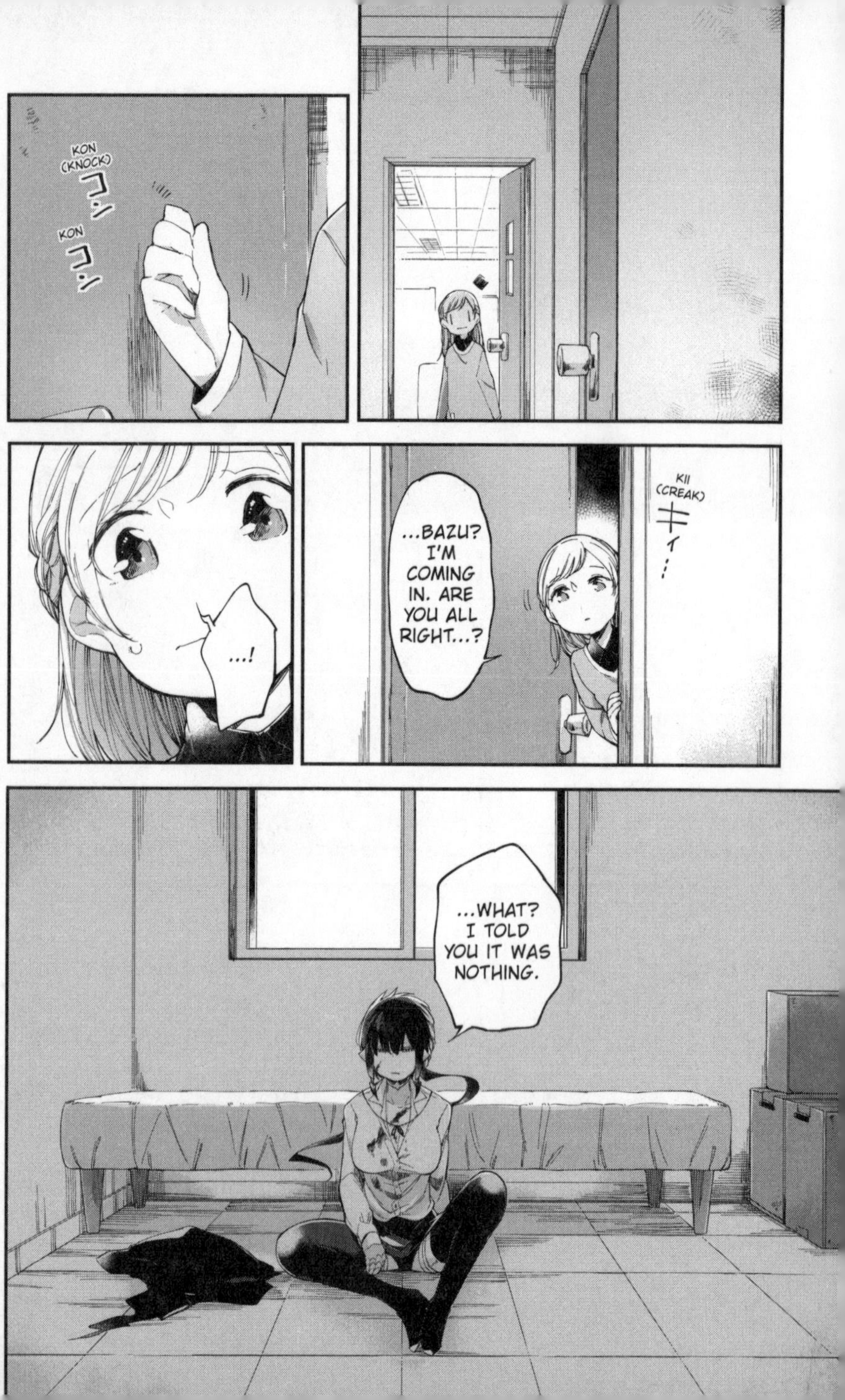
KON (KNOCK)
コン
KON
コン
KII (CREAK)
キイ…
...BAZU? I'M COMING IN. ARE YOU ALL RIGHT...?
...!
...WHAT? I TOLD YOU IT WAS NOTHING.

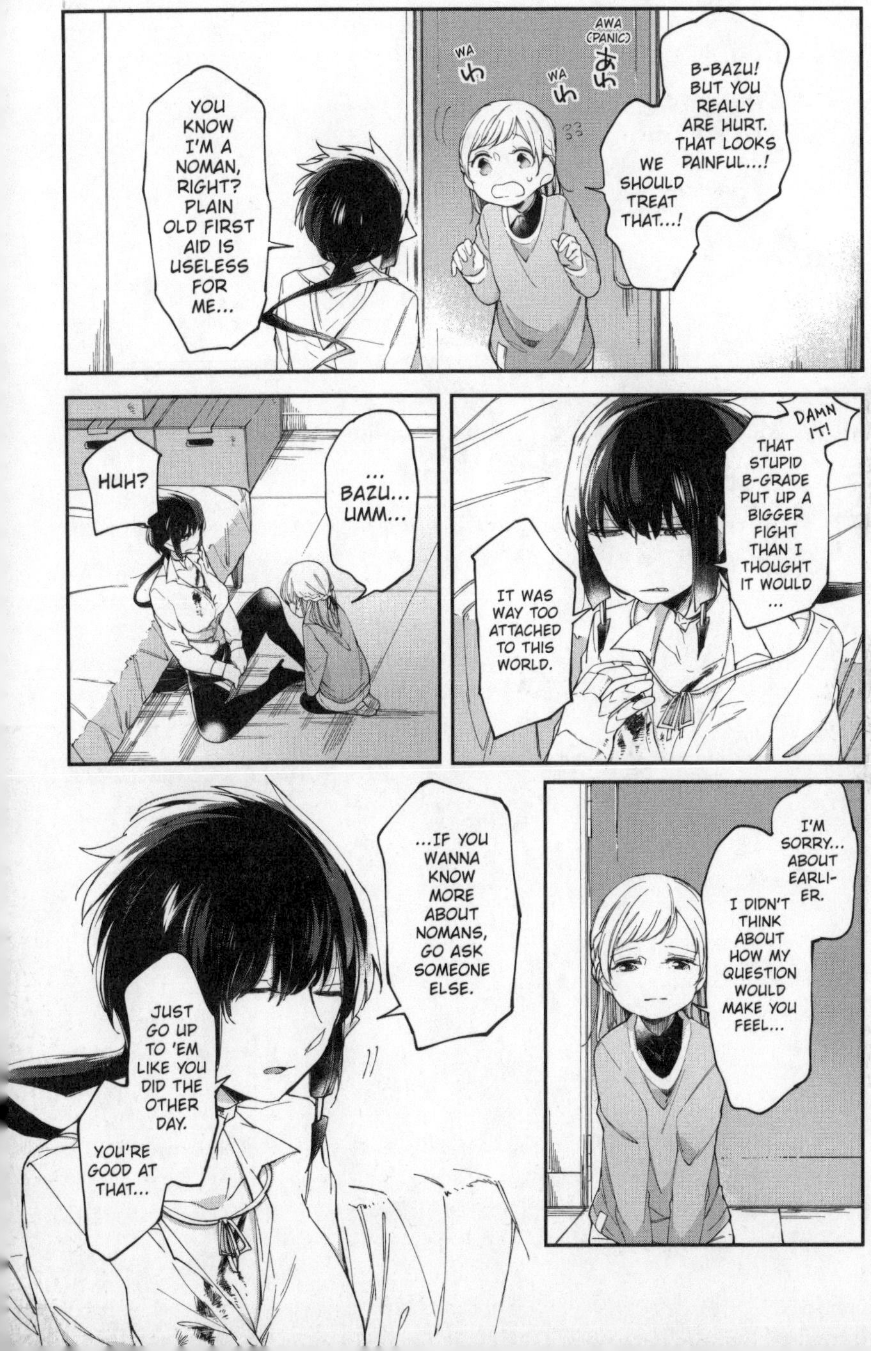
AWA (PANIC)
あわ
WA
わ
WA
わ
B-BAZU! BUT YOU REALLY ARE HURT. THAT LOOKS PAINFUL...!
WE SHOULD TREAT THAT...!
YOU KNOW I'M A NOMAN, RIGHT? PLAIN OLD FIRST AID IS USELESS FOR ME...
DAMN IT!
THAT STUPID B-GRADE PUT UP A BIGGER FIGHT THAN I THOUGHT IT WOULD ...
IT WAS WAY TOO ATTACHED TO THIS WORLD.
... BAZU... UMM...
HUH?
I'M SORRY... ABOUT EARLI-ER.
I DIDN'T THINK ABOUT HOW MY QUESTION WOULD MAKE YOU FEEL...
...IF YOU WANNA KNOW MORE ABOUT NOMANS, GO ASK SOMEONE ELSE.
JUST GO UP TO 'EM LIKE YOU DID THE OTHER DAY.
YOU'RE GOOD AT THAT...

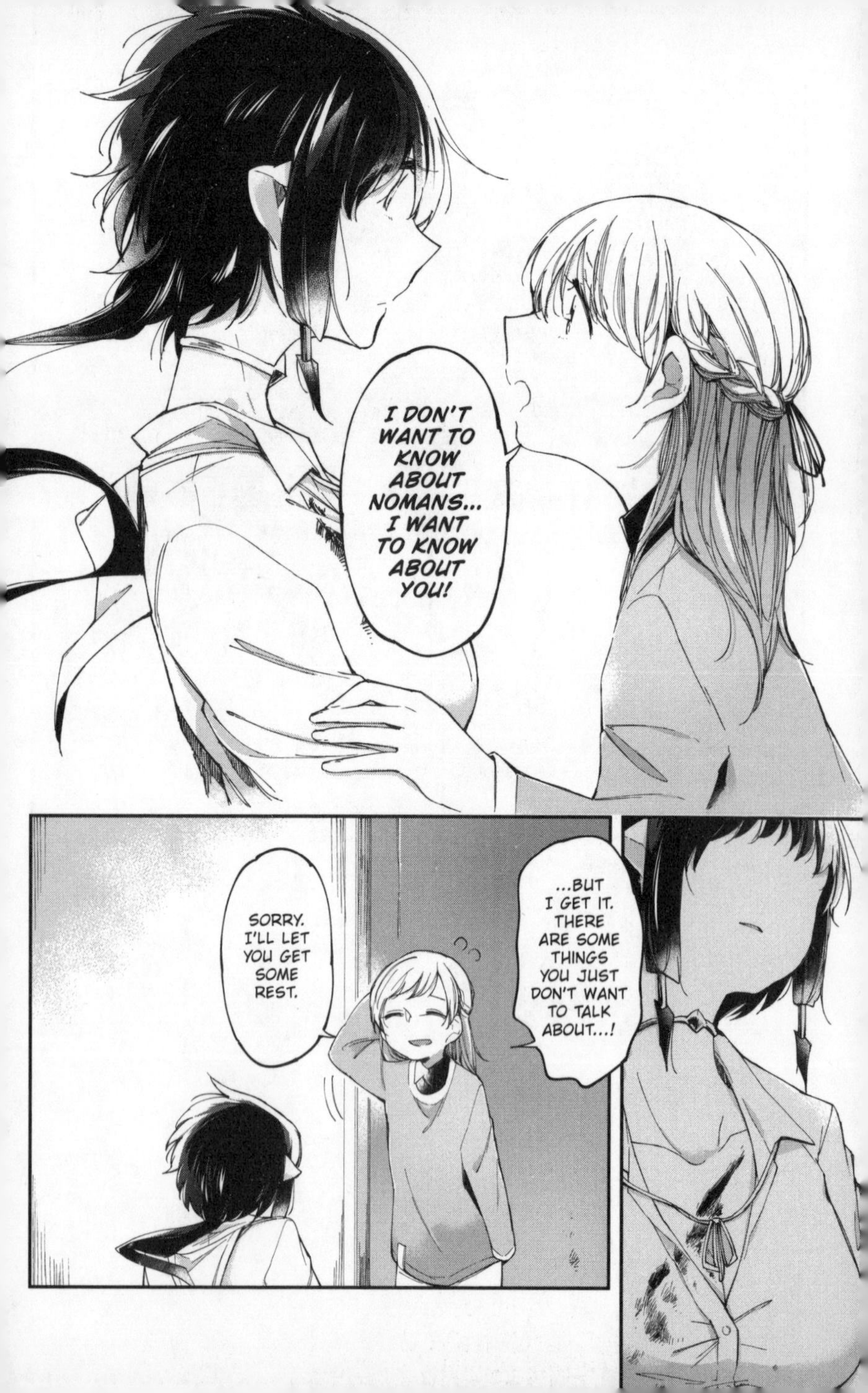
I DON'T WANT TO KNOW ABOUT NOMANS... I WANT TO KNOW ABOUT YOU!
...BUT I GET IT. THERE ARE SOME THINGS YOU JUST DON'T WANT TO TALK ABOUT...!
SORRY. I'LL LET YOU GET SOME REST.

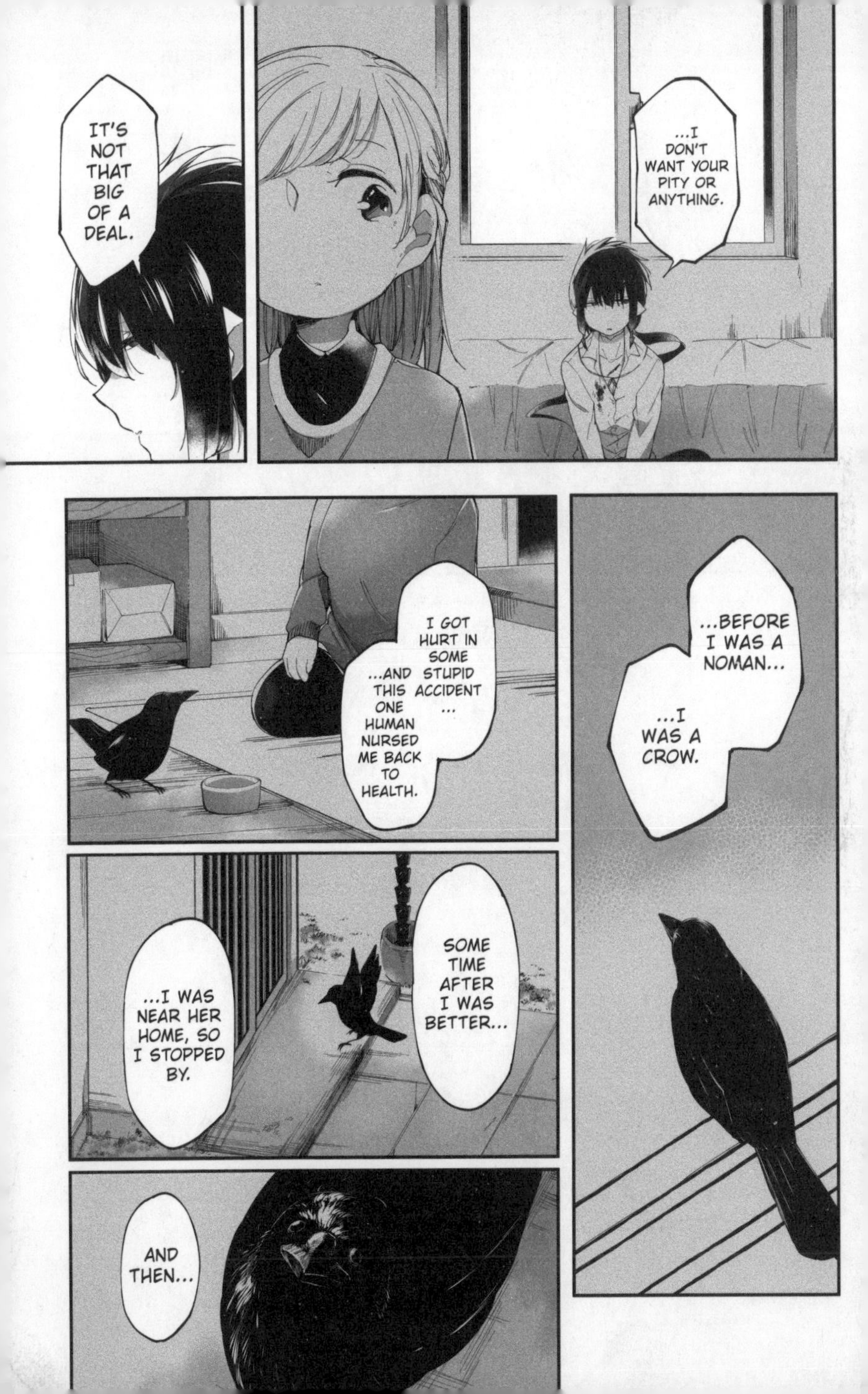
...I DON'T WANT YOUR PITY OR ANYTHING.
IT'S NOT THAT BIG OF A DEAL.
...BEFORE I WAS A NOMAN...
...I WAS A CROW.
I GOT HURT IN SOME STUPID ACCIDENT...
...AND THIS ONE HUMAN NURSED ME BACK TO HEALTH.
SOME TIME AFTER I WAS BETTER...
...I WAS NEAR HER HOME, SO I STOPPED BY.
AND THEN...

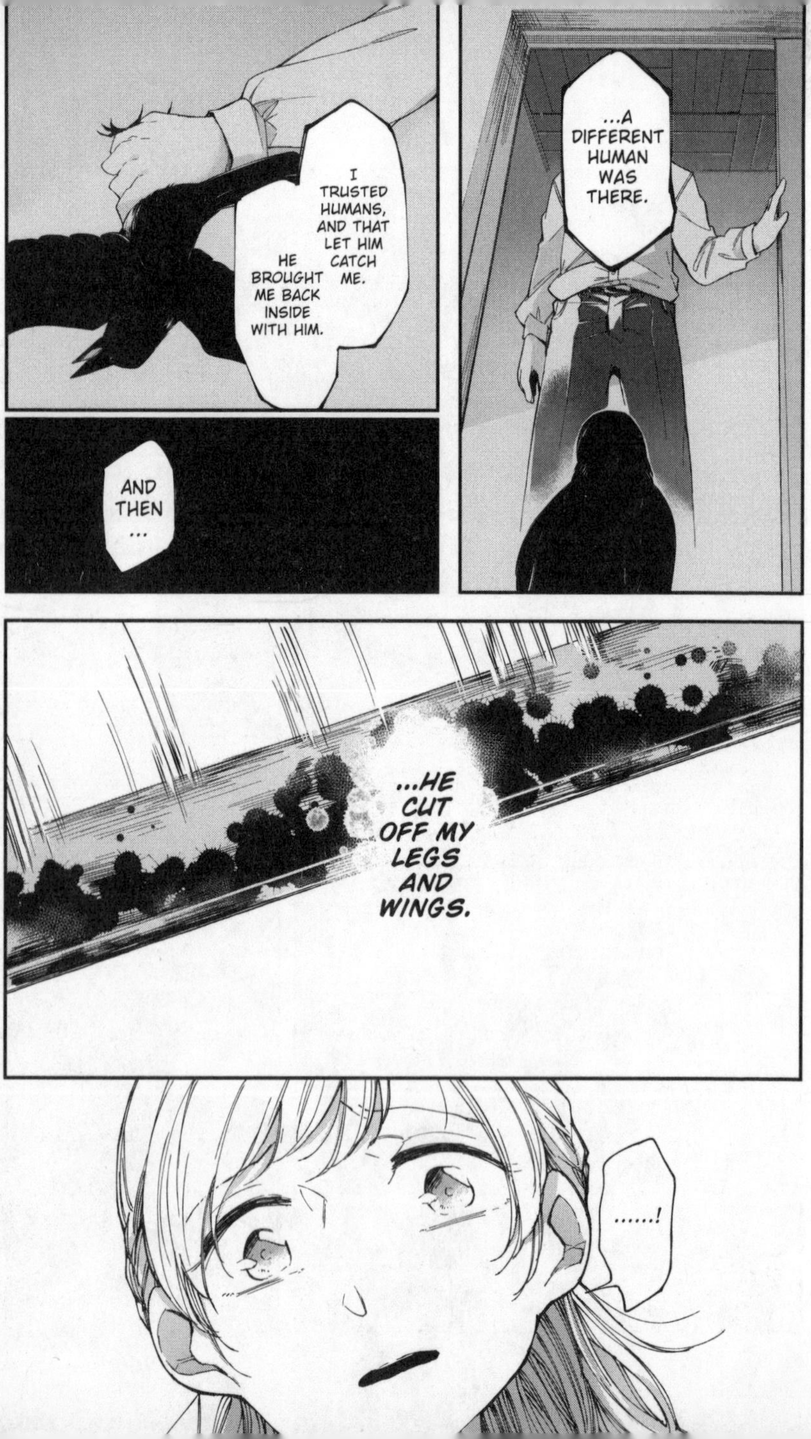
...A DIFFERENT HUMAN WAS THERE.
I TRUSTED HUMANS, AND THAT LET HIM CATCH ME.
HE BROUGHT ME BACK INSIDE WITH HIM.
AND THEN ...
...HE CUT OFF MY LEGS AND WINGS.
......!

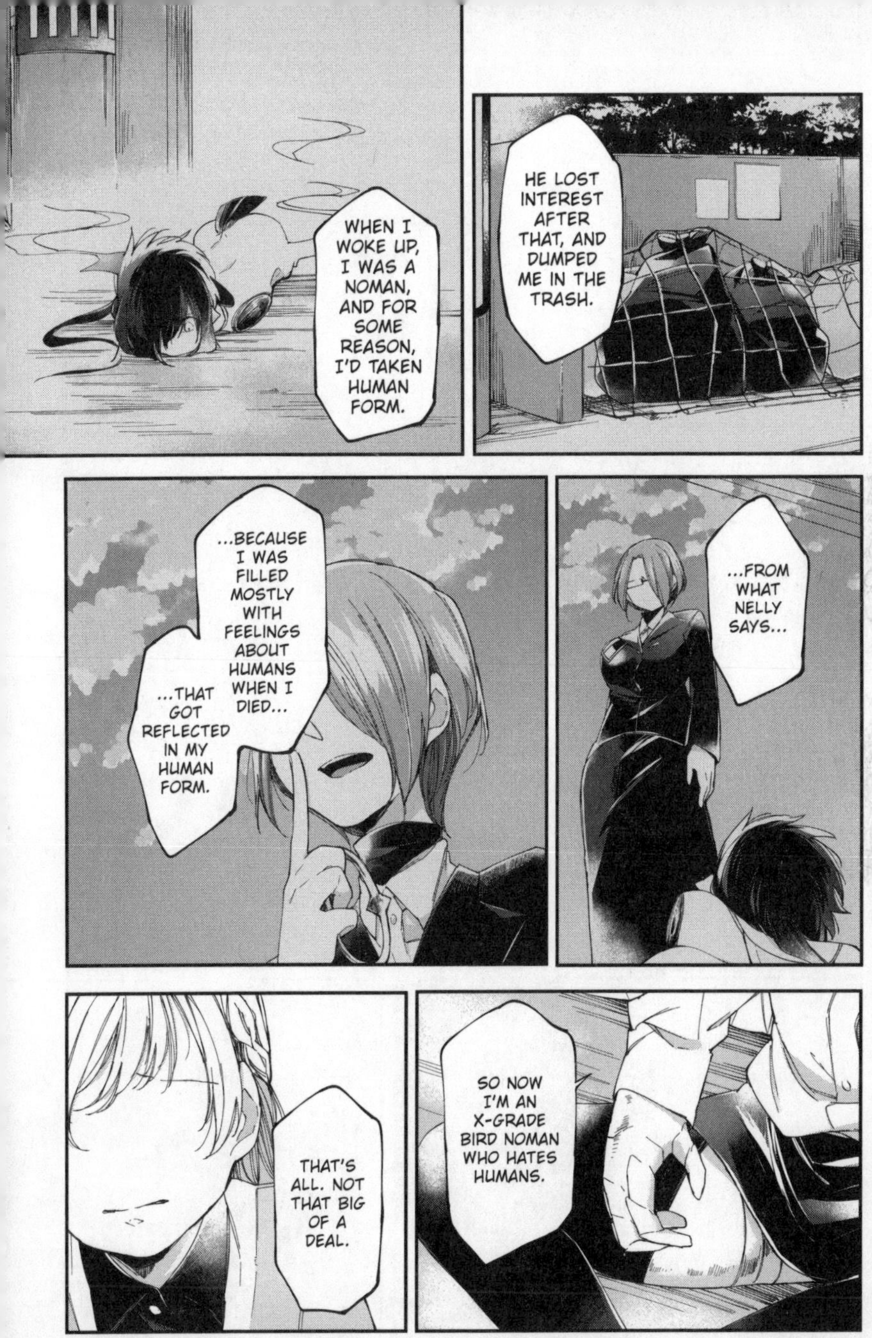
HE LOST INTEREST AFTER THAT, AND DUMPED ME IN THE TRASH.
WHEN I WOKE UP, I WAS A NOMAN, AND FOR SOME REASON, I'D TAKEN HUMAN FORM.
...FROM WHAT NELLY SAYS...
...BECAUSE I WAS FILLED MOSTLY WITH FEELINGS ABOUT HUMANS WHEN I DIED...
...THAT GOT REFLECTED IN MY HUMAN FORM.
SO NOW I'M AN X-GRADE BIRD NOMAN WHO HATES HUMANS.
THAT'S ALL. NOT THAT BIG OF A DEAL.

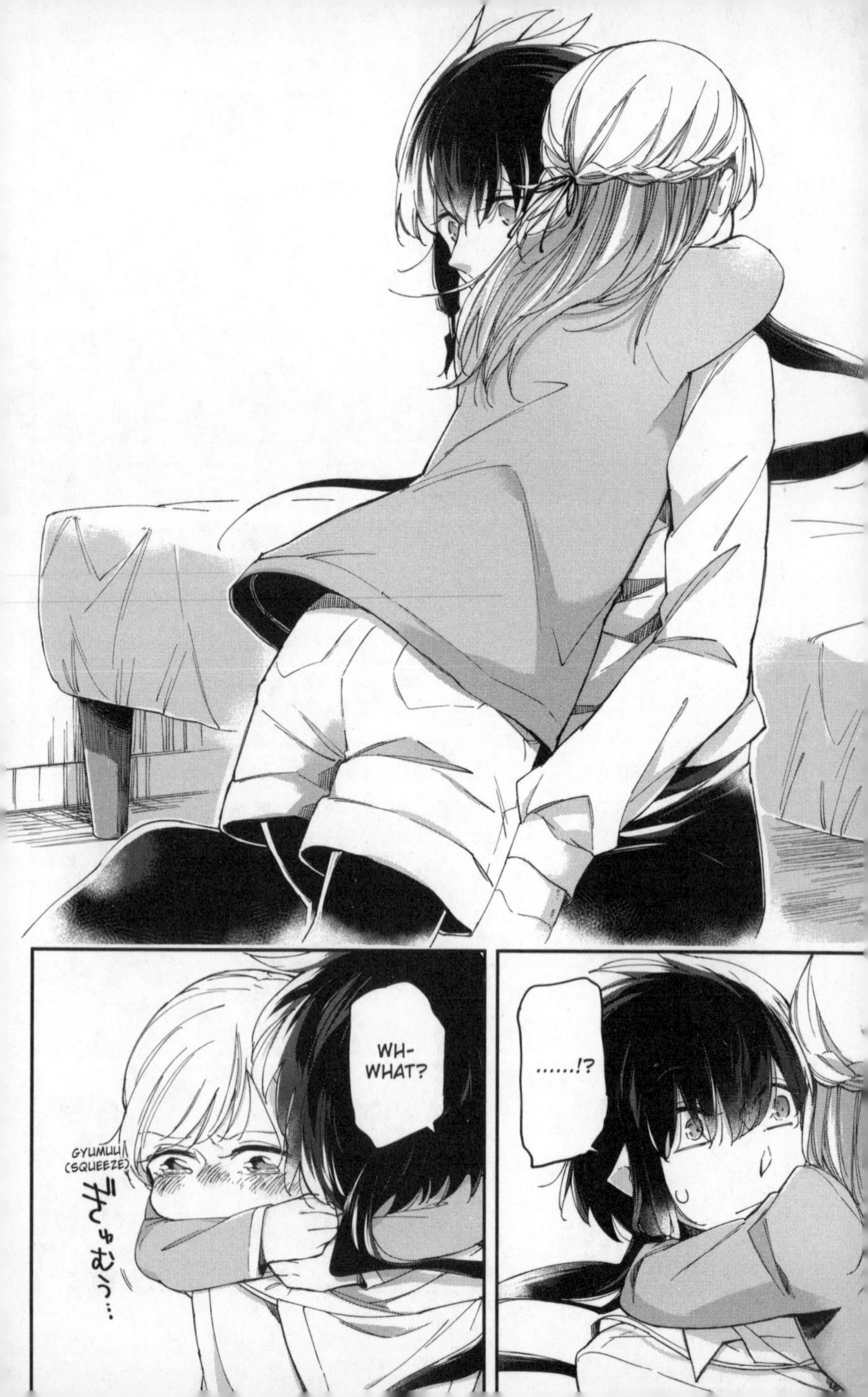
......!?
WH-
WHAT?
GYUMUU
(SQUEEZE)
ぎゅむぅ…

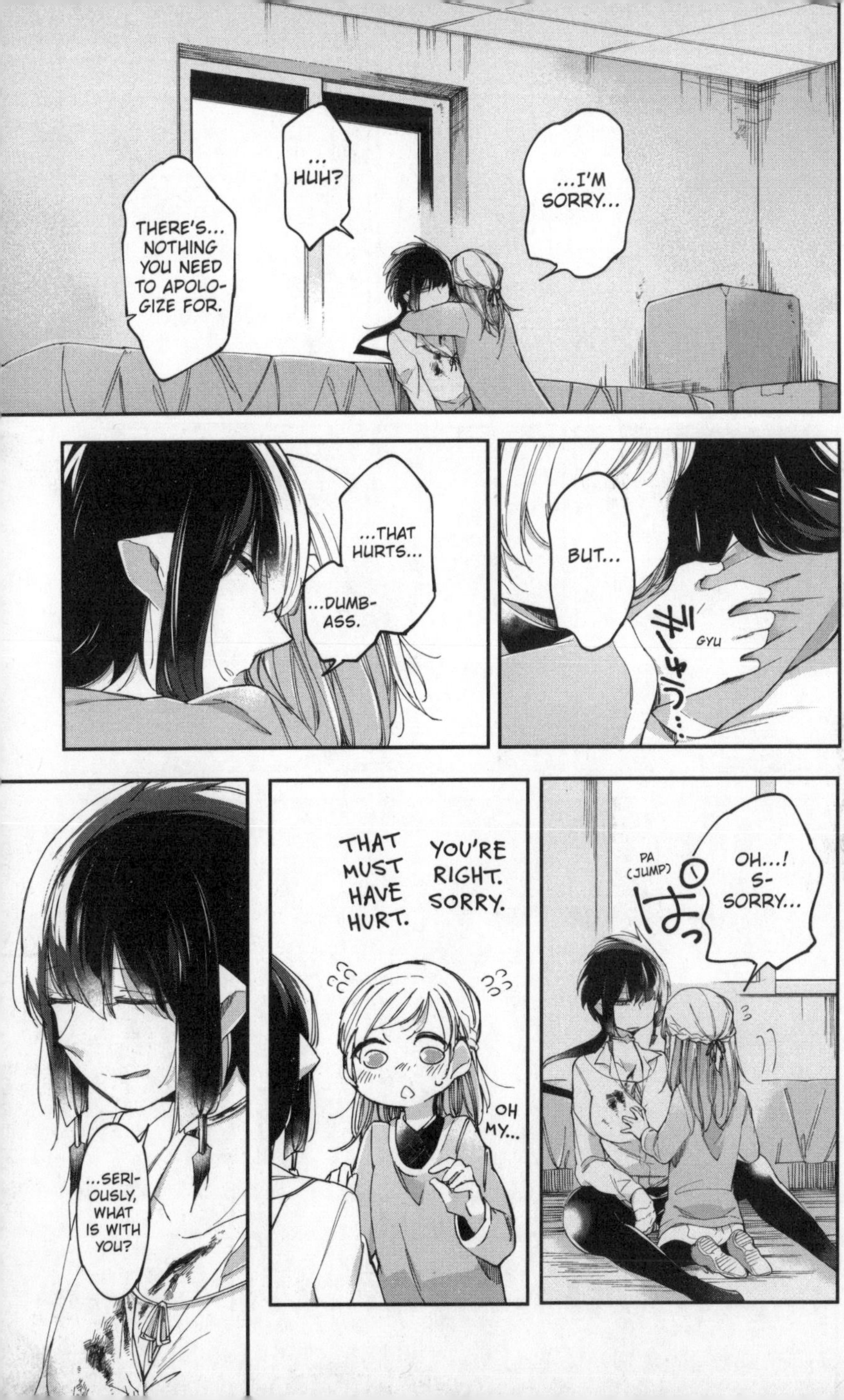
...I'M SORRY...
...
HUH?
THERE'S... NOTHING YOU NEED TO APOLOGIZE FOR.
BUT...
GYU
...THAT HURTS...
...DUMB-ASS.
PA (JUMP)
OH...! S-SORRY...
YOU'RE RIGHT. SORRY.
THAT MUST HAVE HURT.
OH MY...
...SERIOUSLY, WHAT IS WITH YOU?

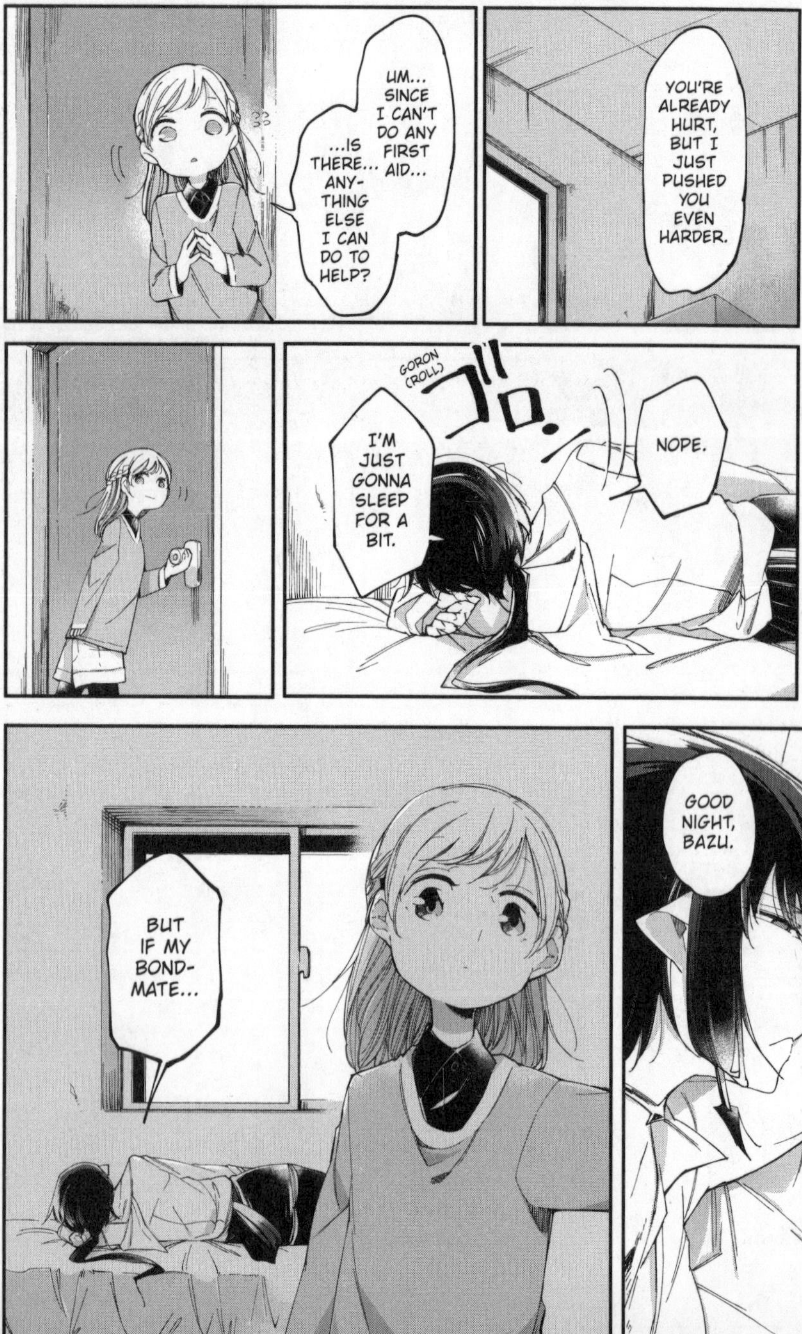
YOU'RE ALREADY HURT, BUT I JUST PUSHED YOU EVEN HARDER.
UM... SINCE I CAN'T DO ANY FIRST AID...
...IS THERE... ANYTHING ELSE I CAN DO TO HELP?
NOPE.
ゴロ
GORON (ROLL)
I'M JUST GONNA SLEEP FOR A BIT.
GOOD NIGHT, BAZU.
BUT IF MY BOND-MATE...

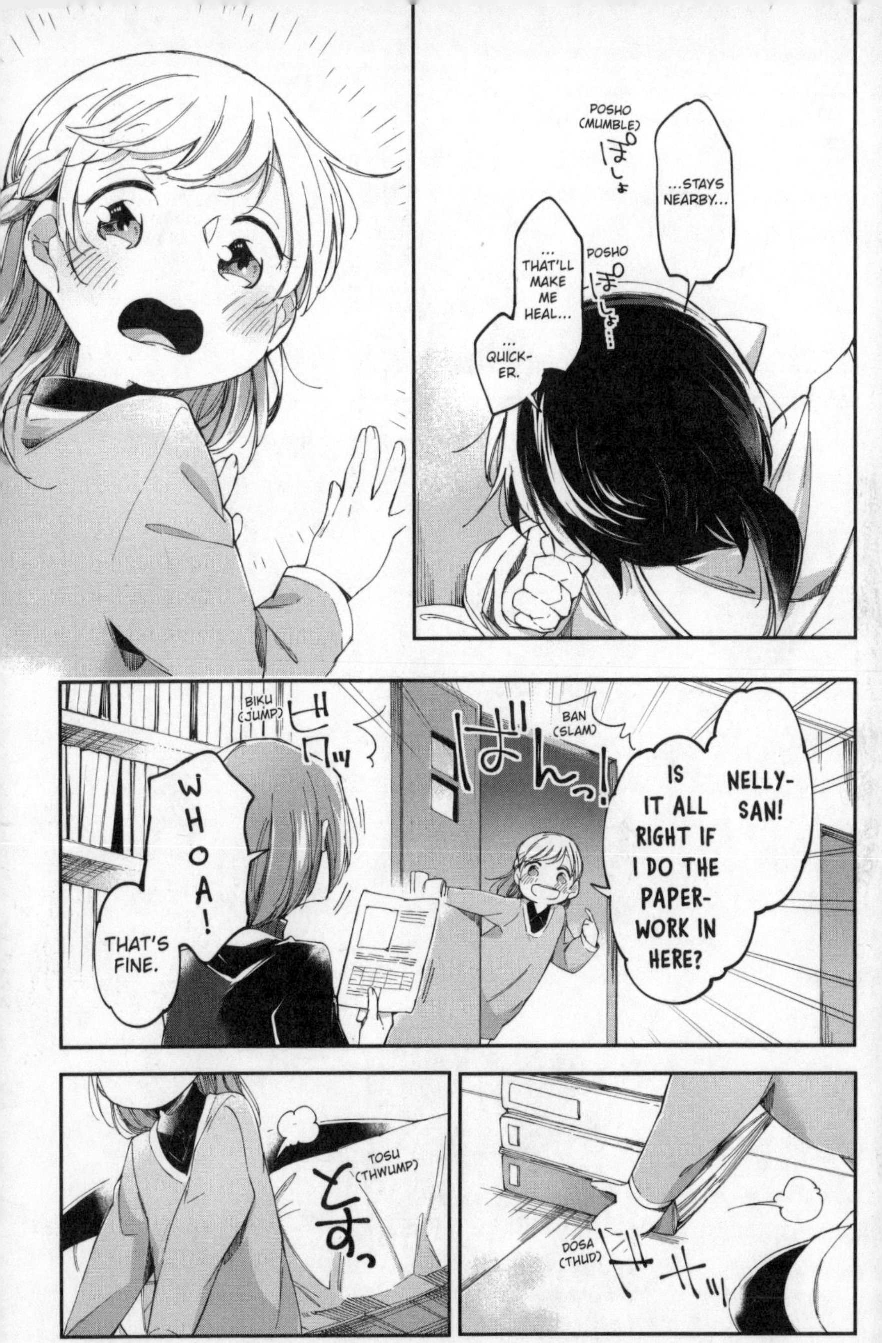
...STAYS NEARBY...
POSHO (MUMBLE)
ぽしょ
POSHO
ぽしょ...
...THAT'LL MAKE ME HEAL...
...QUICKER.
NELLY-SAN!
IS IT ALL RIGHT IF I DO THE PAPERWORK IN HERE?
BAN (SLAM)
ばんっ!
BIKU (JUMP)
ビクッ
WHOA!
THAT'S FINE.
DOSA (THUD)
ドサッ
TOSU (THWUMP)
とすっ

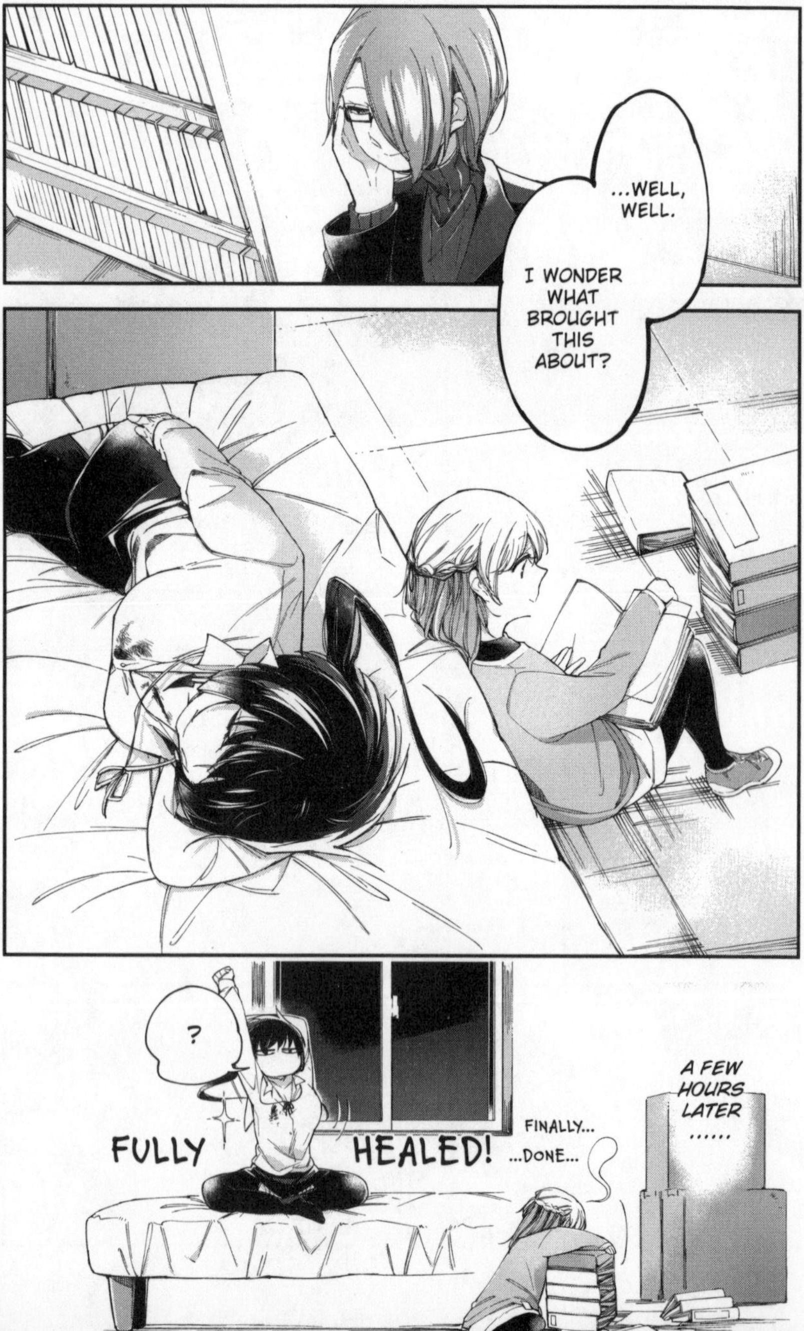
...WELL, WELL.
I WONDER WHAT BROUGHT THIS ABOUT?
A FEW HOURS LATER ......
FINALLY... ...DONE...
FULLY HEALED!
?

PUBLIC SERVANT

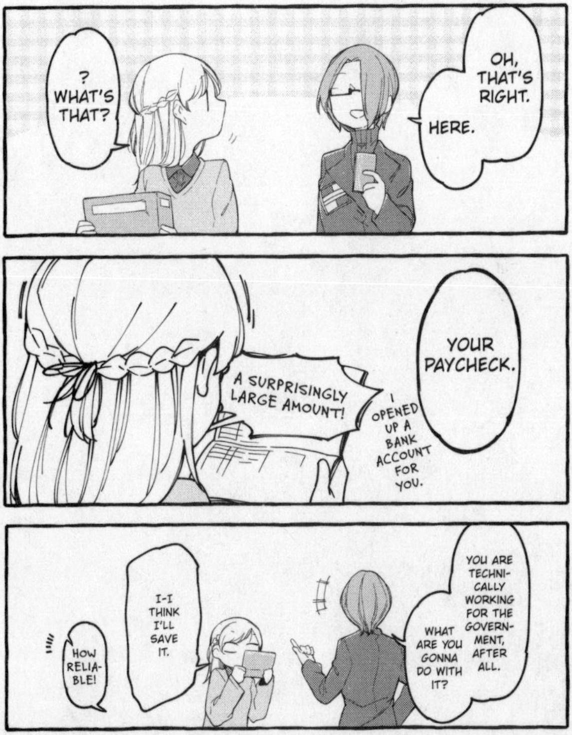
OH, THAT'S RIGHT.
HERE.
? WHAT'S THAT?
YOUR PAYCHECK.
I OPENED UP A BANK ACCOUNT FOR YOU.
A SURPRISINGLY LARGE AMOUNT!
YOU ARE TECHNICALLY WORKING FOR THE GOVERNMENT, AFTER ALL.
WHAT ARE YOU GONNA DO WITH IT?
I-I THINK I'LL SAVE IT.
HOW RELIABLE!

Dear *NOMAN*

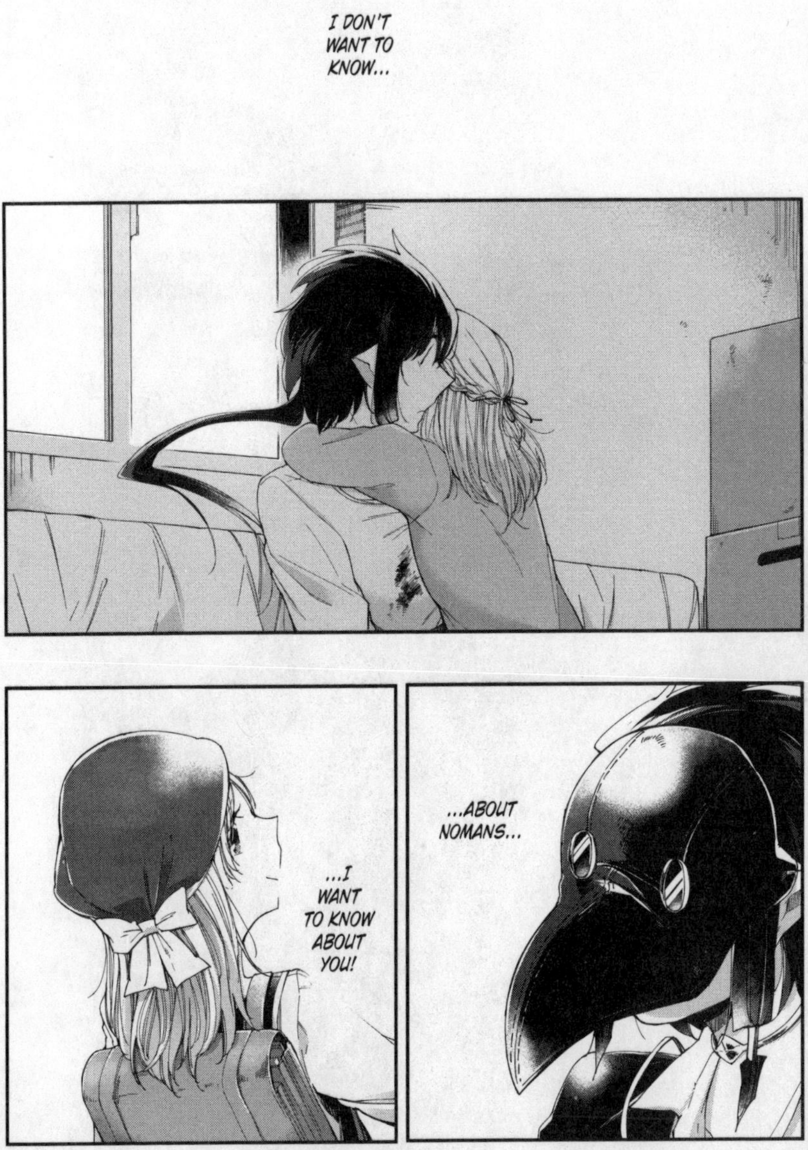
I DON'T WANT TO KNOW...
...ABOUT NOMANS...
...I WANT TO KNOW ABOUT YOU!

LETTER 5

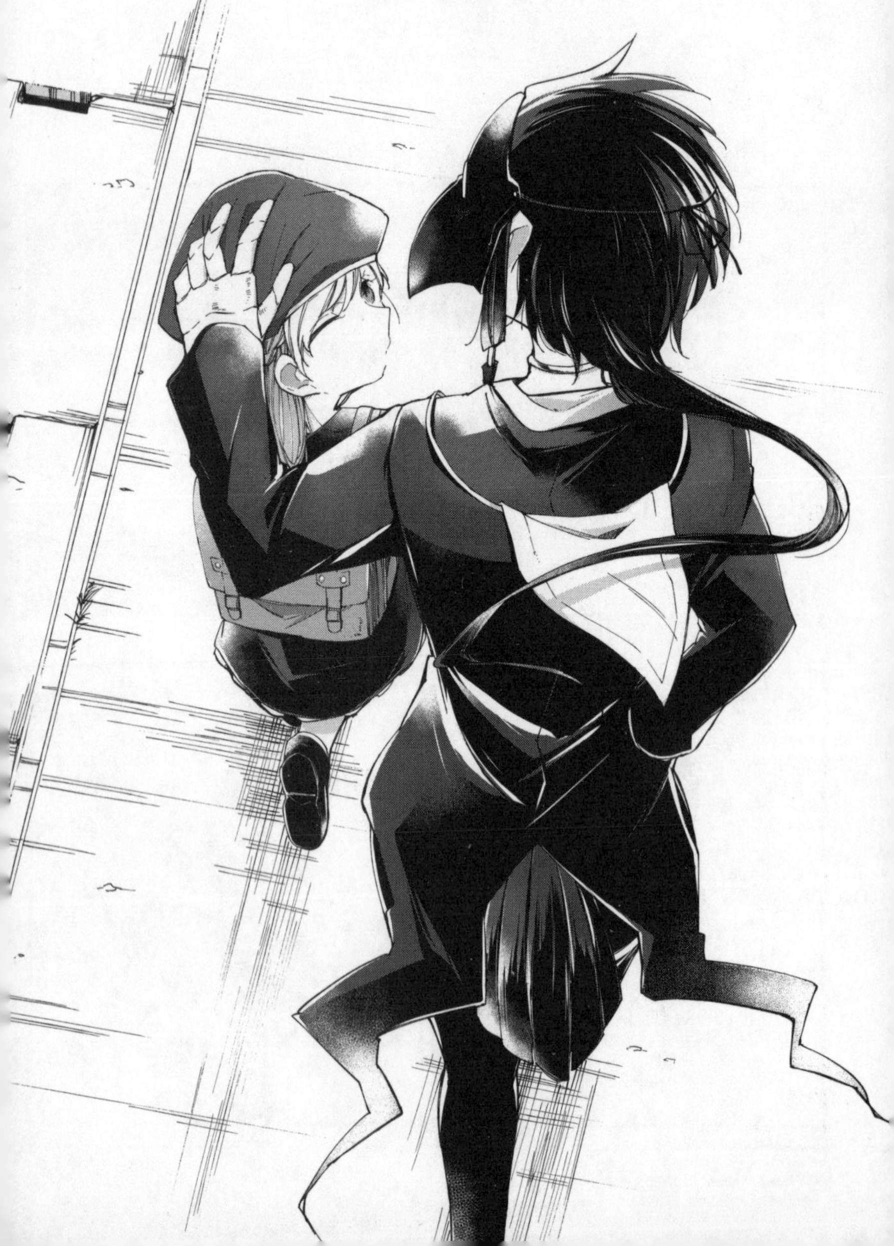

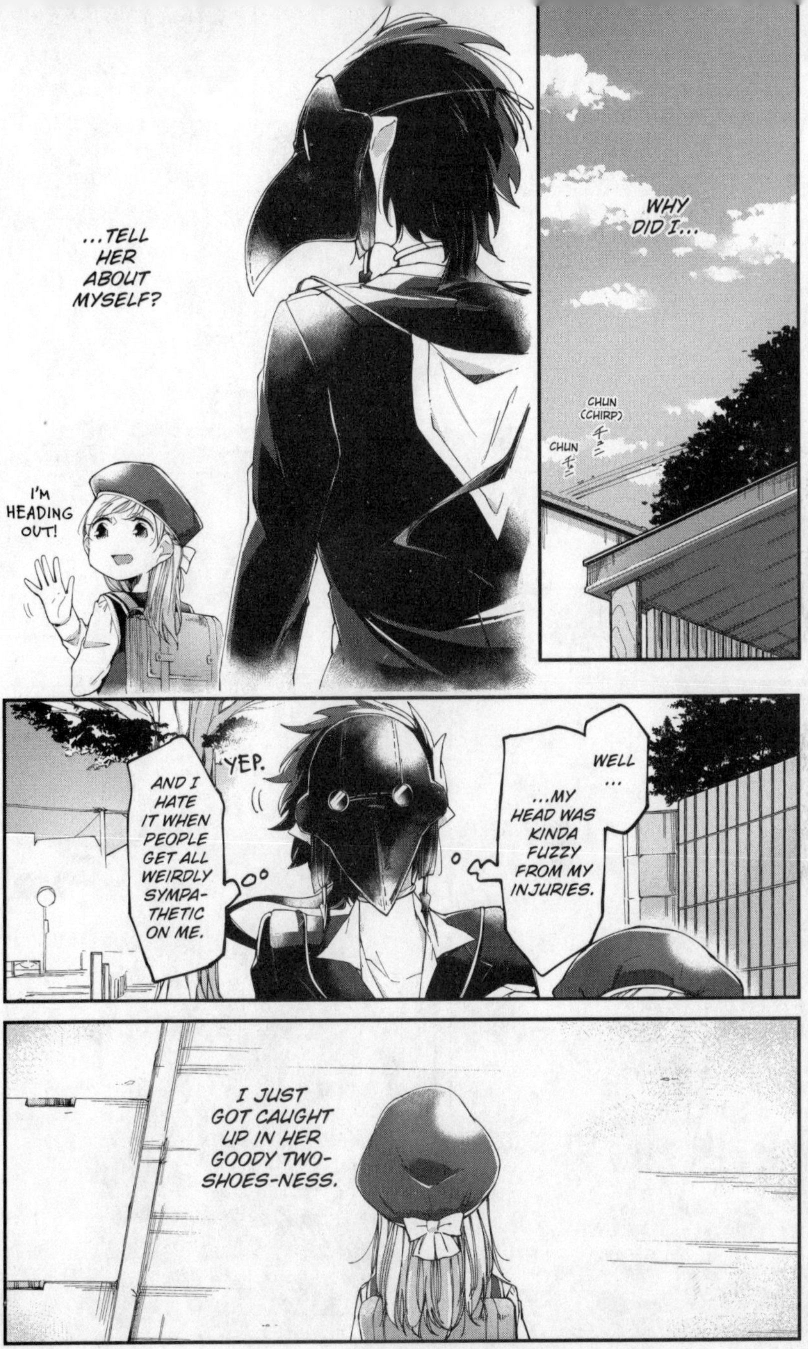
WHY DID I...
CHUN (CHIRP)
CHUN
...TELL HER ABOUT MYSELF?
I'M HEADING OUT!
WELL...
...MY HEAD WAS KINDA FUZZY FROM MY INJURIES.
YEP.
AND I HATE IT WHEN PEOPLE GET ALL WEIRDLY SYMPATHETIC ON ME.
I JUST GOT CAUGHT UP IN HER GOODY TWO-SHOES-NESS.

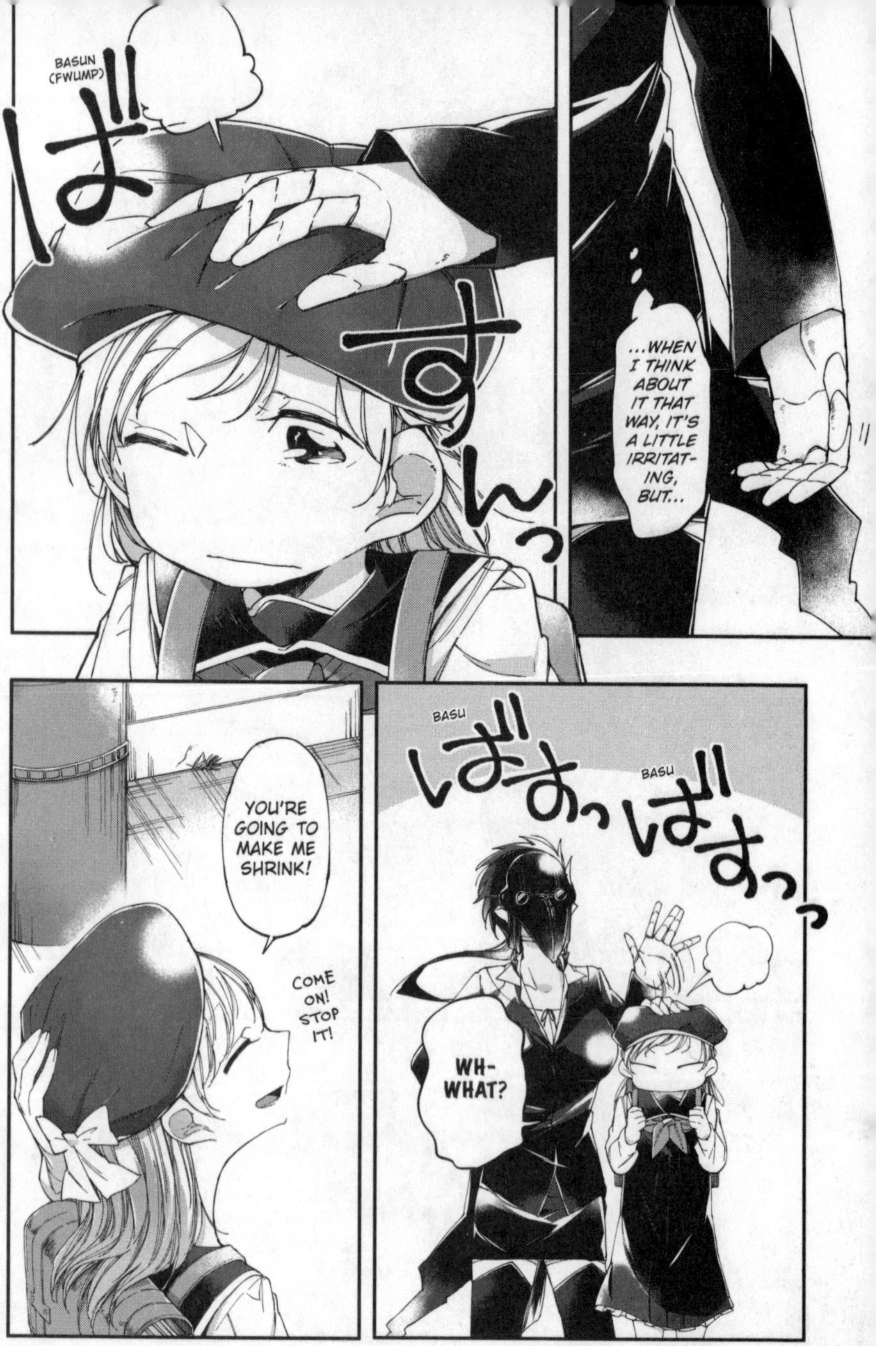
...WHEN I THINK ABOUT IT THAT WAY, IT'S A LITTLE IRRITAT-ING, BUT...
ばすんっ
BASUN (FWUMP)
ばすっばすっ
BASU
BASU
WH-WHAT?
YOU'RE GOING TO MAKE ME SHRINK!
COME ON! STOP IT!

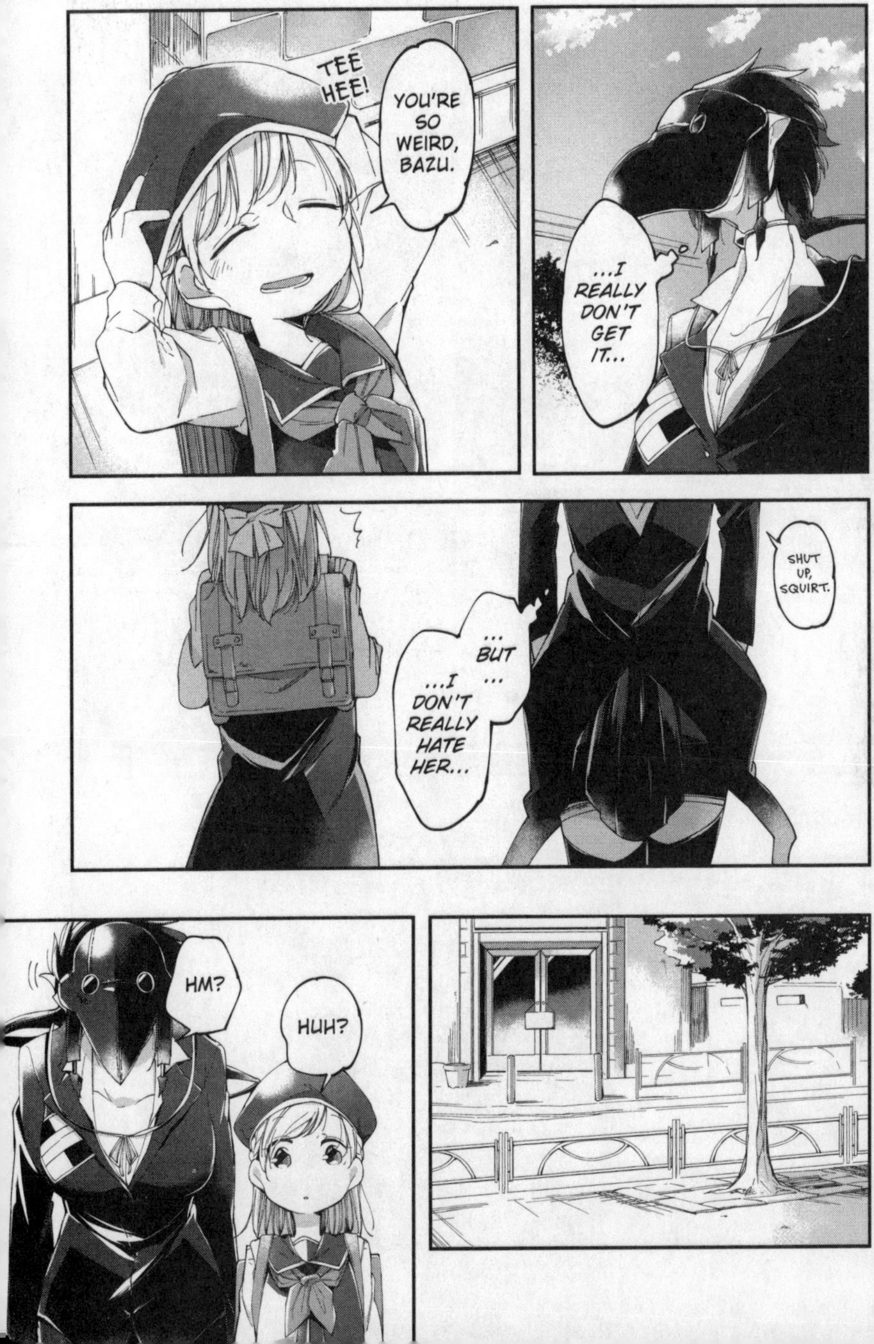
...I REALLY DON'T GET IT...
TEE HEE!
YOU'RE SO WEIRD, BAZU.
SHUT UP, SQUIRT.
...BUT...
...I DON'T REALLY HATE HER...
HM?
HUH?

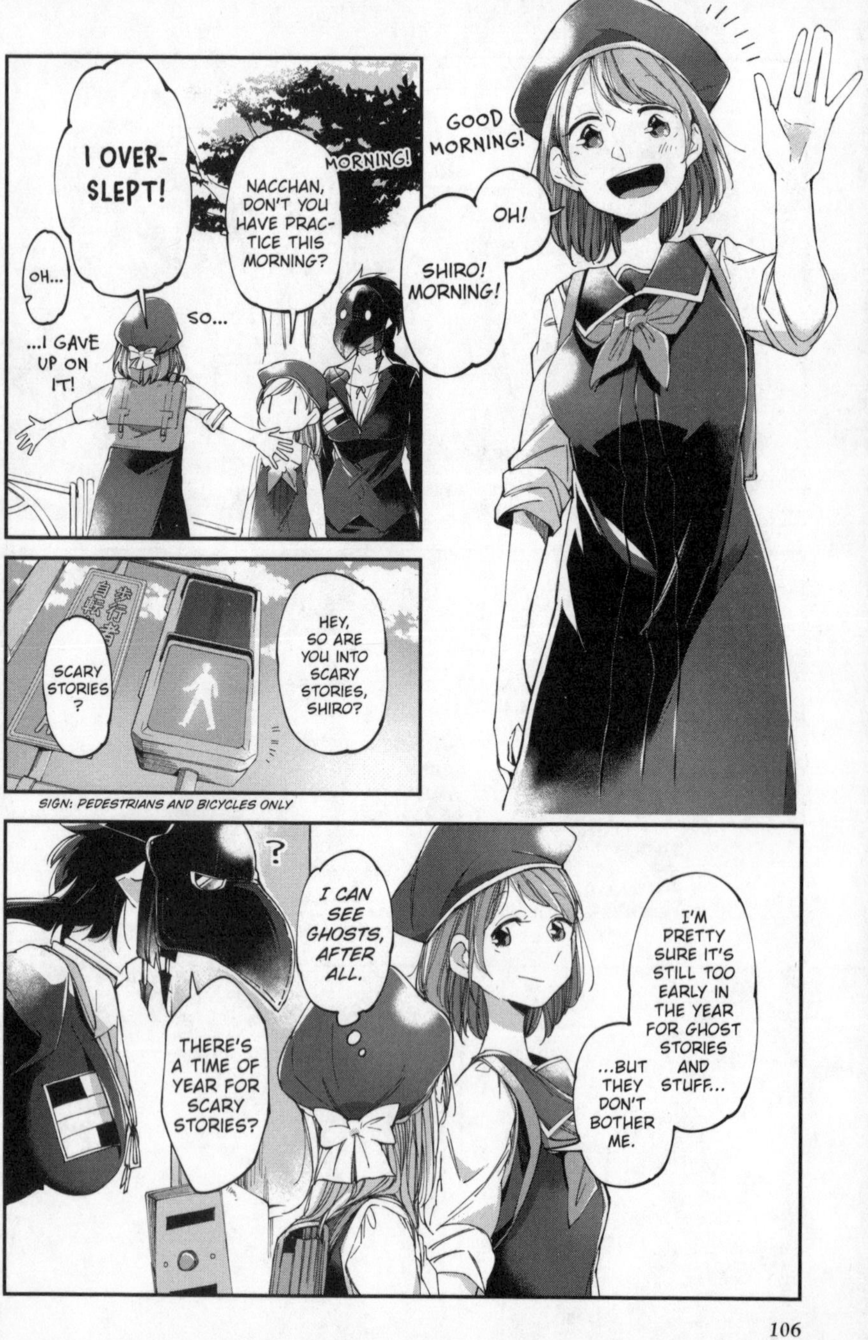
GOOD MORNING!
OH!
SHIRO! MORNING!
MORNING!
NACCHAN, DON'T YOU HAVE PRACTICE THIS MORNING?
I OVERSLEPT!
SO...
OH...
...I GAVE UP ON IT!
HEY, SO ARE YOU INTO SCARY STORIES, SHIRO?
SCARY STORIES?
SIGN: PEDESTRIANS AND BICYCLES ONLY
I'M PRETTY SURE IT'S STILL TOO EARLY IN THE YEAR FOR GHOST STORIES AND STUFF...
...BUT THEY DON'T BOTHER ME.
I CAN SEE GHOSTS, AFTER ALL.
?
THERE'S A TIME OF YEAR FOR SCARY STORIES?

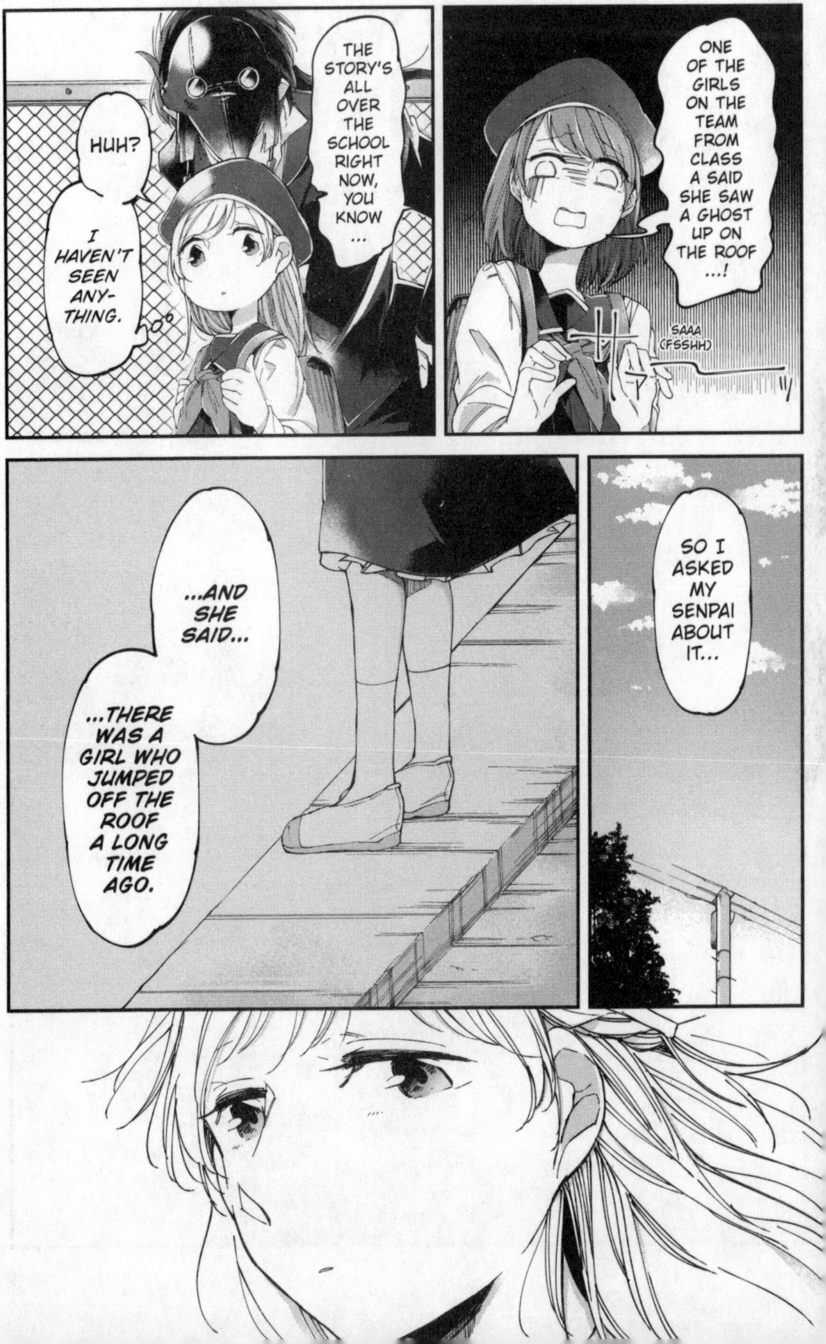
ONE OF THE GIRLS ON THE TEAM FROM CLASS A SAID SHE SAW A GHOST UP ON THE ROOF ...!
SAAA (FSSHH)
THE STORY'S ALL OVER THE SCHOOL RIGHT NOW, YOU KNOW ...
HUH?
I HAVEN'T SEEN ANY-THING.
SO I ASKED MY SENPAI ABOUT IT...
...AND SHE SAID...
...THERE WAS A GIRL WHO JUMPED OFF THE ROOF A LONG TIME AGO.

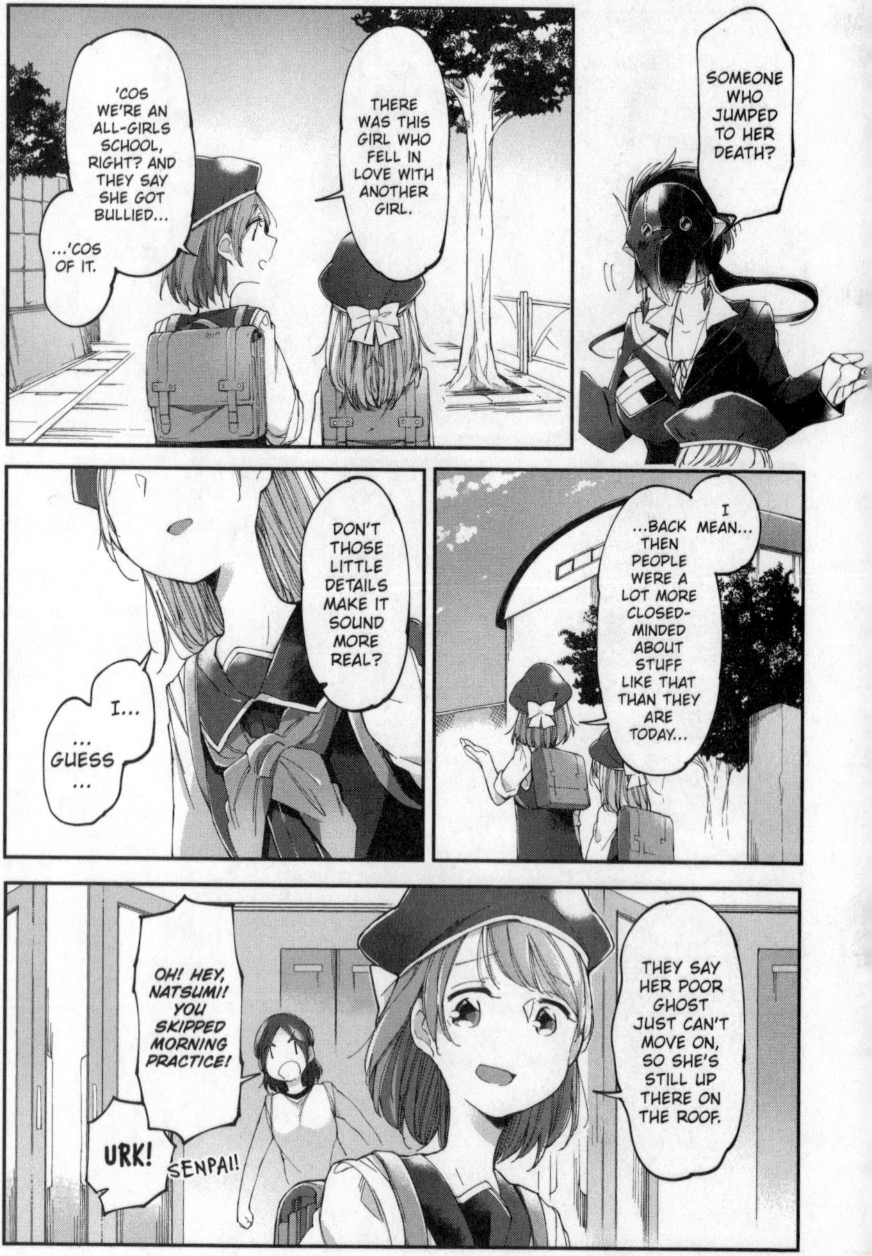
SOMEONE WHO JUMPED TO HER DEATH?
THERE WAS THIS GIRL WHO FELL IN LOVE WITH ANOTHER GIRL.
'COS WE'RE AN ALL-GIRLS SCHOOL, RIGHT? AND THEY SAY SHE GOT BULLIED...
...'COS OF IT.
I MEAN... ...BACK THEN PEOPLE WERE A LOT MORE CLOSED-MINDED ABOUT STUFF LIKE THAT THAN THEY ARE TODAY...
DON'T THOSE LITTLE DETAILS MAKE IT SOUND MORE REAL?
I... ...GUESS...
THEY SAY HER POOR GHOST JUST CAN'T MOVE ON, SO SHE'S STILL UP THERE ON THE ROOF.
OH! HEY, NATSUMI! YOU SKIPPED MORNING PRACTICE!
SENPAI!
URK!

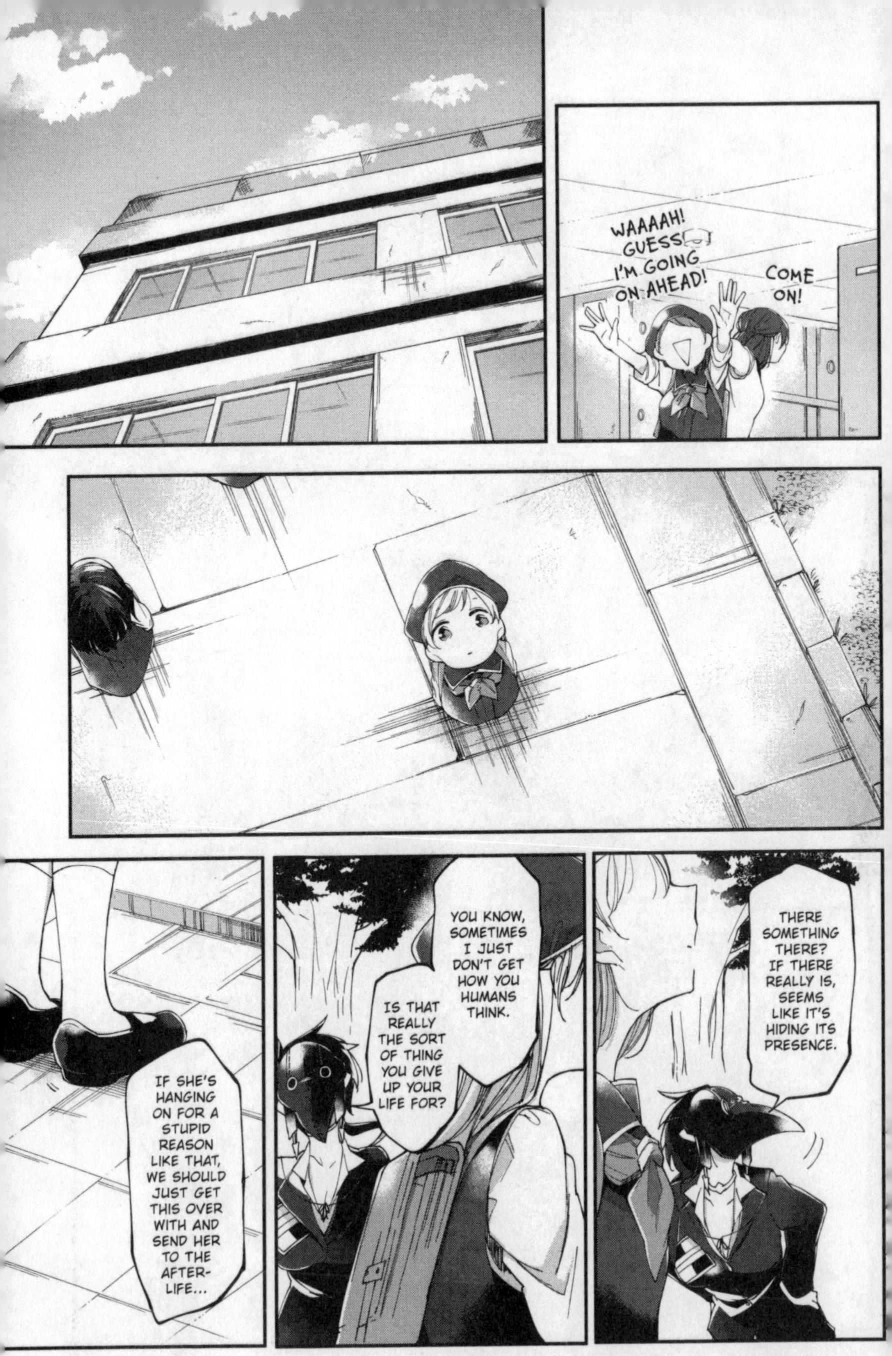
COME ON!
WAAAAH! GUESS I'M GOING ON AHEAD!
THERE SOMETHING THERE? IF THERE REALLY IS, SEEMS LIKE IT'S HIDING ITS PRESENCE.
YOU KNOW, SOMETIMES I JUST DON'T GET HOW YOU HUMANS THINK.
IS THAT REALLY THE SORT OF THING YOU GIVE UP YOUR LIFE FOR?
IF SHE'S HANGING ON FOR A STUPID REASON LIKE THAT, WE SHOULD JUST GET THIS OVER WITH AND SEND HER TO THE AFTER-LIFE...

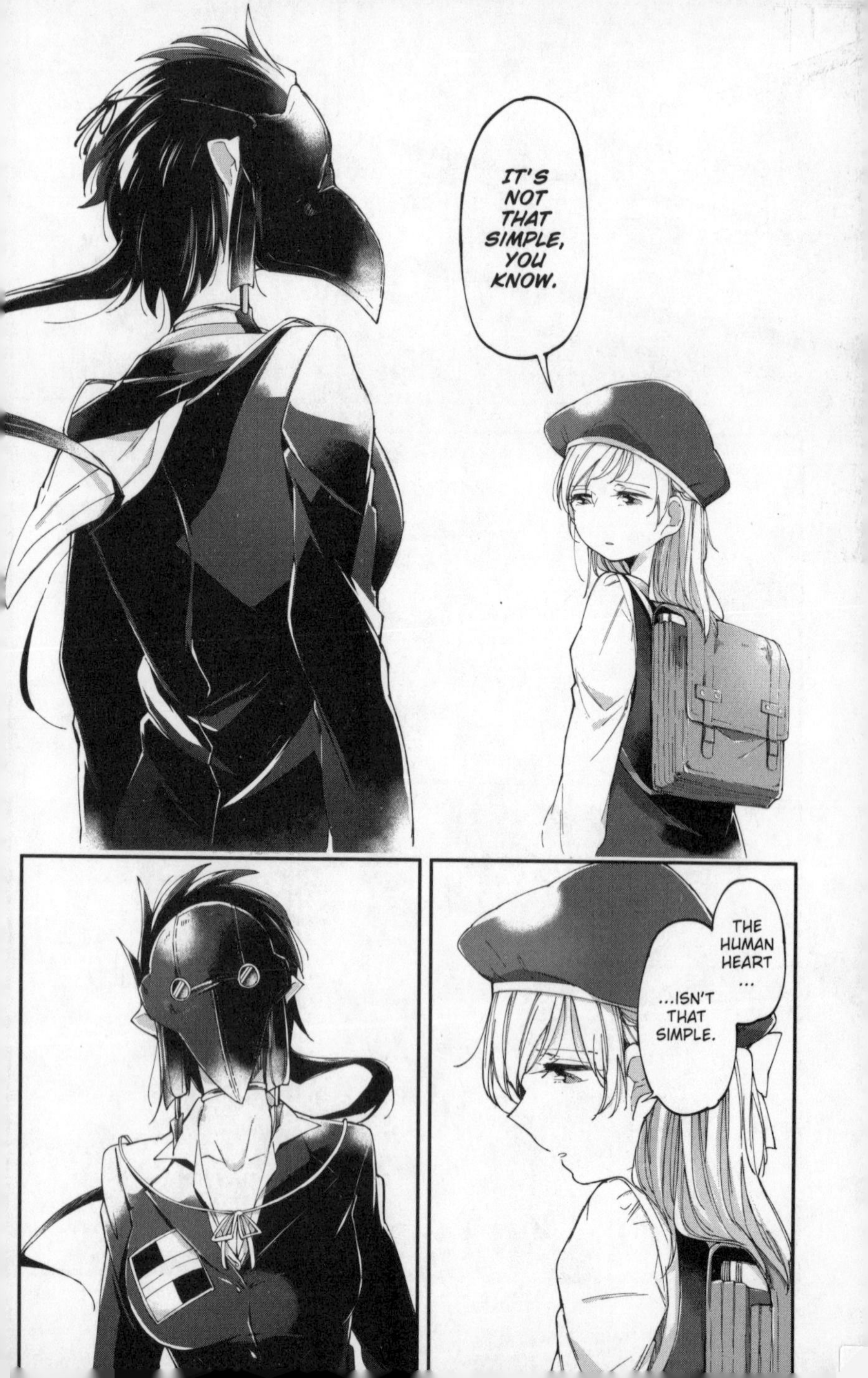
IT'S NOT THAT SIMPLE, YOU KNOW.
THE HUMAN HEART...
...ISN'T THAT SIMPLE.

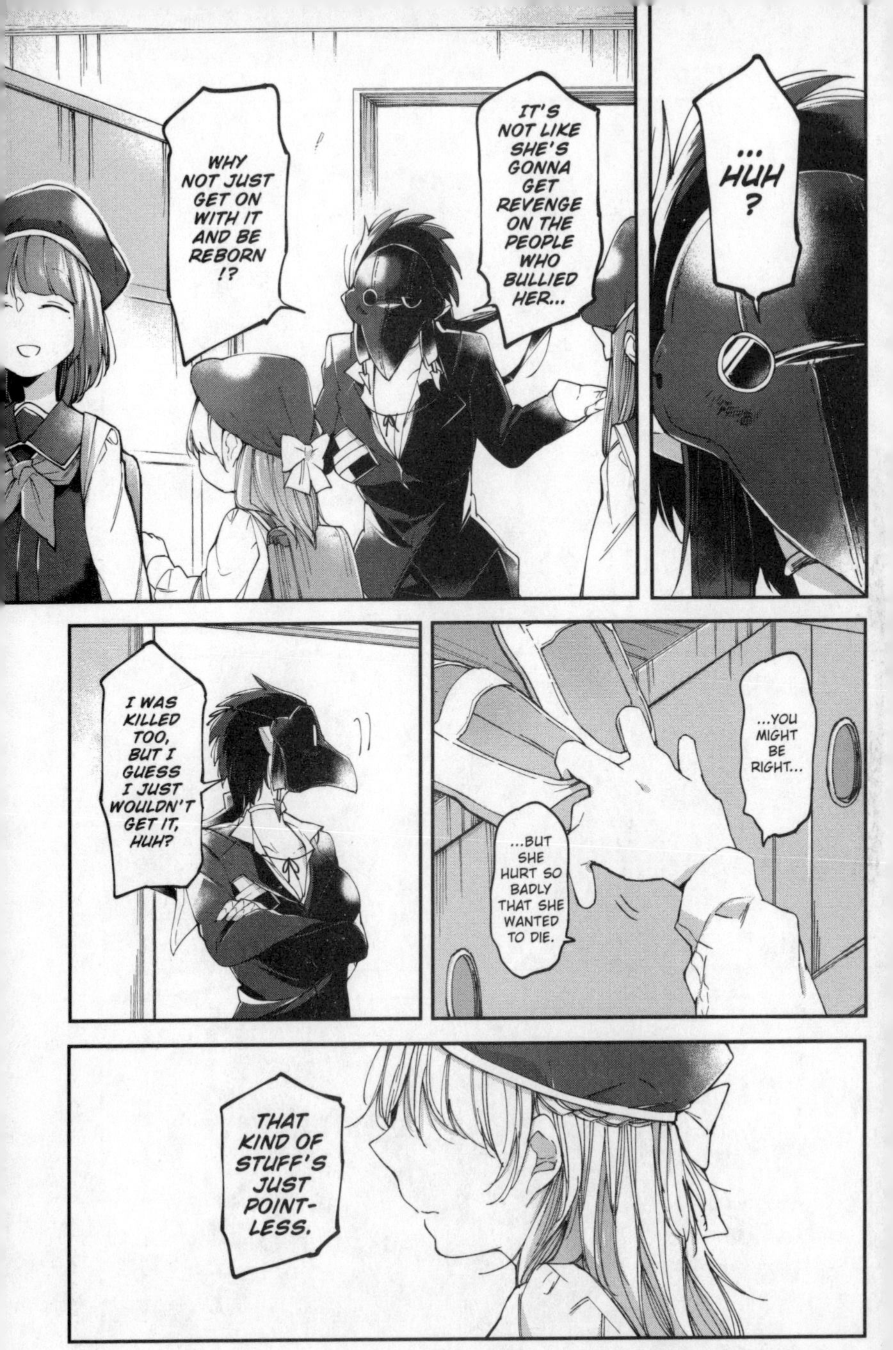
...HÜH?
IT'S NOT LIKE SHE'S GONNA GET REVENGE ON THE PEOPLE WHO BULLIED HER...
WHY NOT JUST GET ON WITH IT AND BE REBORN!?
...YOU MIGHT BE RIGHT...
...BUT SHE HURT SO BADLY THAT SHE WANTED TO DIE.
I WAS KILLED TOO, BUT I GUESS I JUST WOULDN'T GET IT, HUH?
THAT KIND OF STUFF'S JUST POINTLESS.

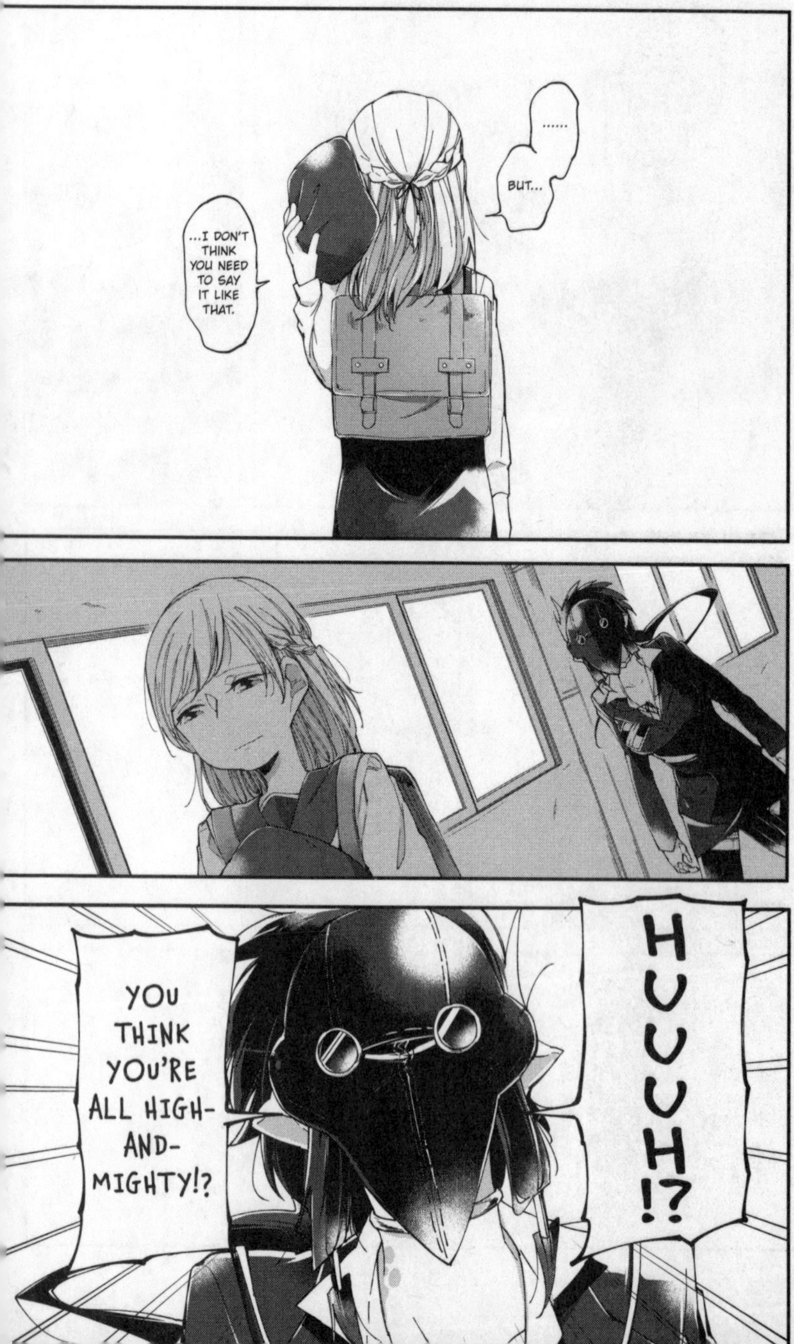
......
BUT...
...I DON'T THINK YOU NEED TO SAY IT LIKE THAT.
HUUUH!?
YOU THINK YOU'RE ALL HIGH-AND-MIGHTY!?

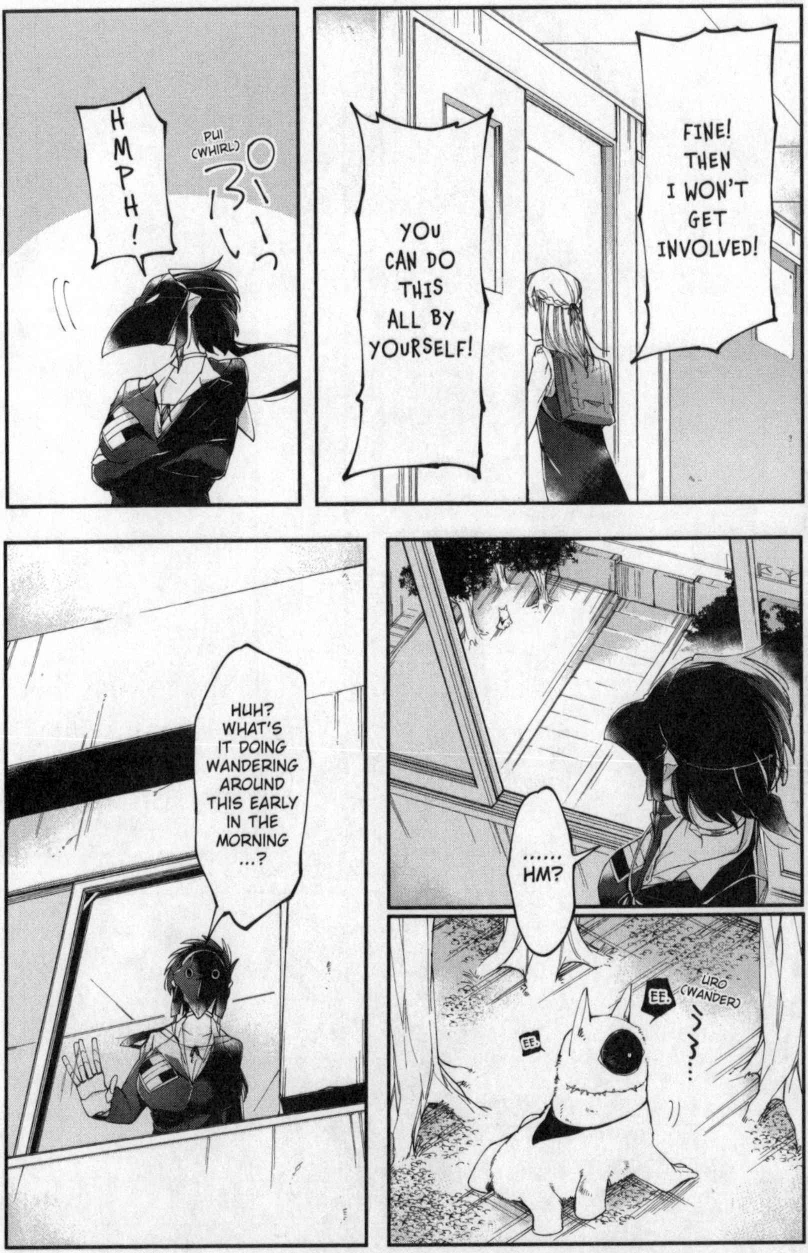
FINE! THEN I WON'T GET INVOLVED!
YOU CAN DO THIS ALL BY YOURSELF!
HMPH!
PUI (WHIRL)
......HM?
HUH? WHAT'S IT DOING WANDERING AROUND THIS EARLY IN THE MORNING ...?
URO (WANDER)
EE.
EE.

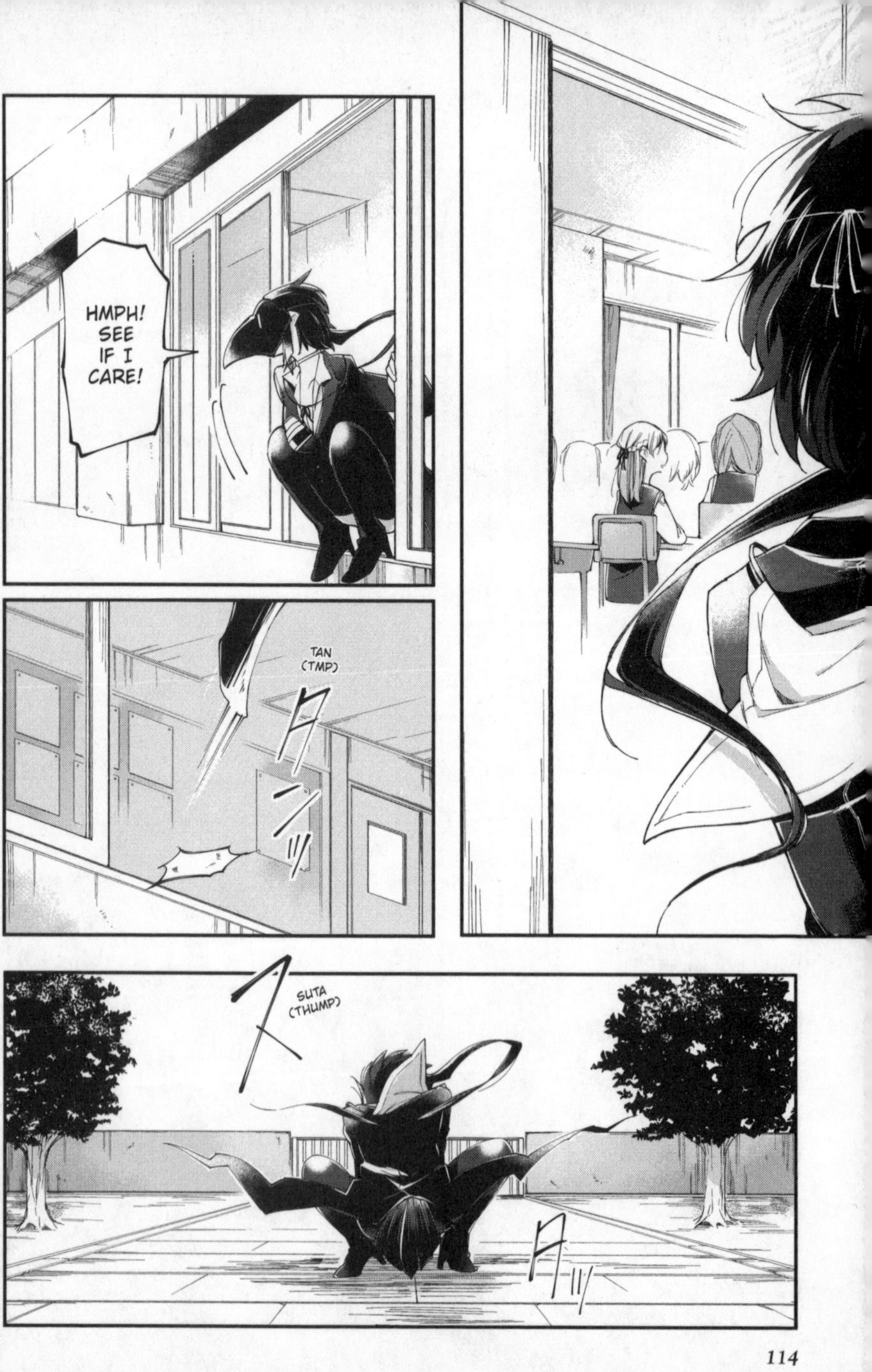
HMPH! SEE IF I CARE!
TAN (TMP)
SUTA (THUMP)

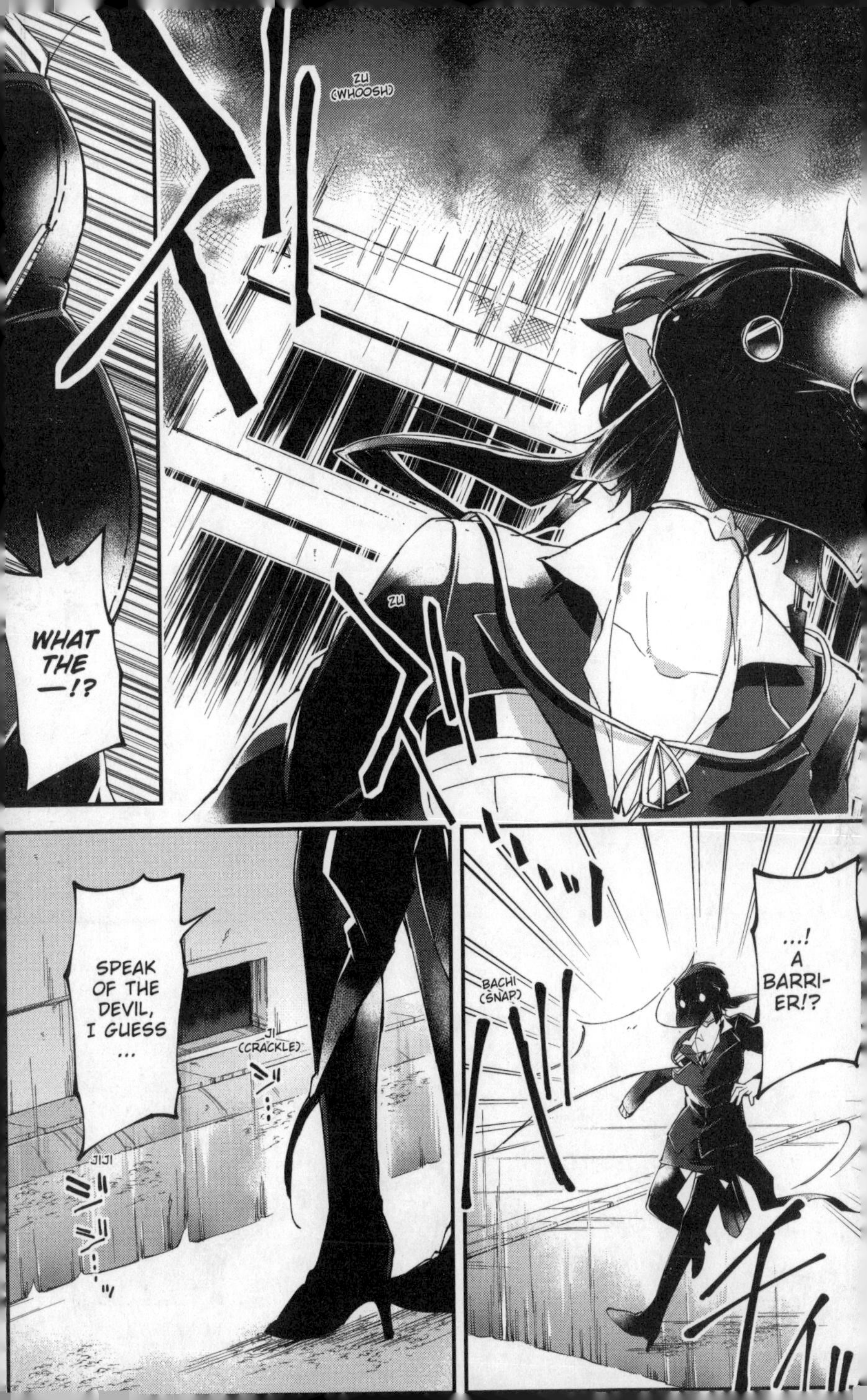
ZU (WHOOSH)
ZU
WHAT THE—!?
...! A BARRIER!?
BACHI (SNAP)
SPEAK OF THE DEVIL, I GUESS ...
JI (CRACKLE)
JIJI

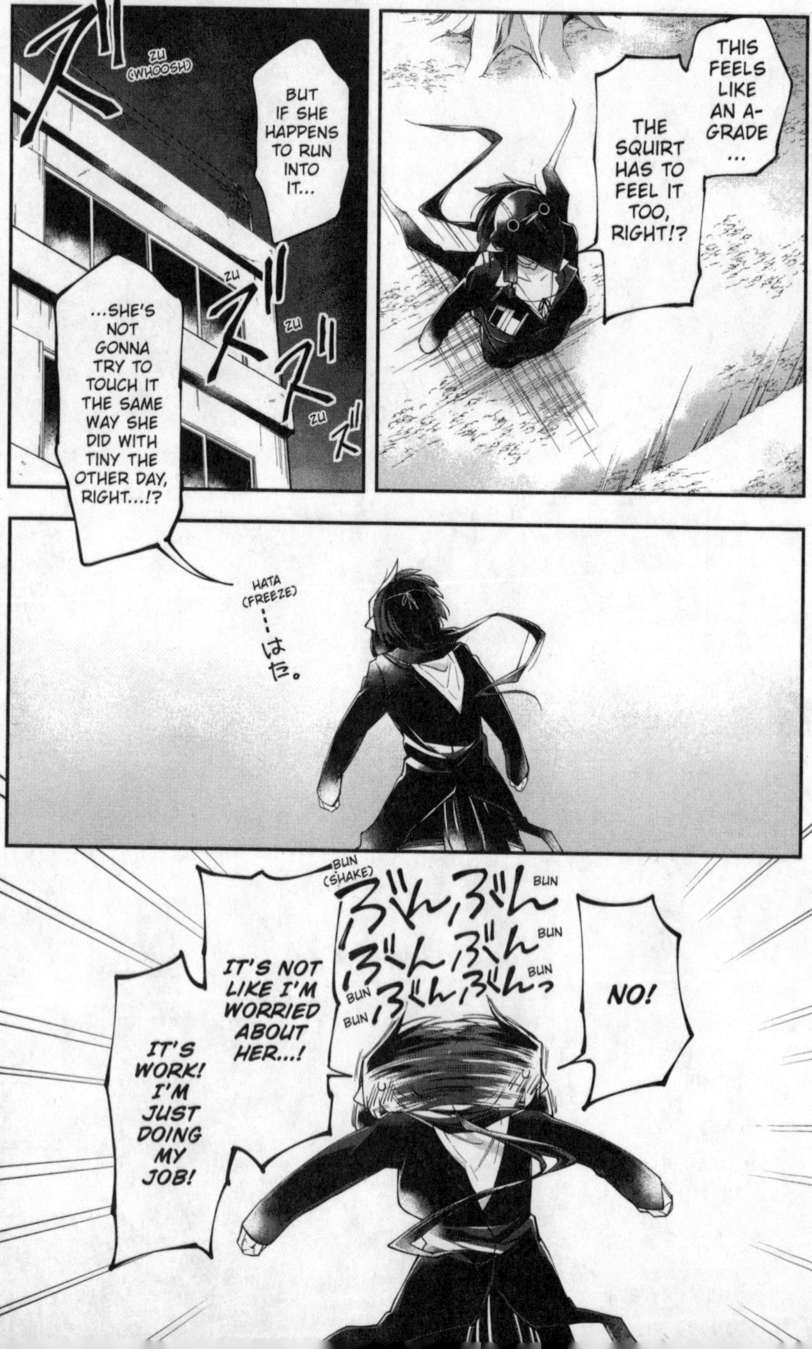
THIS FEELS LIKE AN A-GRADE...
THE SQUIRT HAS TO FEEL IT TOO, RIGHT!?
ZU (WHOOSH)
BUT IF SHE HAPPENS TO RUN INTO IT...
ZU
ZU
ZU
...SHE'S NOT GONNA TRY TO TOUCH IT THE SAME WAY SHE DID WITH TINY THE OTHER DAY, RIGHT...!?
HATA (FREEZE)
...はた。
NO!
BUN (SHAKE)
BUN
BUN
BUN
BUN
BUN
ぶんぶんぶんぶんぶんぶんっ
IT'S NOT LIKE I'M WORRIED ABOUT HER...!
IT'S WORK! I'M JUST DOING MY JOB!

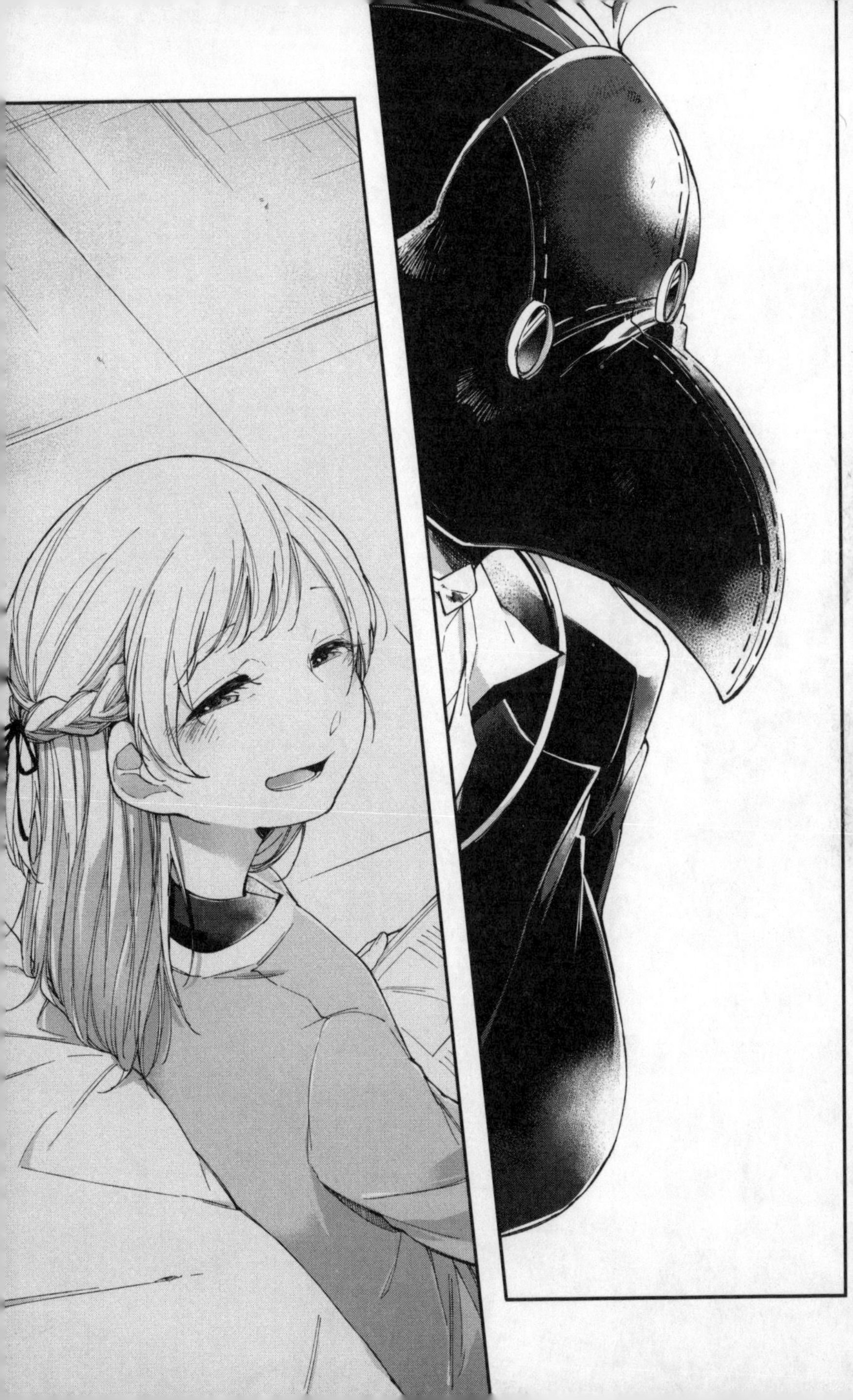

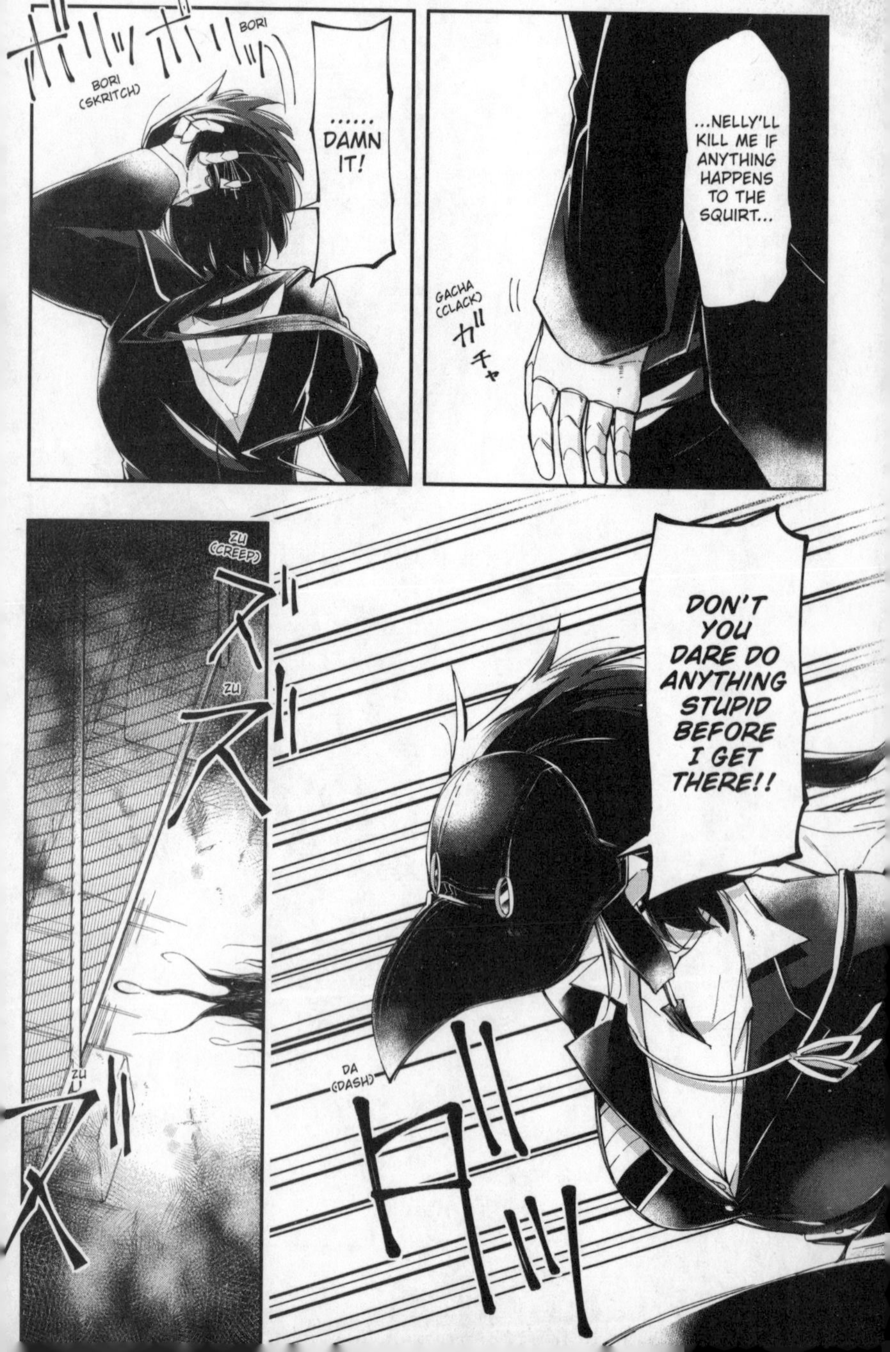
...NELLY'LL KILL ME IF ANYTHING HAPPENS TO THE SQUIRT...
GACHA (CLACK)
BORI
BORI (SKRITCH)
...... DAMN IT!
DON'T YOU DARE DO ANYTHING STUPID BEFORE I GET THERE!!
DA (DASH)
ZU (CREEP)
ZU
ZU

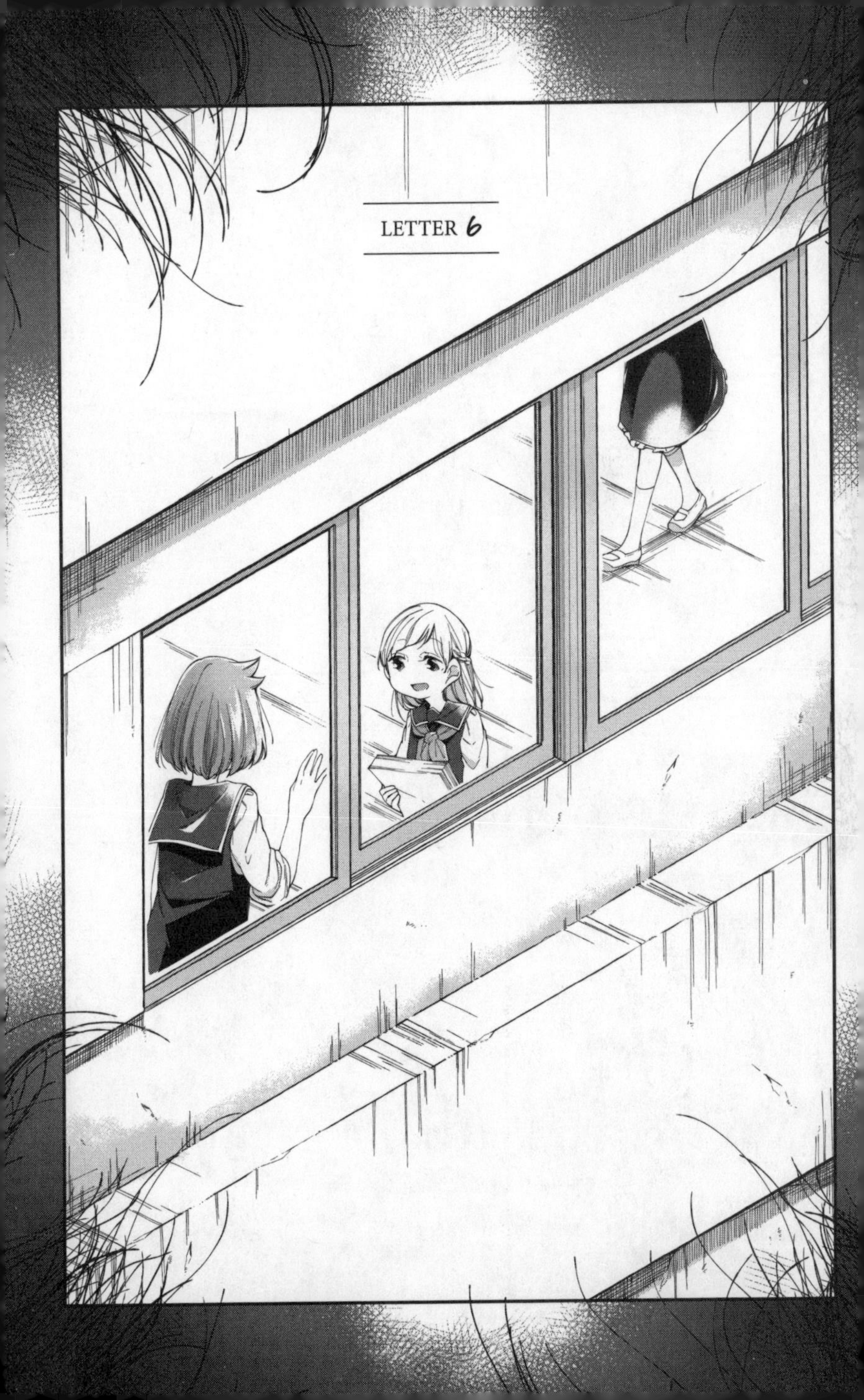
LETTER 6

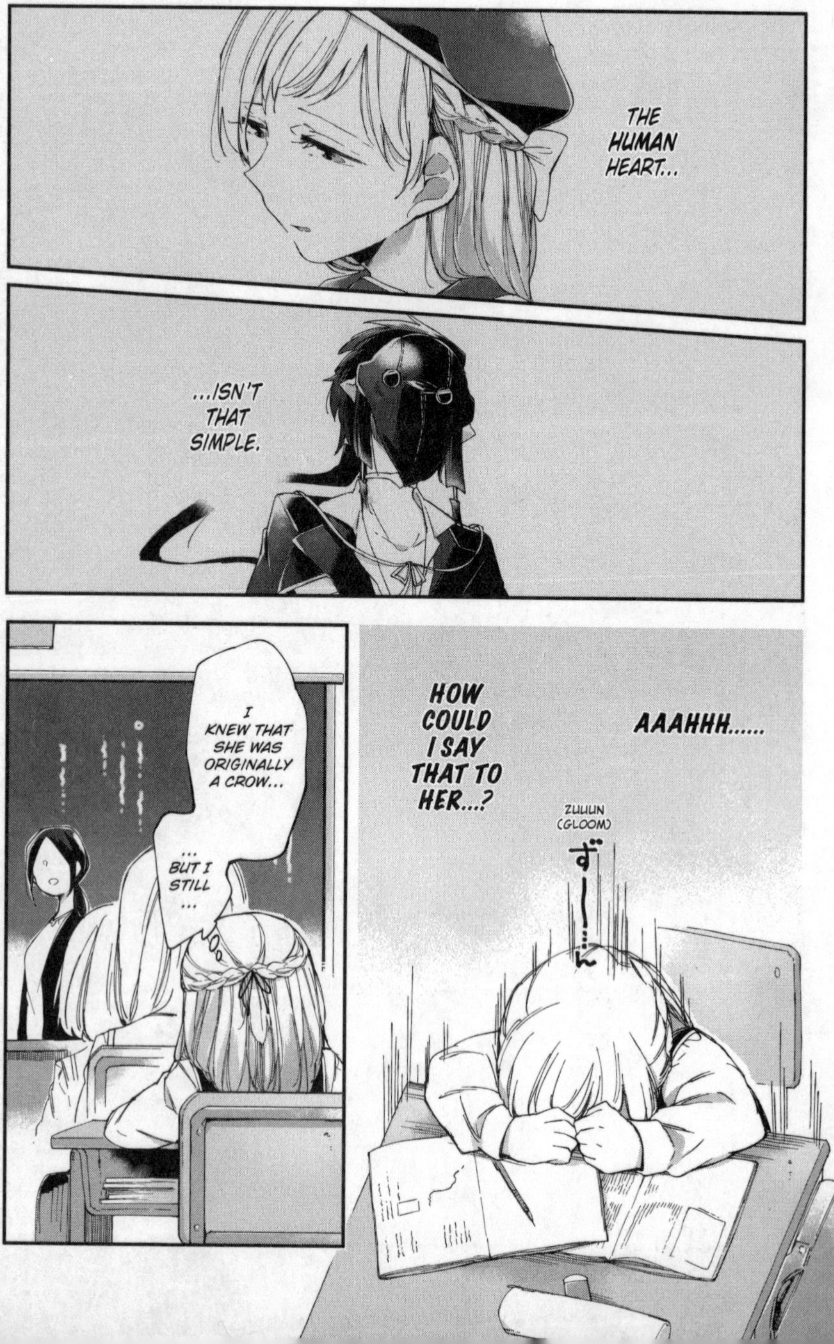
THE HUMAN HEART...
...ISN'T THAT SIMPLE.
AAAHHH......
HOW COULD I SAY THAT TO HER...?
ZUUUN (GLOOM)
ず～…ん
I KNEW THAT SHE WAS ORIGINALLY A CROW...
...BUT I STILL...

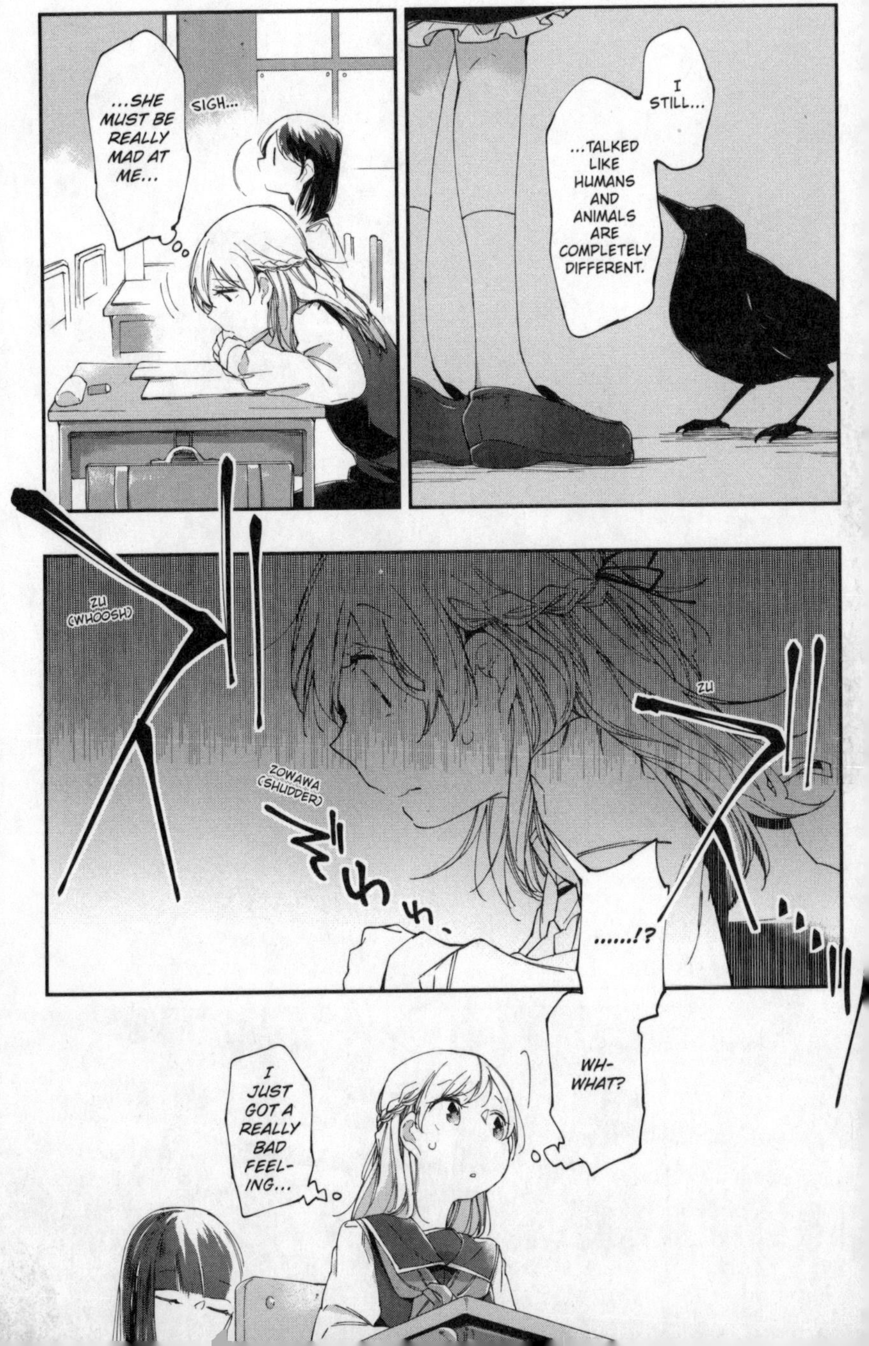
I STILL...
...TALKED LIKE HUMANS AND ANIMALS ARE COMPLETELY DIFFERENT.
...SHE MUST BE REALLY MAD AT ME...
SIGH...
ZU
ZU (WHOOSH)
......!?
ZOWAWA (SHUDDER)
WH-WHAT?
I JUST GOT A REALLY BAD FEEL-ING...

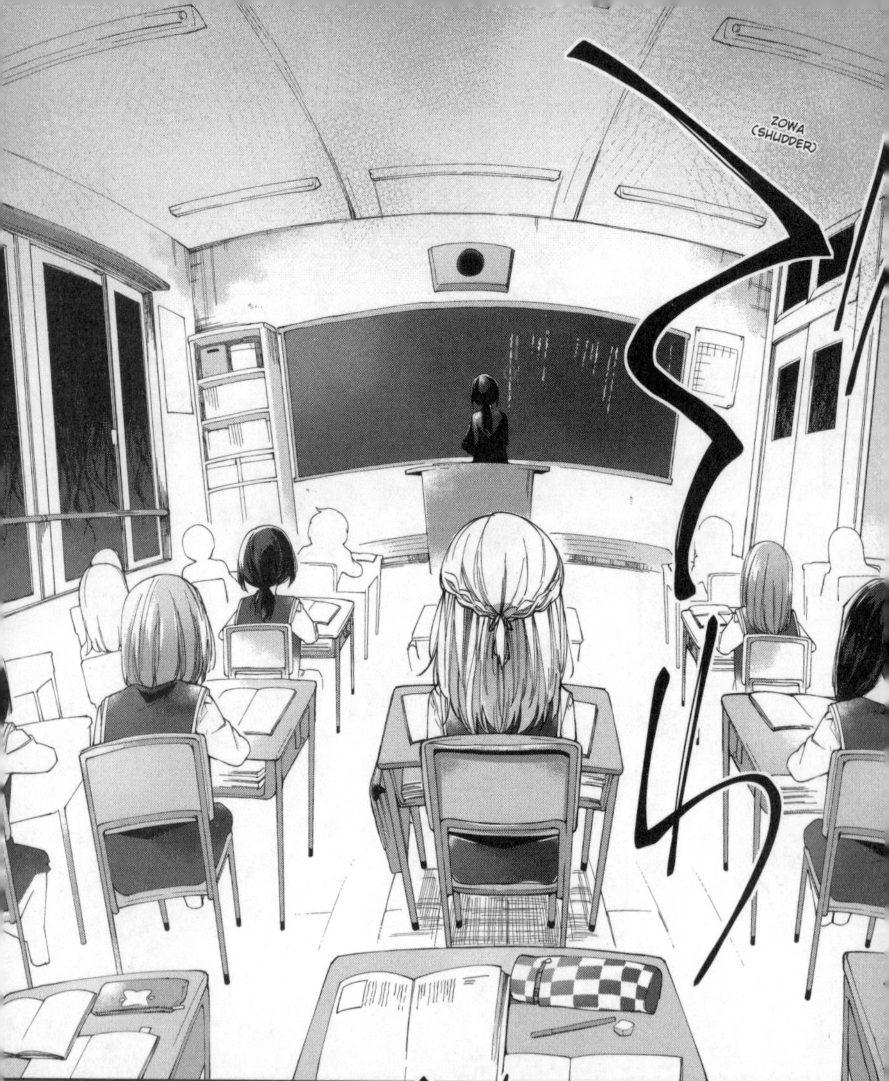
ZOWA
(SHUDDER)
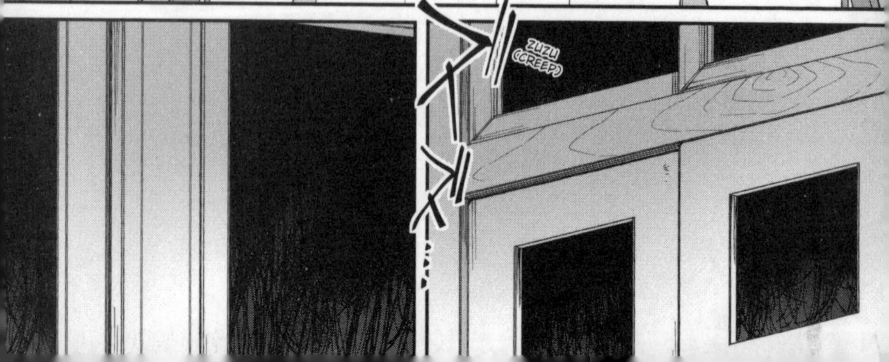
ZUZU
(CREEP)

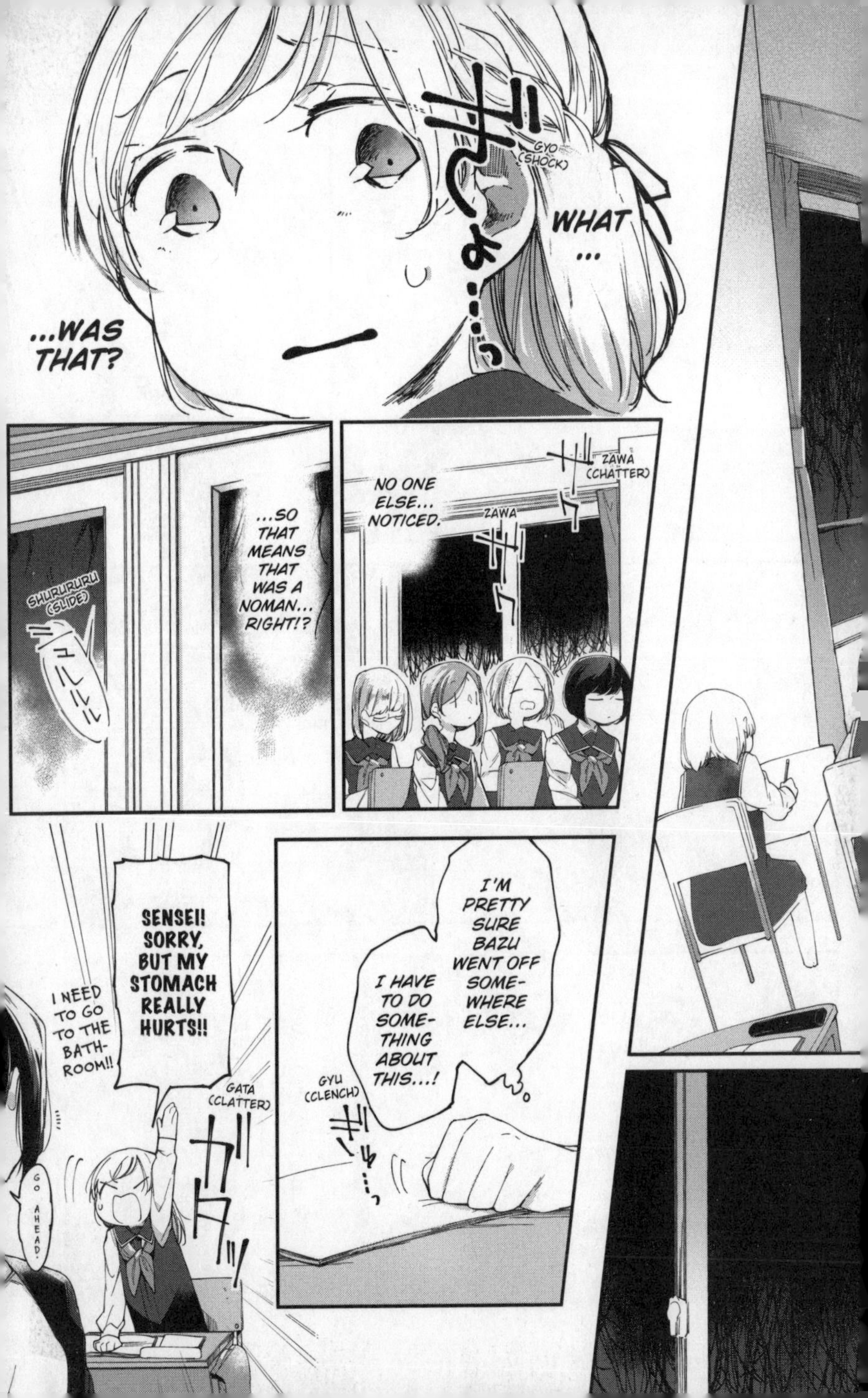
GYO (SHOCK)
WHAT...
...WAS THAT?
ZAWA (CHATTER)
ZAWA
NO ONE ELSE... NOTICED.
...SO THAT MEANS THAT WAS A NOMAN... RIGHT!?
SHURURURU (SLIDE)
I'M PRETTY SURE BAZU WENT OFF SOMEWHERE ELSE...
I HAVE TO DO SOMETHING ABOUT THIS...!
GYU (CLENCH)
SENSEI! SORRY, BUT MY STOMACH REALLY HURTS!!
I NEED TO GO TO THE BATHROOM!!
GATA (CLATTER)
GO AHEAD.

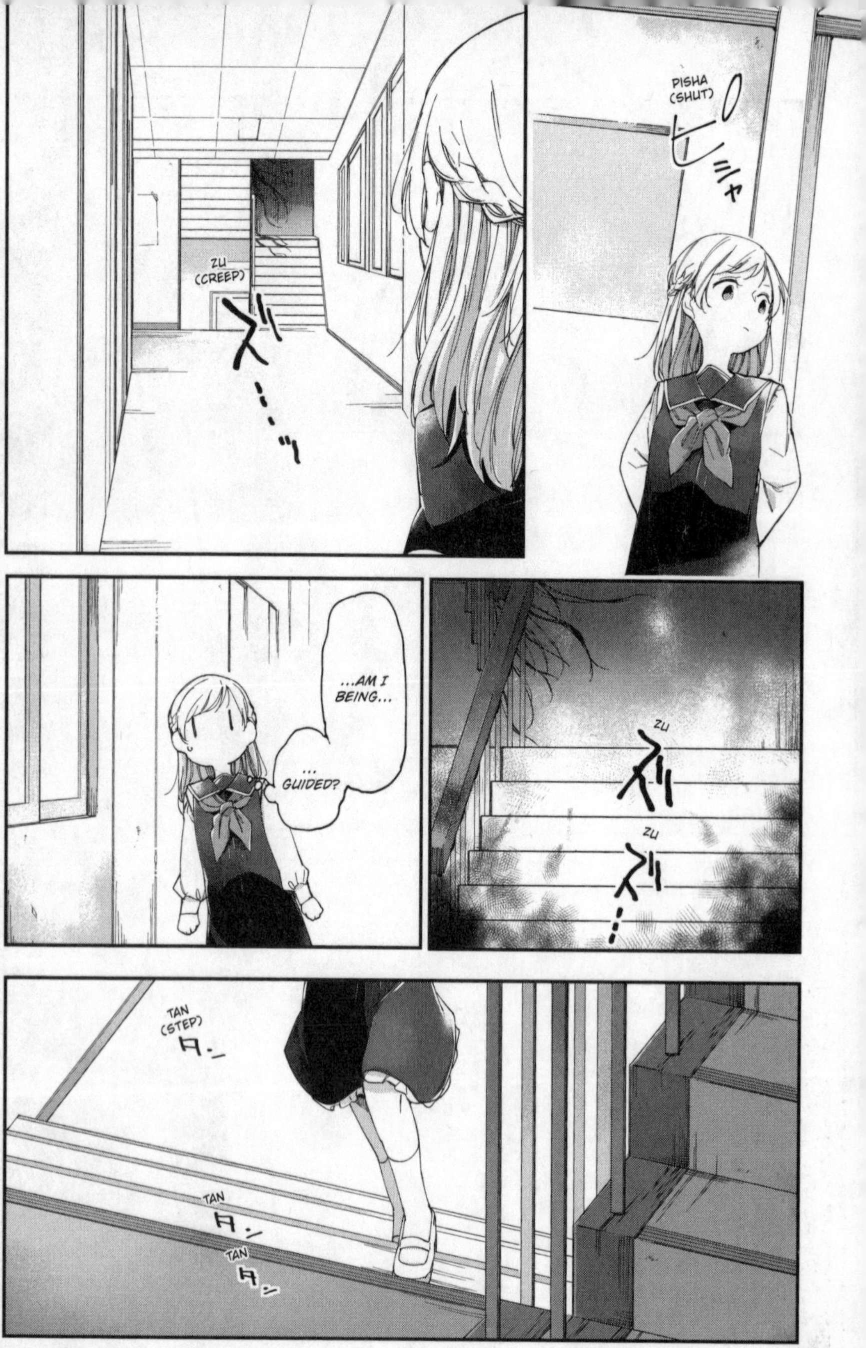
PISHA (SHUT)
ZU (CREEP)
ZU
ZU
...AM I BEING...
... GUIDED?
TAN (STEP)
TAN
TAN

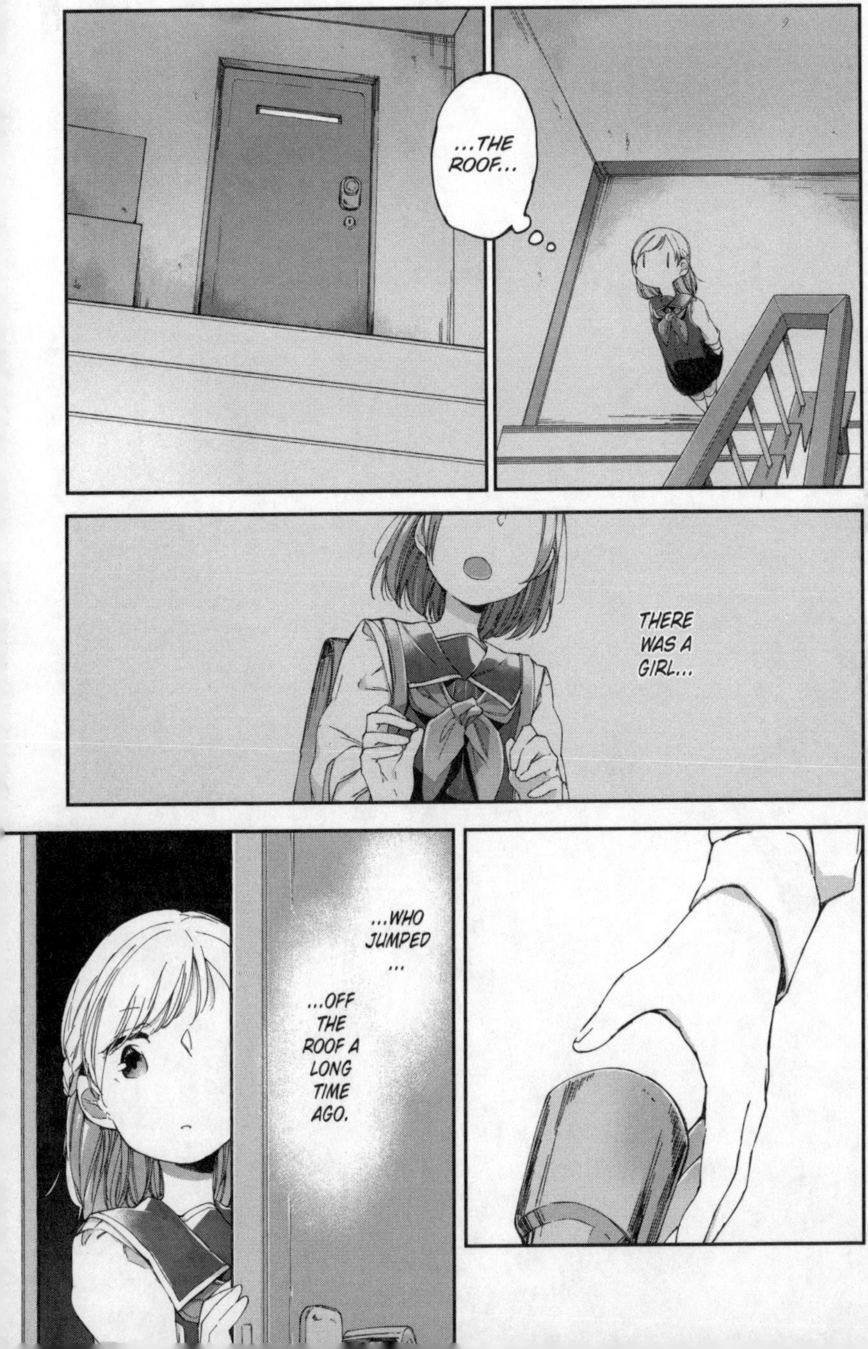
...THE ROOF...
THERE WAS A GIRL...
...WHO JUMPED ...
...OFF THE ROOF A LONG TIME AGO.

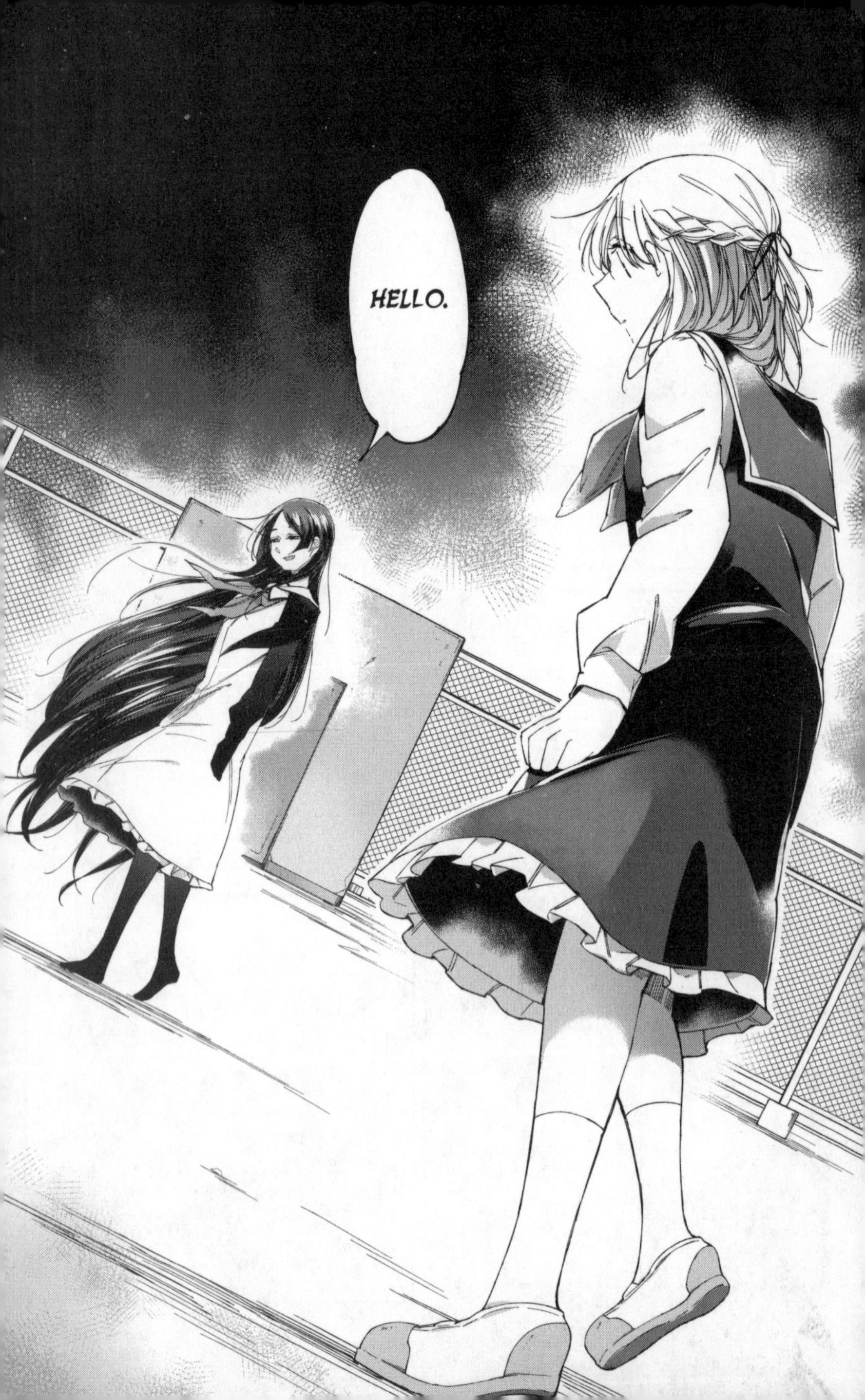
HELLO.

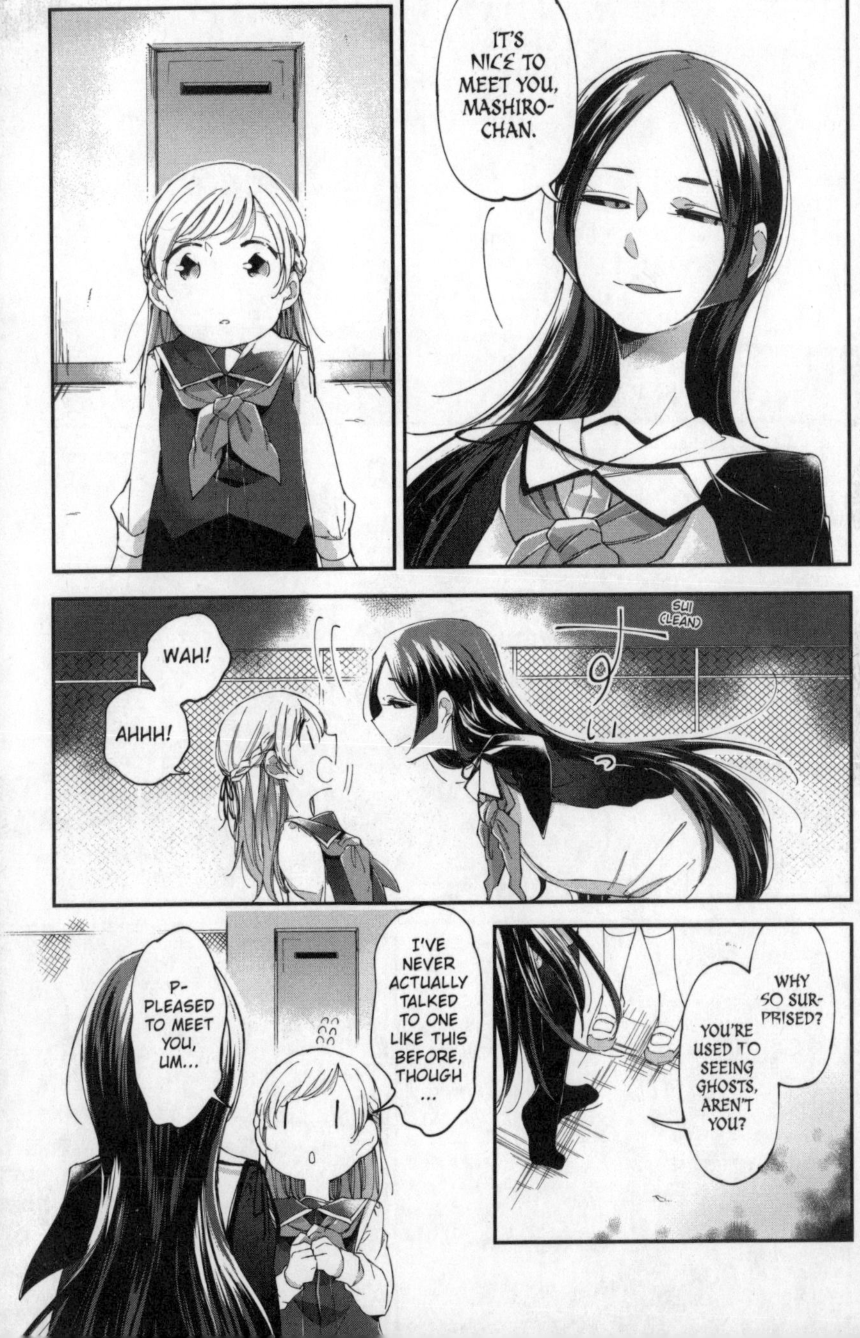
IT'S NICE TO MEET YOU, MASHIRO-CHAN.
SUI (LEAN)
WAH!
AHHH!
WHY SO SURPRISED?
YOU'RE USED TO SEEING GHOSTS, AREN'T YOU?
I'VE NEVER ACTUALLY TALKED TO ONE LIKE THIS BEFORE, THOUGH...
P-PLEASED TO MEET YOU, UM...

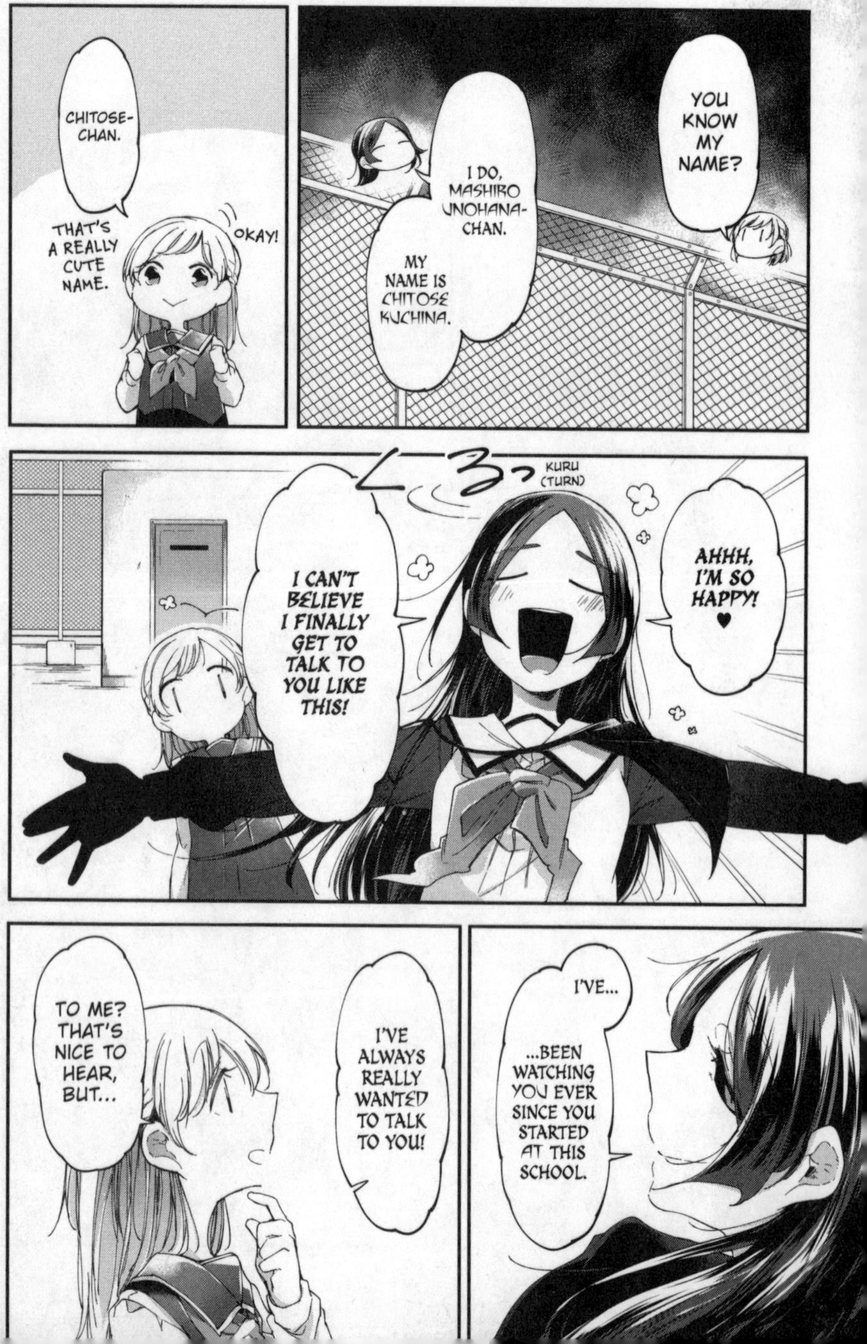
YOU KNOW MY NAME?
I DO, MASHIRO UNOHANA-CHAN.
MY NAME IS CHITOSE KUCHINA.
CHITOSE-CHAN.
OKAY!
THAT'S A REALLY CUTE NAME.
くるっ
KURU (TURN)
AHHH, I'M SO HAPPY! ♥
I CAN'T BELIEVE I FINALLY GET TO TALK TO YOU LIKE THIS!
I'VE...
...BEEN WATCHING YOU EVER SINCE YOU STARTED AT THIS SCHOOL.
I'VE ALWAYS REALLY WANTED TO TALK TO YOU!
TO ME? THAT'S NICE TO HEAR, BUT...

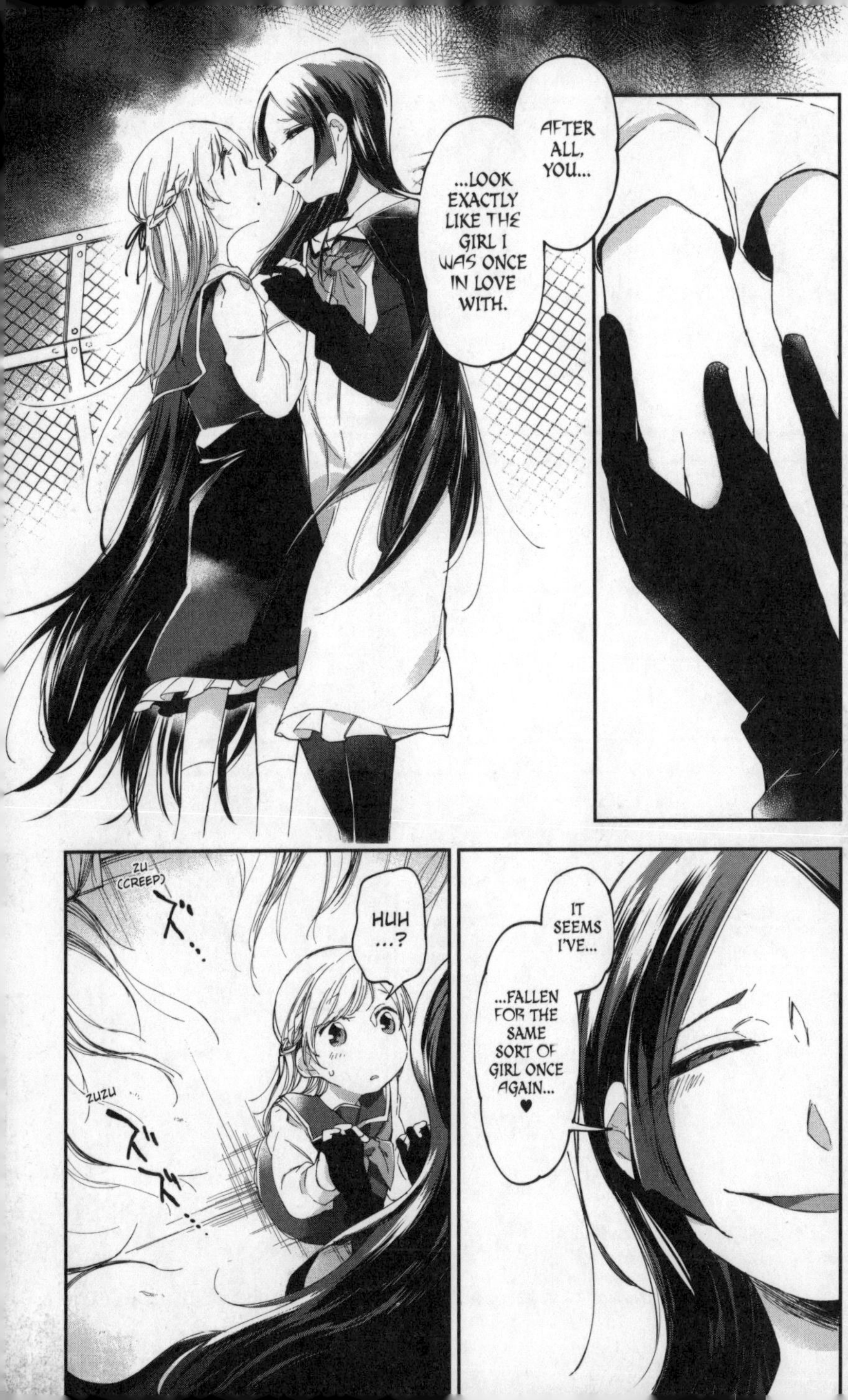
AFTER ALL, YOU...
...LOOK EXACTLY LIKE THE GIRL I WAS ONCE IN LOVE WITH.
IT SEEMS I'VE...
...FALLEN FOR THE SAME SORT OF GIRL ONCE AGAIN...♥
ZU (CREEP)
ズ...
HUH...?
ZUZU
ズズ...

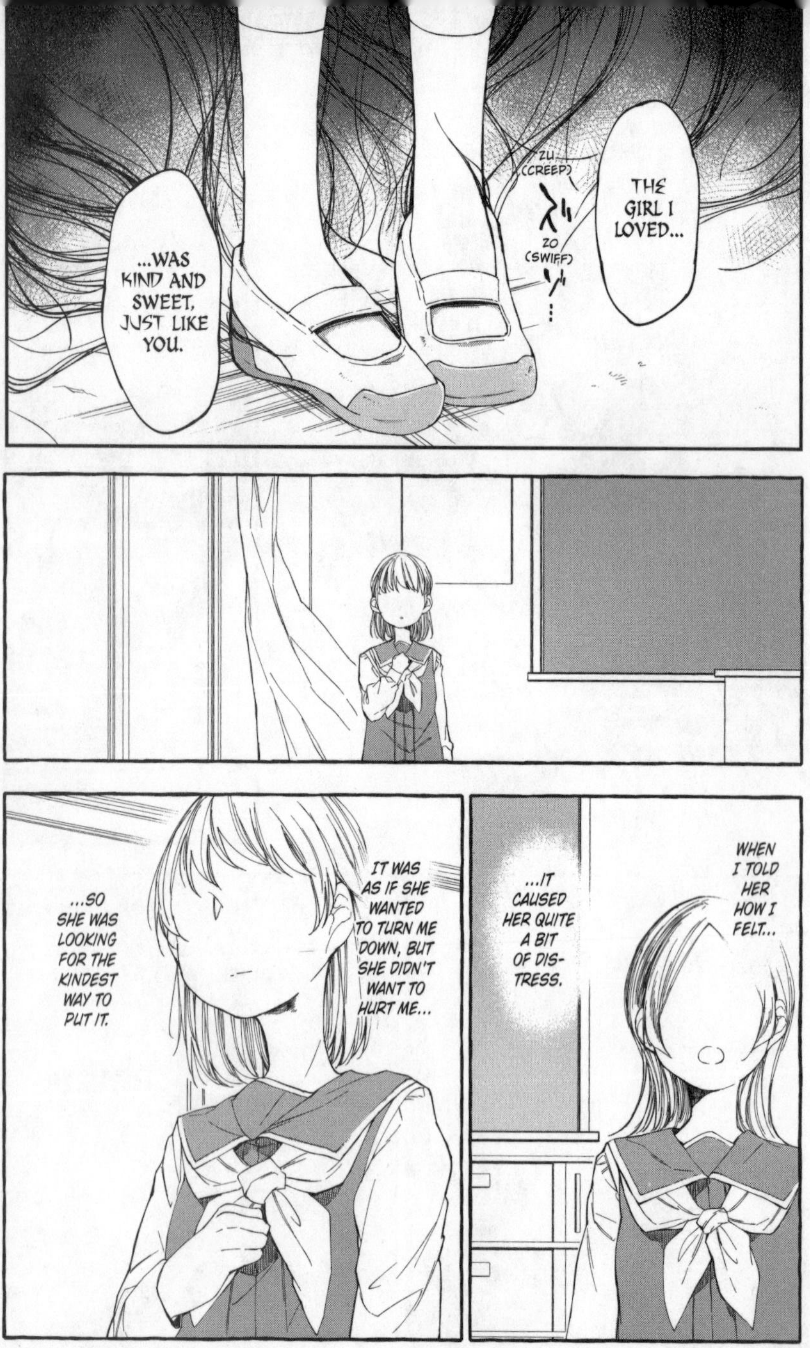
THE GIRL I LOVED...
ZU (CREEP) ズ
ZO (SWIFF) ゾ...
...WAS KIND AND SWEET, JUST LIKE YOU.
WHEN I TOLD HER HOW I FELT...
...IT CAUSED HER QUITE A BIT OF DIS-TRESS.
IT WAS AS IF SHE WANTED TO TURN ME DOWN, BUT SHE DIDN'T WANT TO HURT ME...
...SO SHE WAS LOOKING FOR THE KINDEST WAY TO PUT IT.

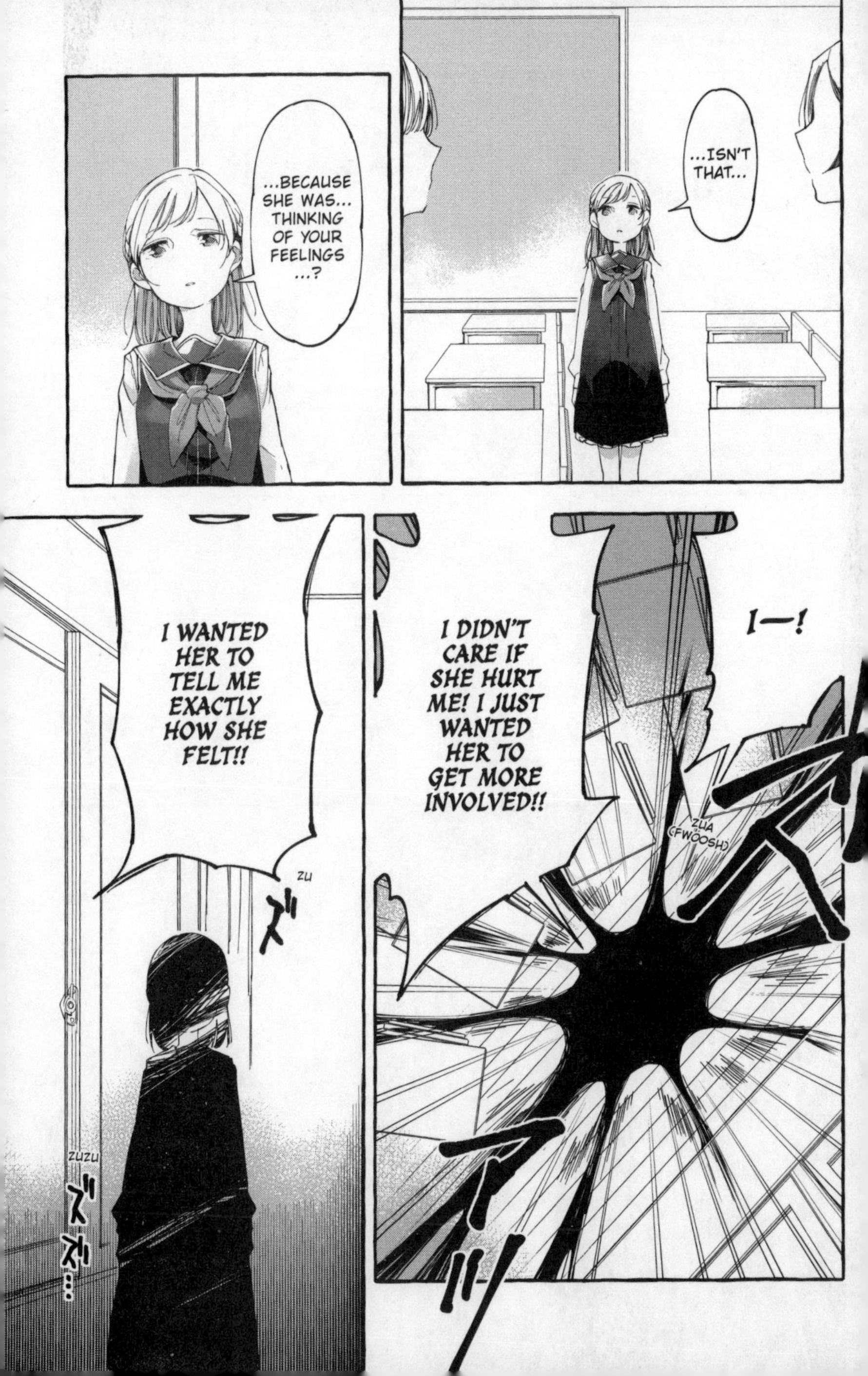
...ISN'T THAT...
...BECAUSE SHE WAS... THINKING OF YOUR FEELINGS ...?
I—!
I DIDN'T CARE IF SHE HURT ME! I JUST WANTED HER TO GET MORE INVOLVED!!
ZUA (FWOOSH)
I WANTED HER TO TELL ME EXACTLY HOW SHE FELT!!
ZU
ZUZU

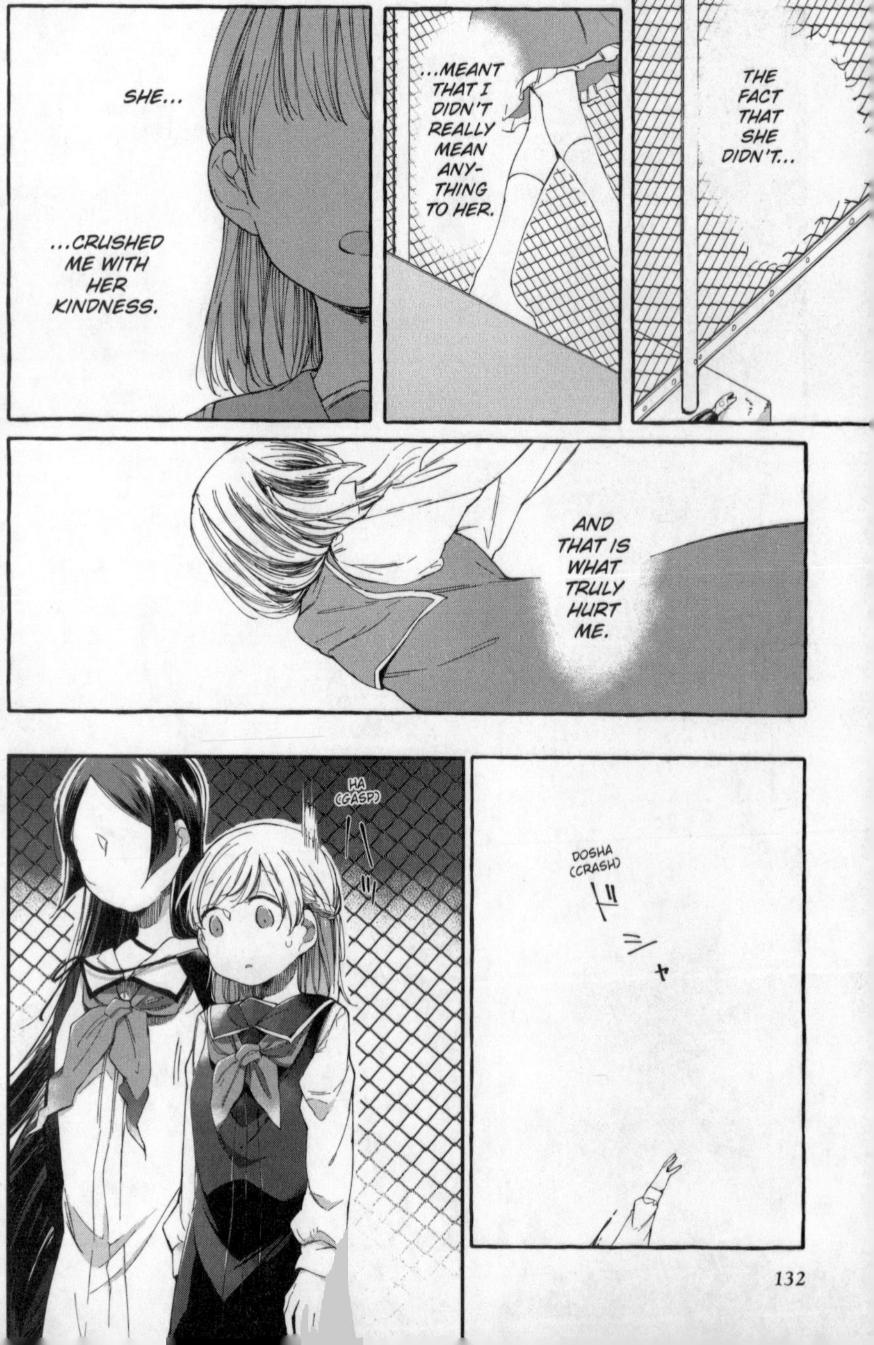
THE FACT THAT SHE DIDN'T...
...MEANT THAT I DIDN'T REALLY MEAN ANY-THING TO HER.
SHE...
...CRUSHED ME WITH HER KINDNESS.
AND THAT IS WHAT TRULY HURT ME.
DOSHA (CRASH)
HA (GASP)

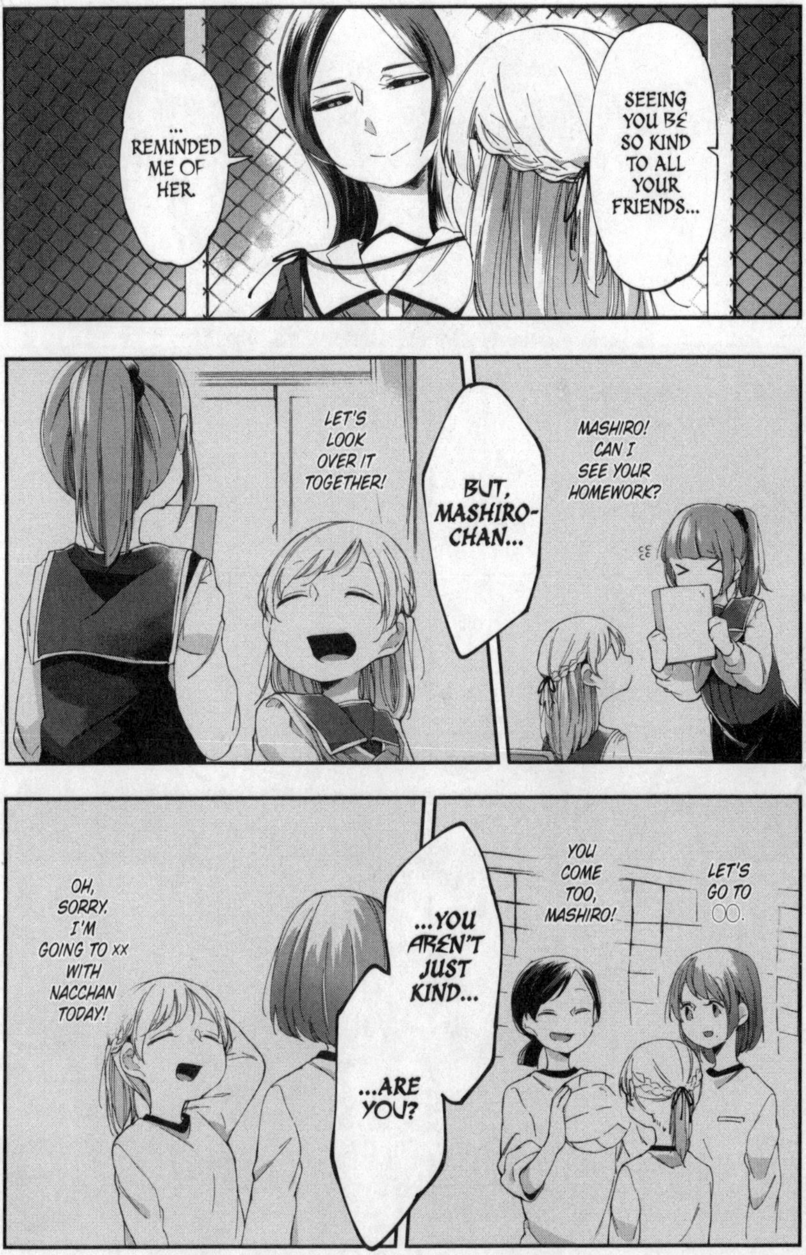
SEEING YOU BE SO KIND TO ALL YOUR FRIENDS...
...REMINDED ME OF HER.
MASHIRO! CAN I SEE YOUR HOMEWORK?
BUT, MASHIRO-CHAN...
LET'S LOOK OVER IT TOGETHER!
LET'S GO TO ○○.
YOU COME TOO, MASHIRO!
...YOU AREN'T JUST KIND...
...ARE YOU?
OH, SORRY. I'M GOING TO xx WITH NACCHAN TODAY!

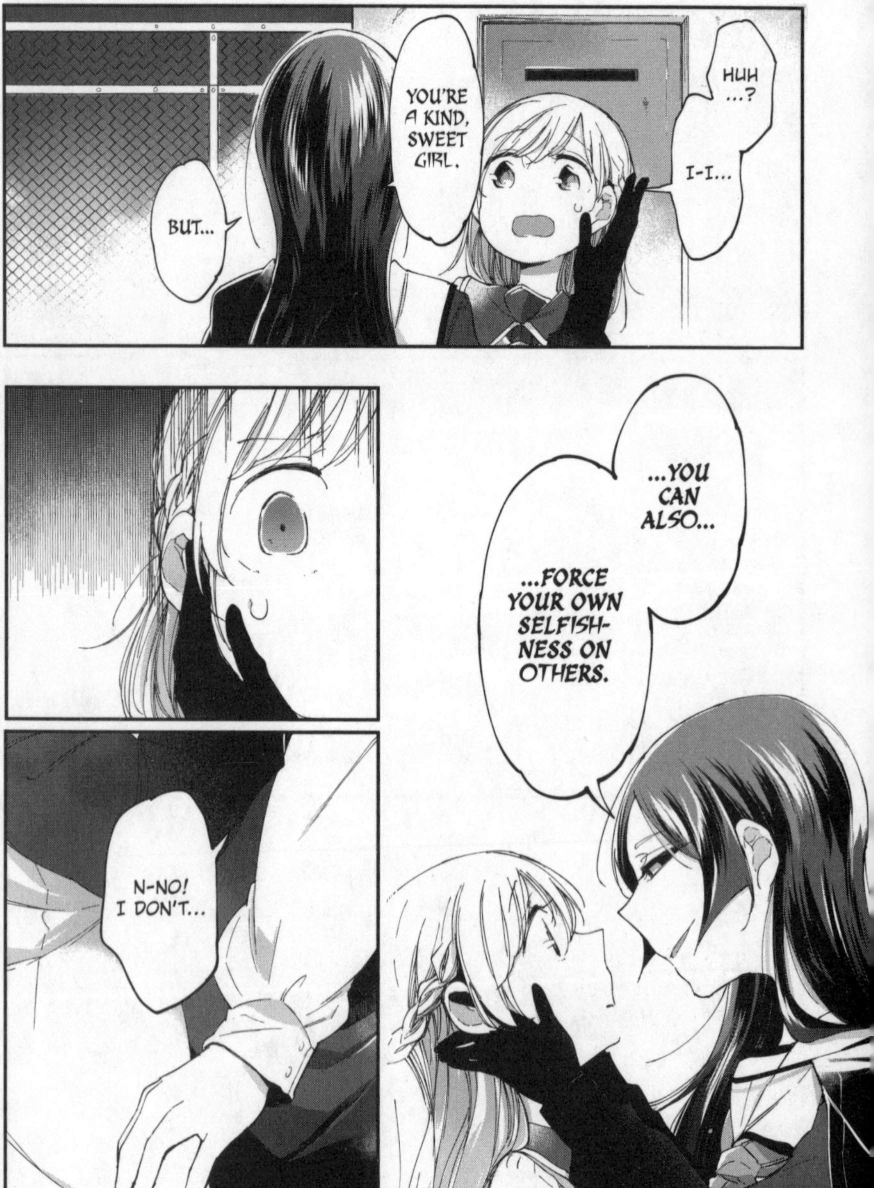
HUH ...?
I-I...
YOU'RE A KIND, SWEET GIRL.
BUT...
...YOU CAN ALSO...
...FORCE YOUR OWN SELFISH-NESS ON OTHERS.
N-NO! I DON'T...

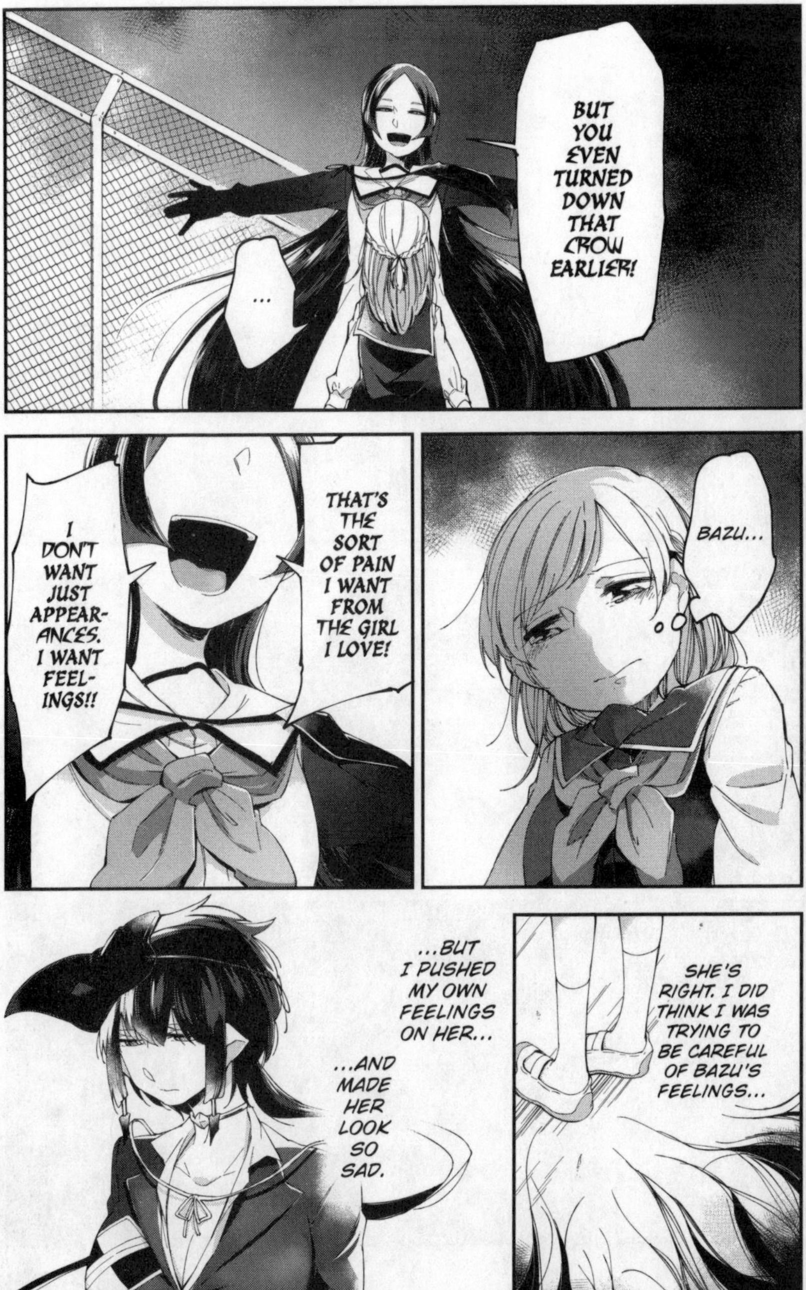
BUT YOU EVEN TURNED DOWN THAT CROW EARLIER!
...
BAZU...
THAT'S THE SORT OF PAIN I WANT FROM THE GIRL I LOVE!
I DON'T WANT JUST APPEARANCES. I WANT FEELINGS!!
SHE'S RIGHT. I DID THINK I WAS TRYING TO BE CAREFUL OF BAZU'S FEELINGS...
...BUT I PUSHED MY OWN FEELINGS ON HER...
...AND MADE HER LOOK SO SAD.

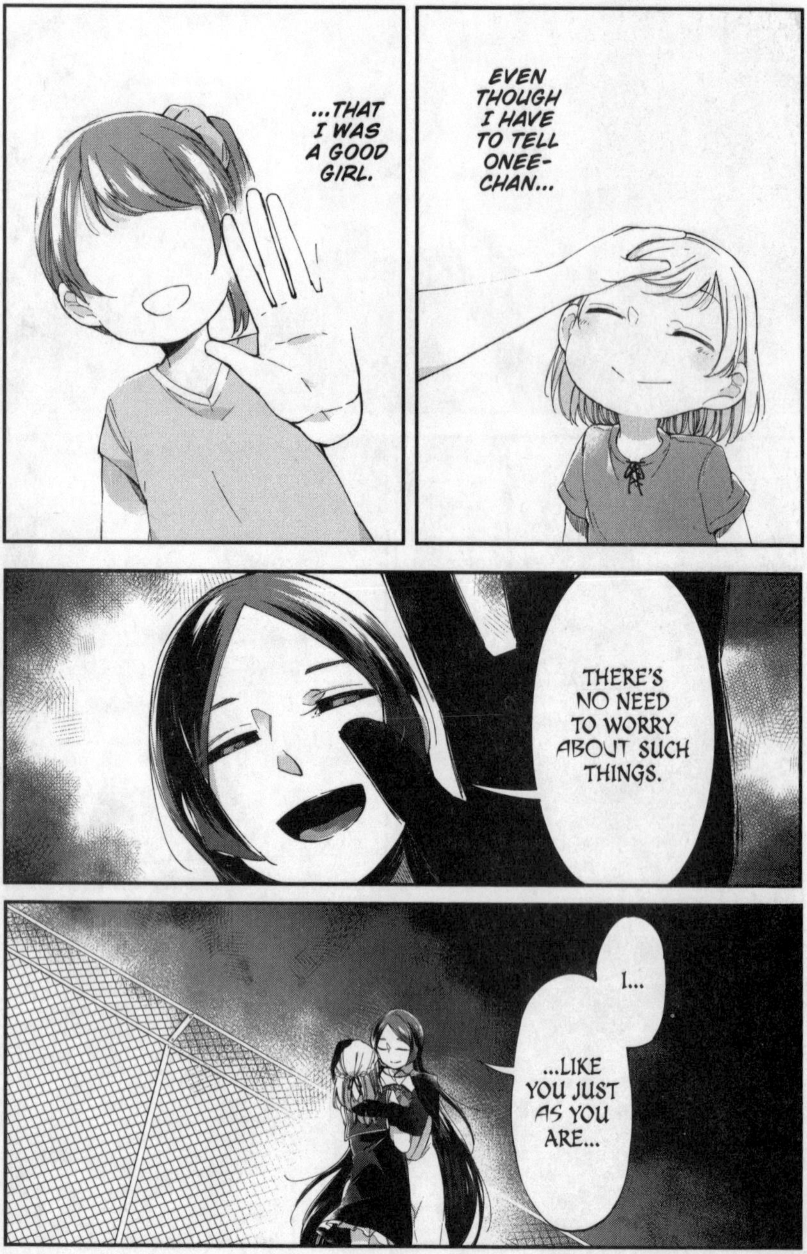
EVEN THOUGH I HAVE TO TELL ONEE-CHAN...
...THAT I WAS A GOOD GIRL.
THERE'S NO NEED TO WORRY ABOUT SUCH THINGS.
I...
...LIKE YOU JUST AS YOU ARE...

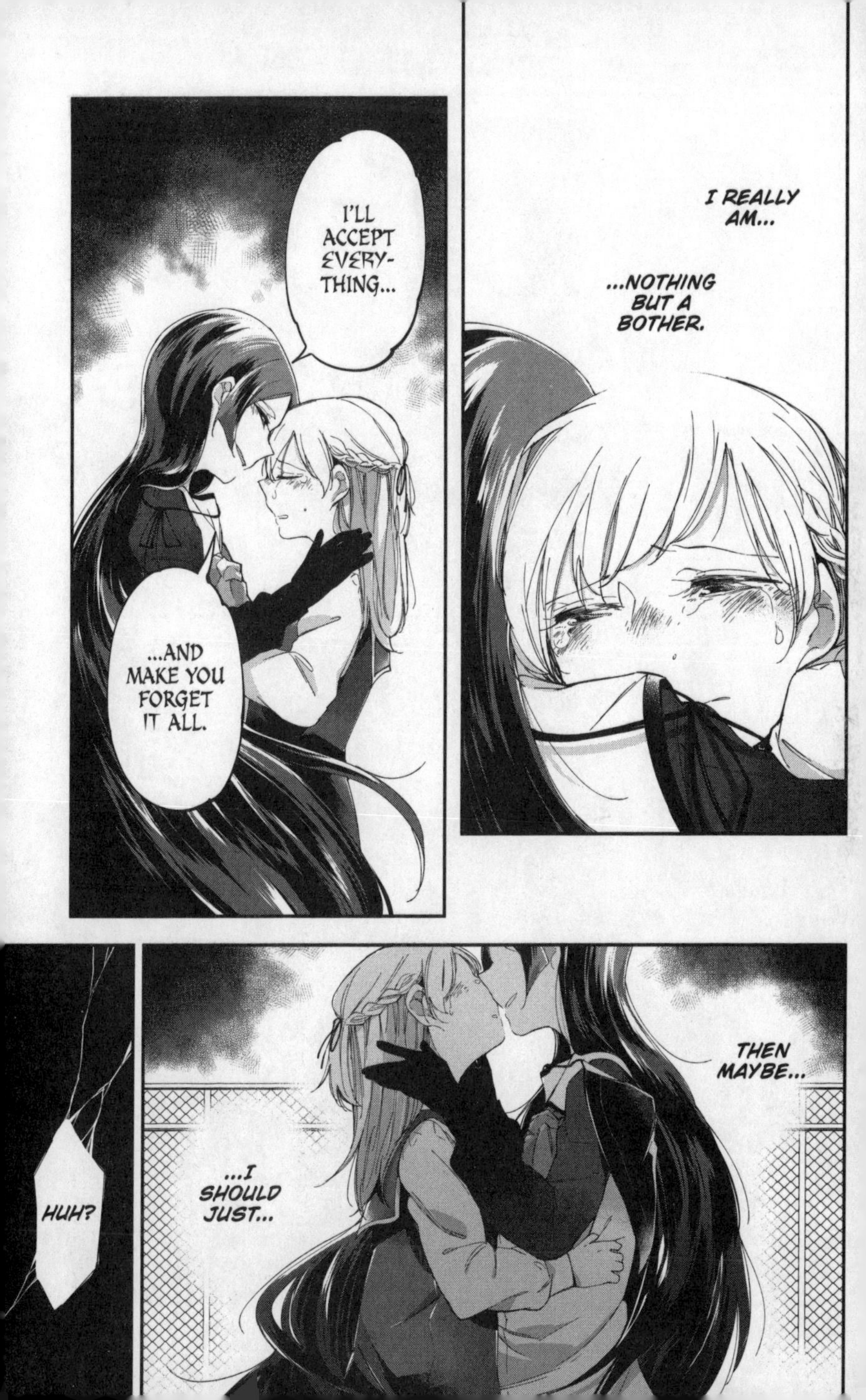
I REALLY AM...
...NOTHING BUT A BOTHER.
I'LL ACCEPT EVERY-THING...
...AND MAKE YOU FORGET IT ALL.
THEN MAYBE...
...I SHOULD JUST...
HUH?

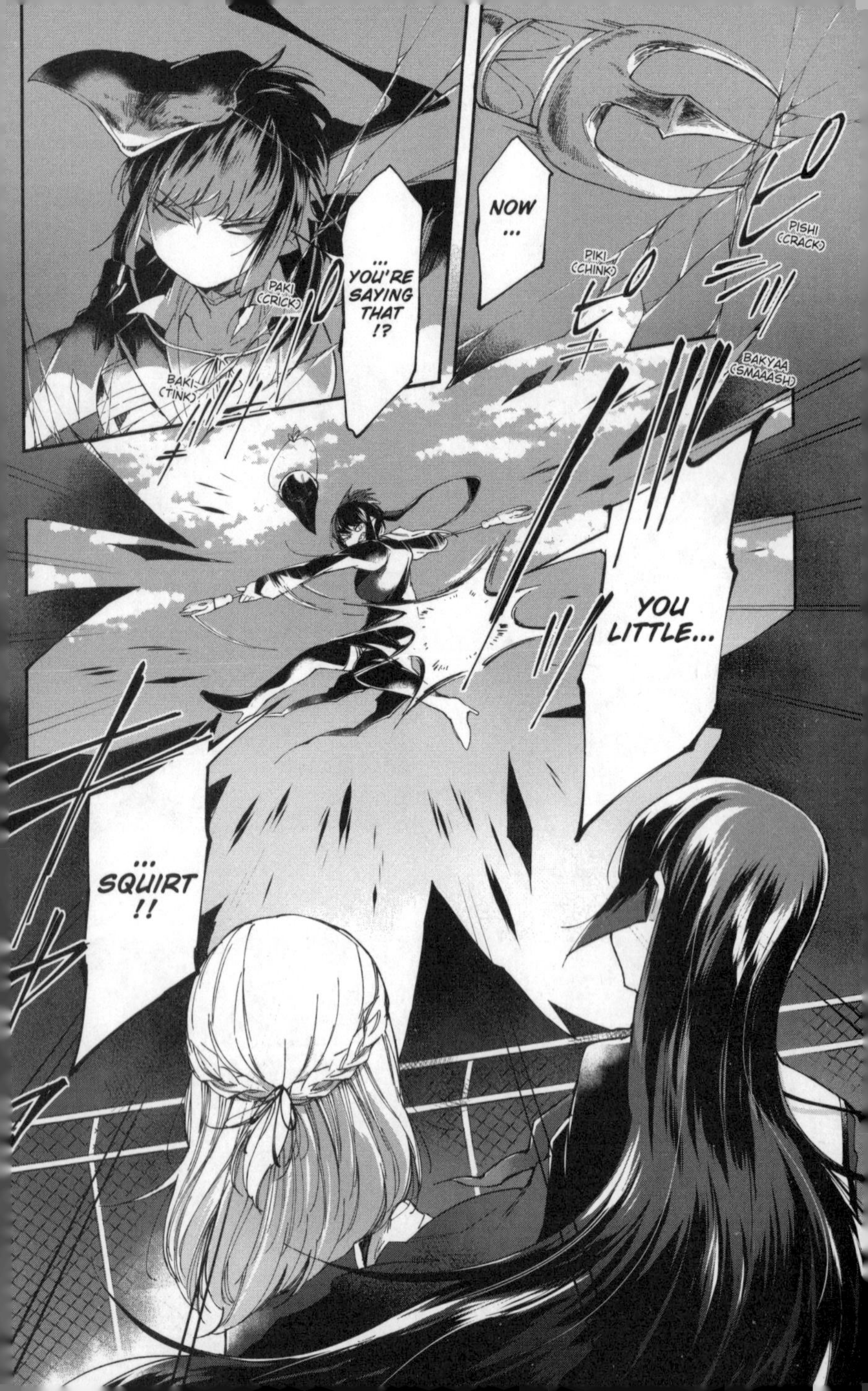
PISHI
(CRACK)
NOW ...
PIKI
(CHINK)
BAKYAA
(SMAAASH)
... YOU'RE SAYING THAT !?
PAKI
(CRICK)
BAKI
(TINK)
YOU LITTLE...
... SQUIRT !!

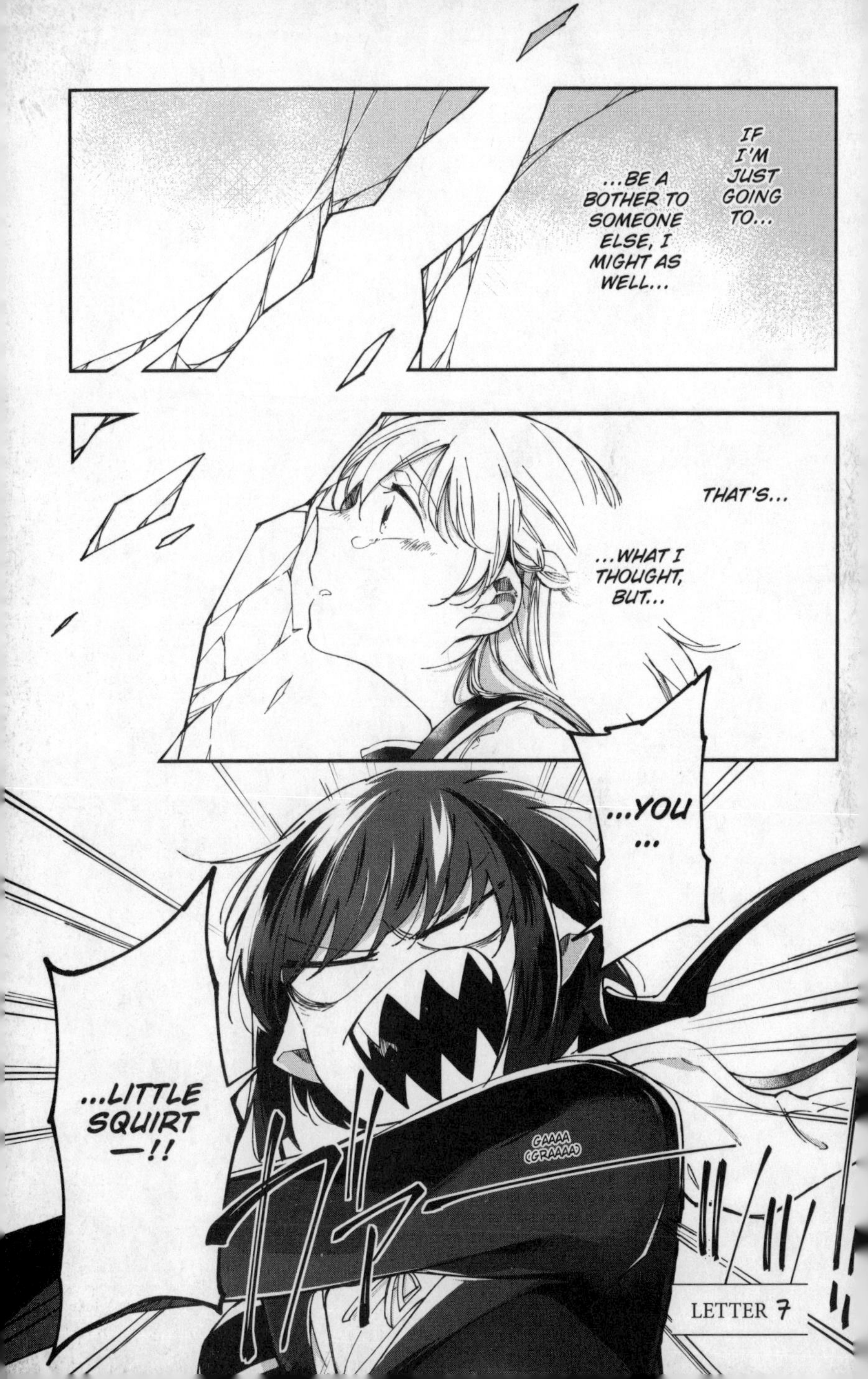
IF I'M JUST GOING TO...
...BE A BOTHER TO SOMEONE ELSE, I MIGHT AS WELL...
THAT'S...
...WHAT I THOUGHT, BUT...
...YOU ...
...LITTLE SQUIRT—!!
GAAAA (GRAAAA)
LETTER 7

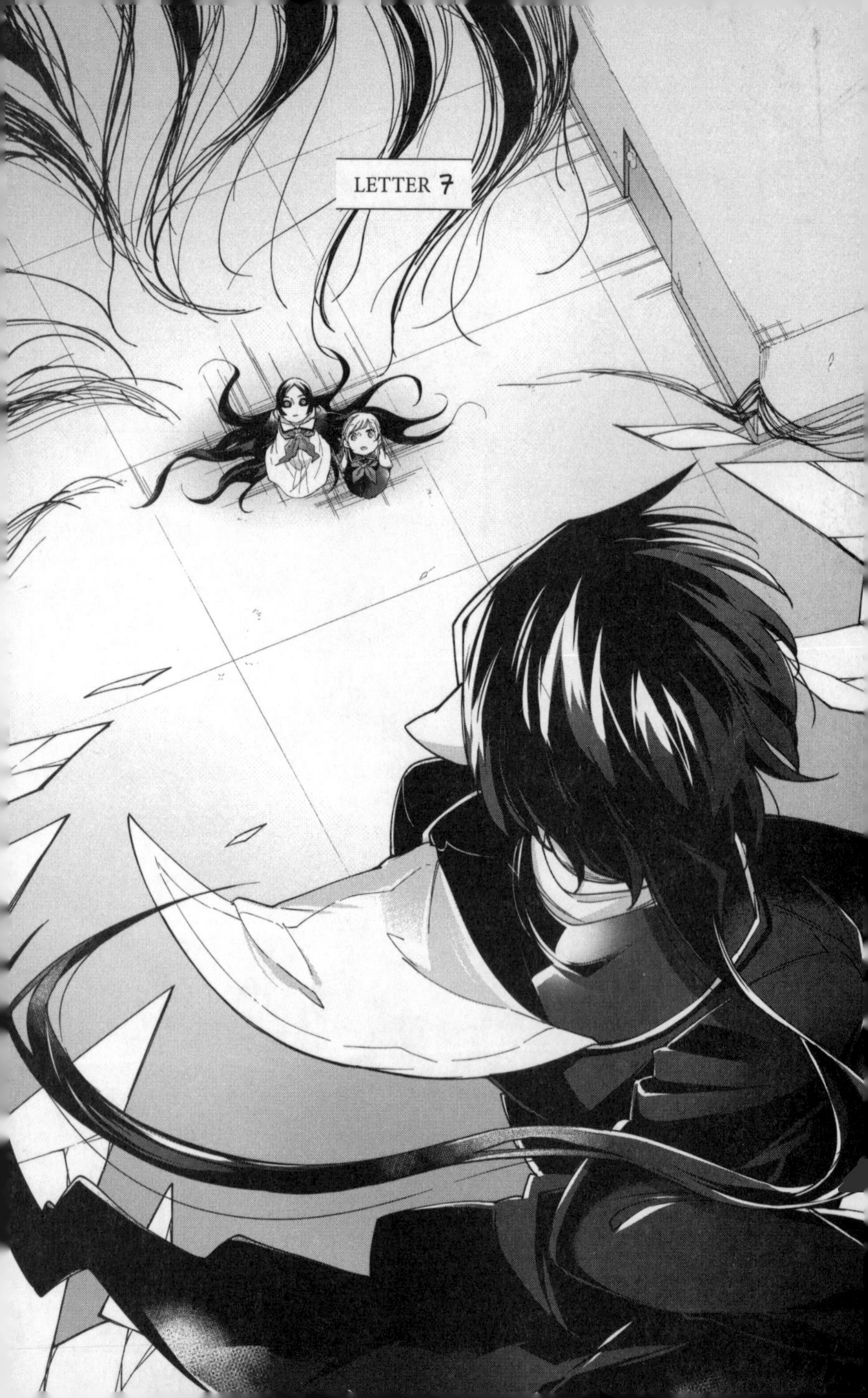
LETTER 7

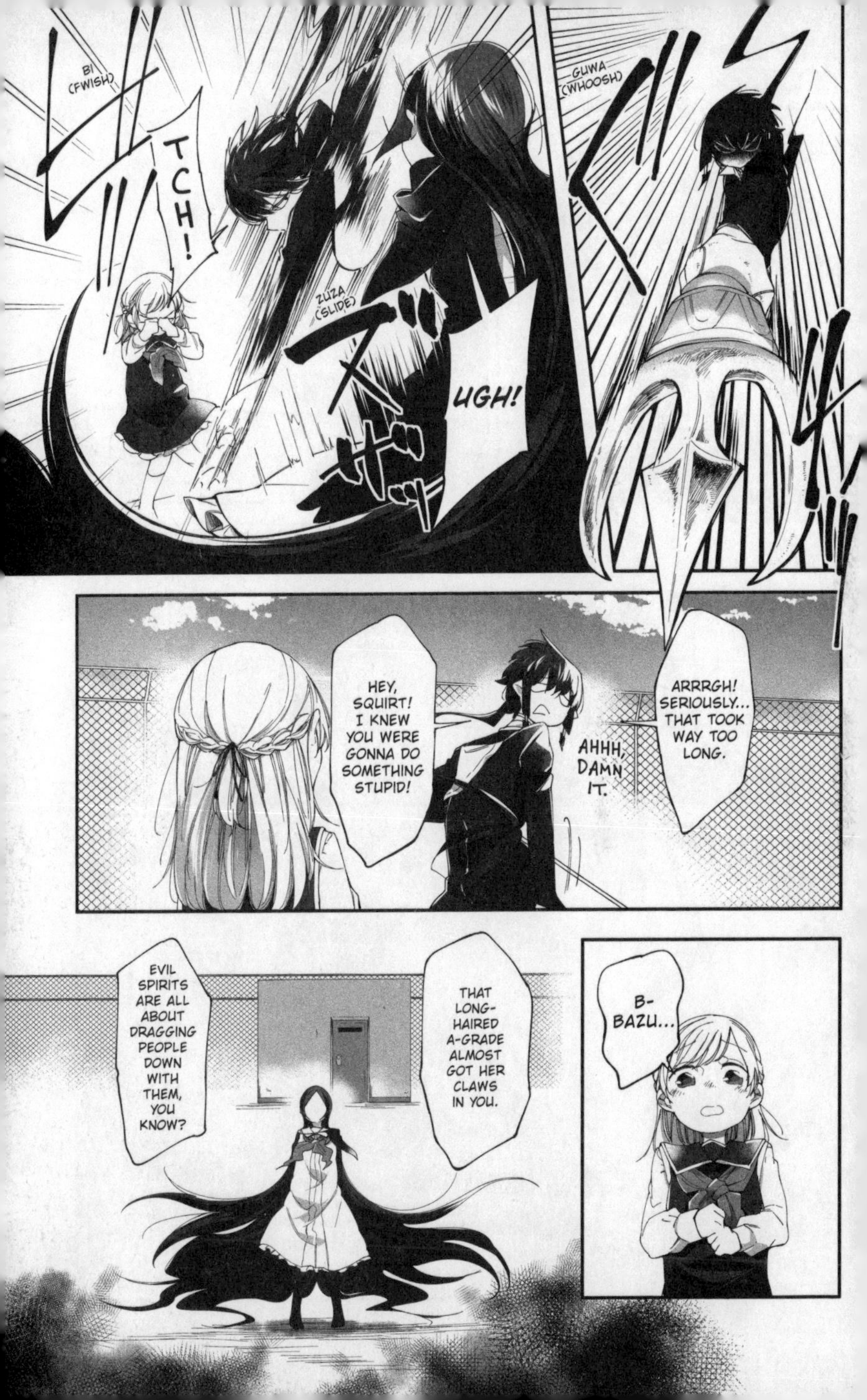
GUWA (WHOOSH)
BI (FWISH)
TCH!
ZUZA (SLIDE)
UGH!
ARRRGH! SERIOUSLY... THAT TOOK WAY TOO LONG.
AHHH, DAMN IT.
HEY, SQUIRT! I KNEW YOU WERE GONNA DO SOMETHING STUPID!
B-BAZU...
THAT LONG-HAIRED A-GRADE ALMOST GOT HER CLAWS IN YOU.
EVIL SPIRITS ARE ALL ABOUT DRAGGING PEOPLE DOWN WITH THEM, YOU KNOW?

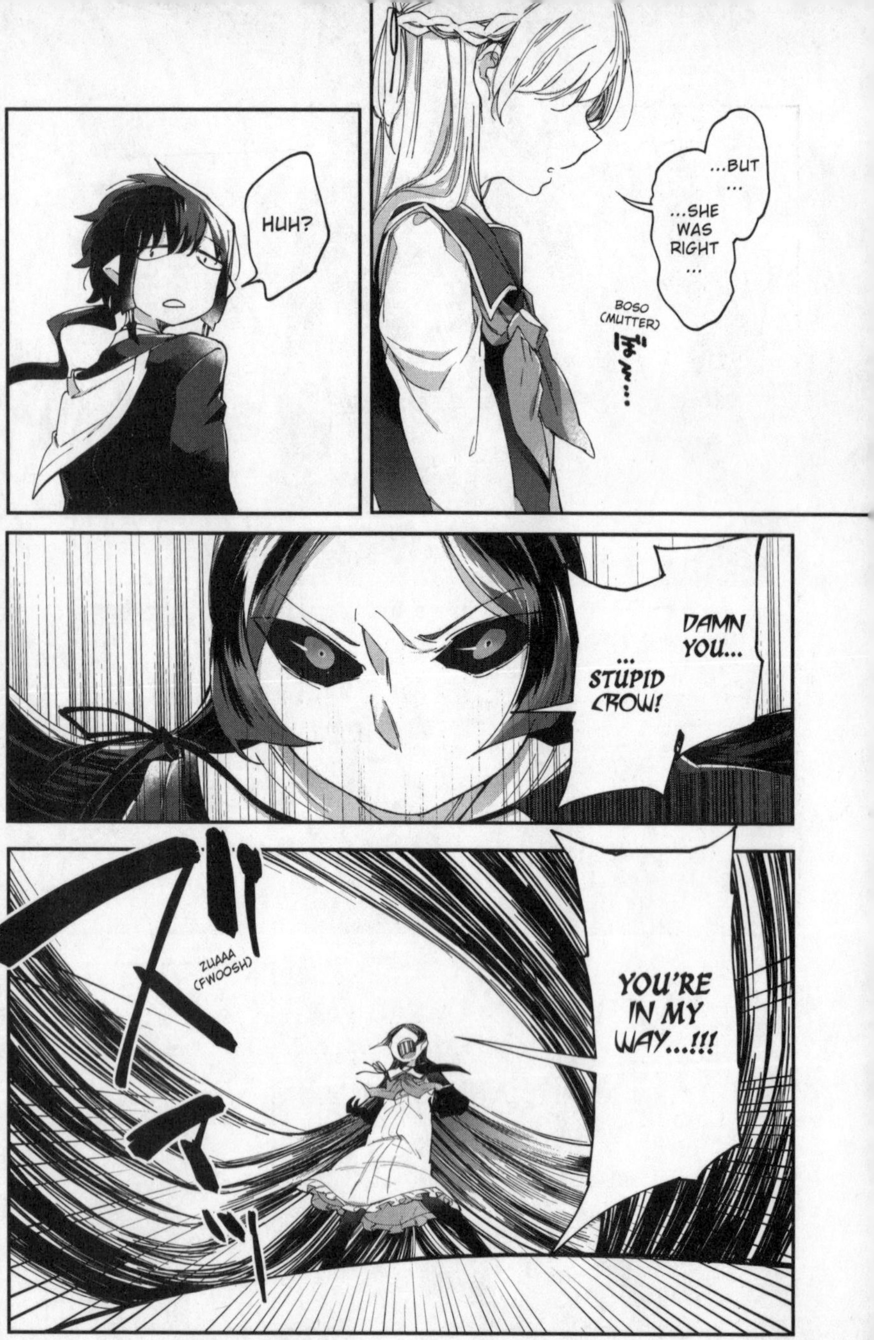

...BUT ... ...SHE WAS RIGHT ...
BOSO (MUTTER)
HUH?
DAMN YOU... ... STUPID CROW!
ZUAAA (FWOOSH)
YOU'RE IN MY WAY...!!!

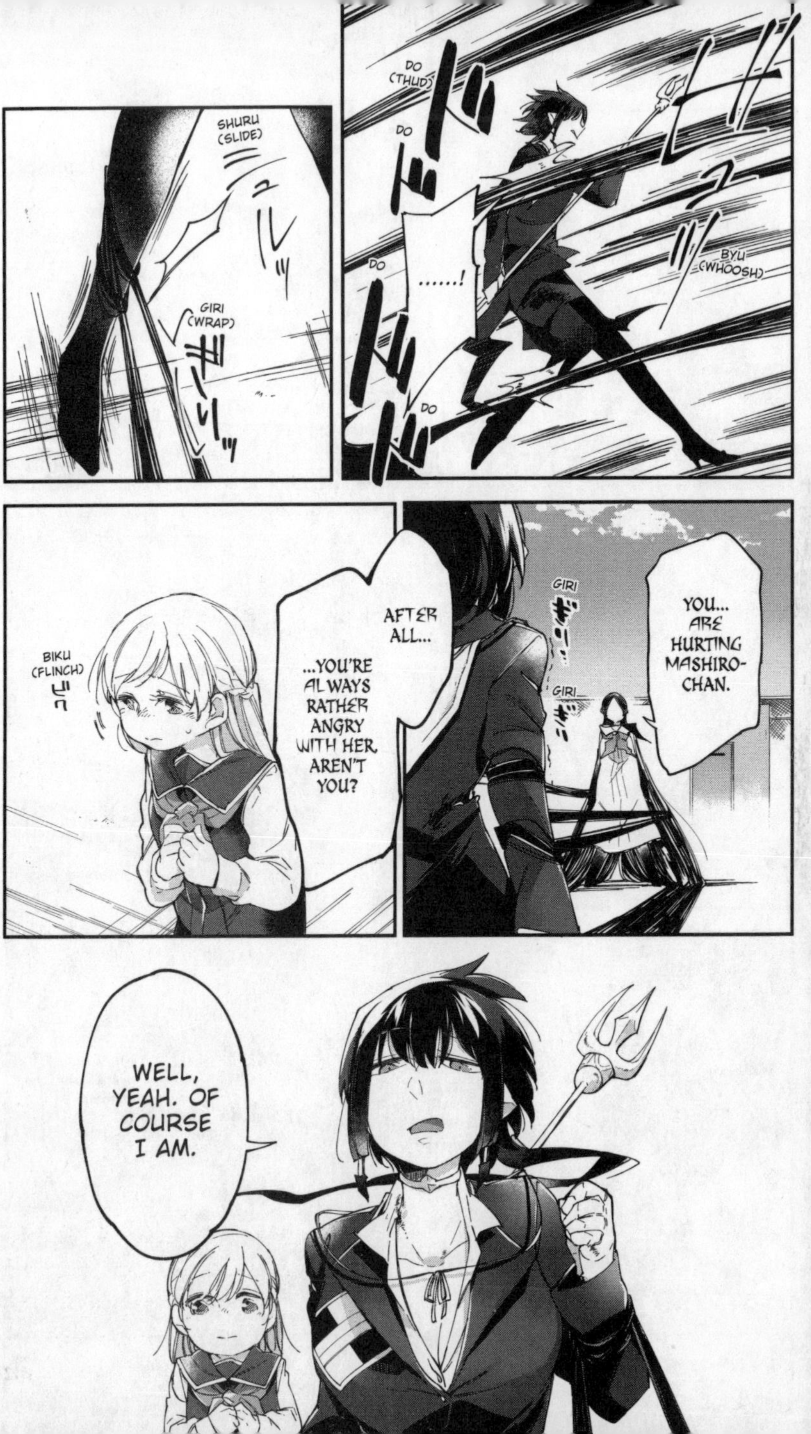
DO (THUD)
DO
BYU (WHOOSH)
......!
DO
DO
SHURU (SLIDE)
GIRI (WRAP)
YOU... ARE HURTING MASHIRO-CHAN.
GIRI
GIRI
AFTER ALL...
...YOU'RE ALWAYS RATHER ANGRY WITH HER AREN'T YOU?
BIKU (FLINCH)
WELL, YEAH. OF COURSE I AM.

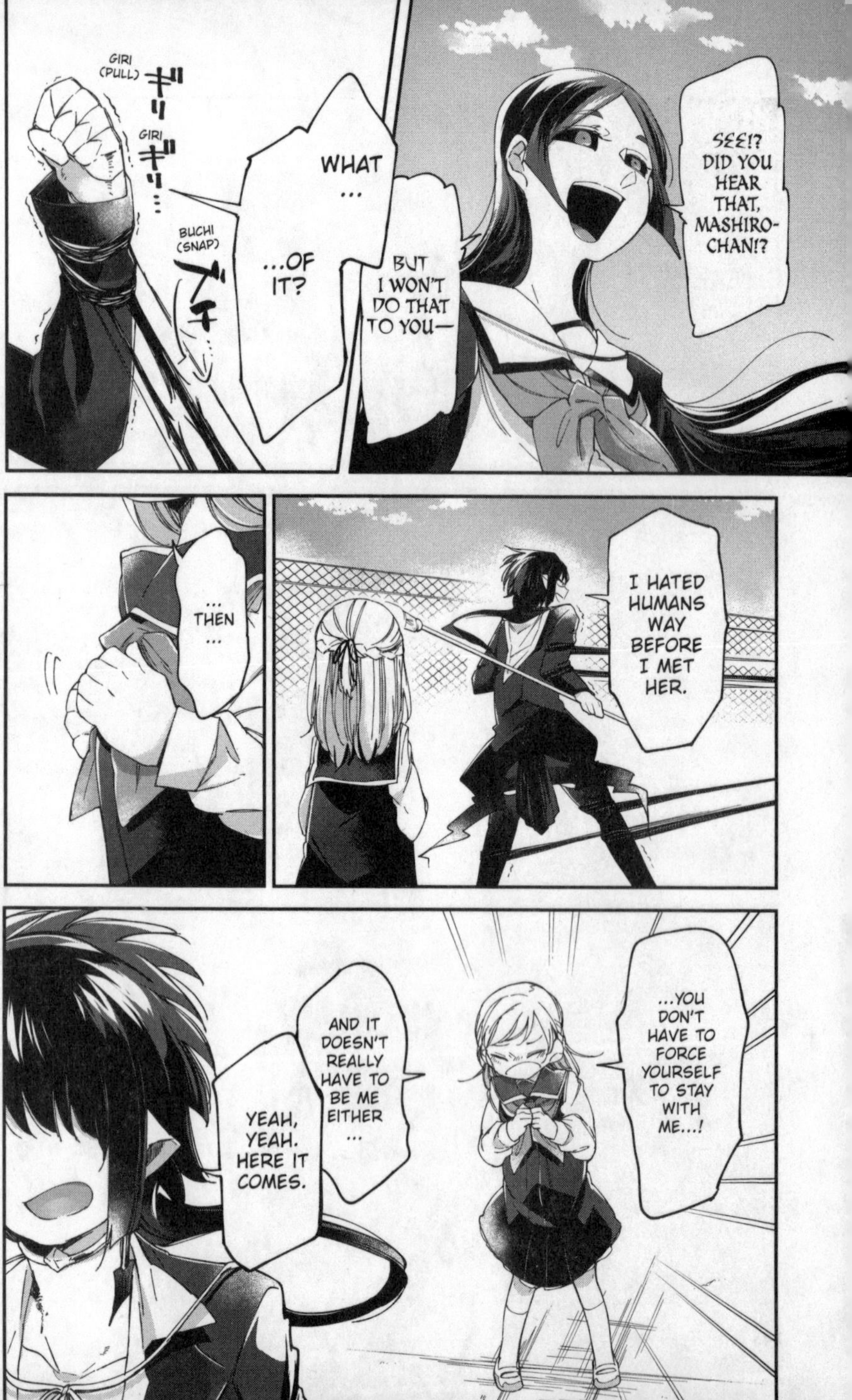
SEE!? DID YOU HEAR THAT, MASHIRO-CHAN!?
BUT I WON'T DO THAT TO YOU—
WHAT ...
...OF IT?
GIRI (PULL) ギリ
GIRI ギリ...
BUCHI (SNAP) ブチ
I HATED HUMANS WAY BEFORE I MET HER.
... THEN ...
...YOU DON'T HAVE TO FORCE YOURSELF TO STAY WITH ME...!
AND IT DOESN'T REALLY HAVE TO BE ME EITHER ...
YEAH, YEAH. HERE IT COMES.

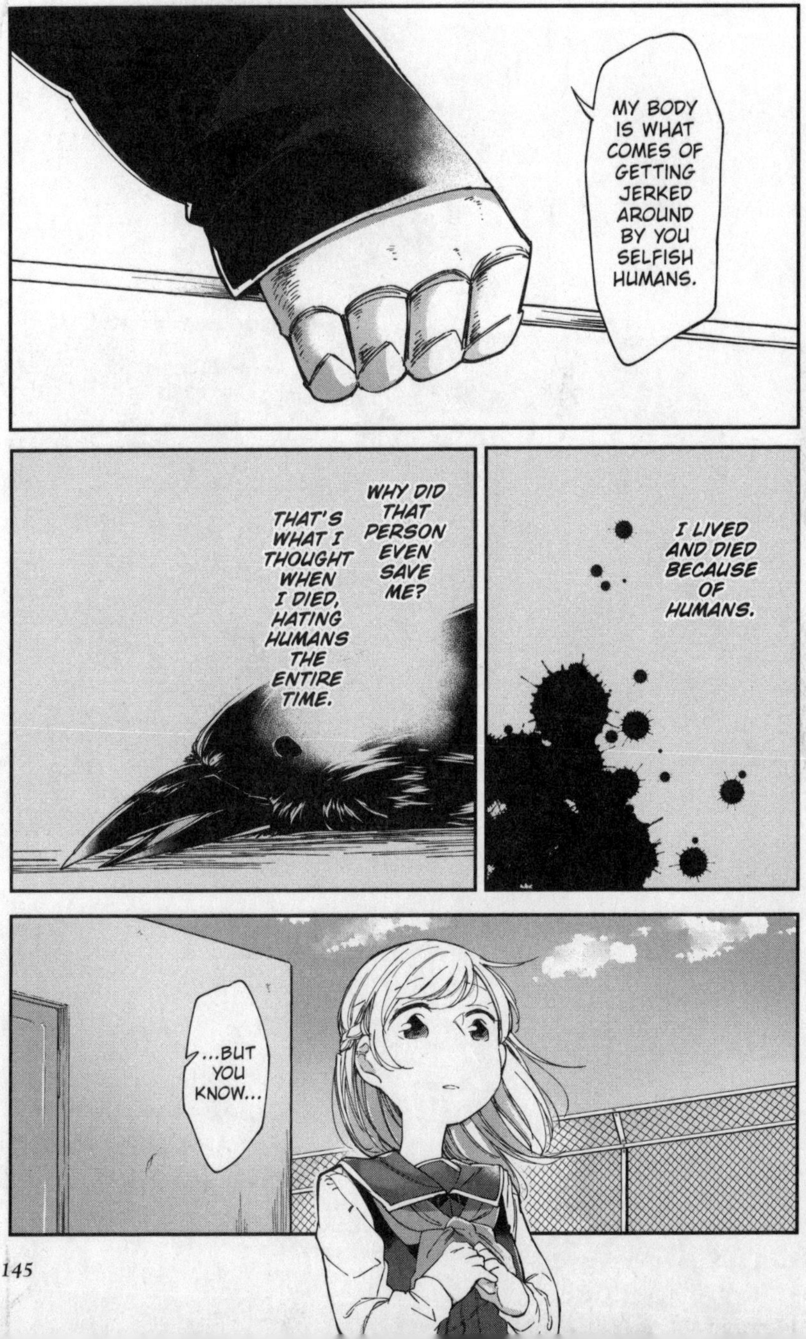
MY BODY IS WHAT COMES OF GETTING JERKED AROUND BY YOU SELFISH HUMANS.
I LIVED AND DIED BECAUSE OF HUMANS.
WHY DID THAT PERSON EVEN SAVE ME?
THAT'S WHAT I THOUGHT WHEN I DIED, HATING HUMANS THE ENTIRE TIME.
...BUT YOU KNOW...

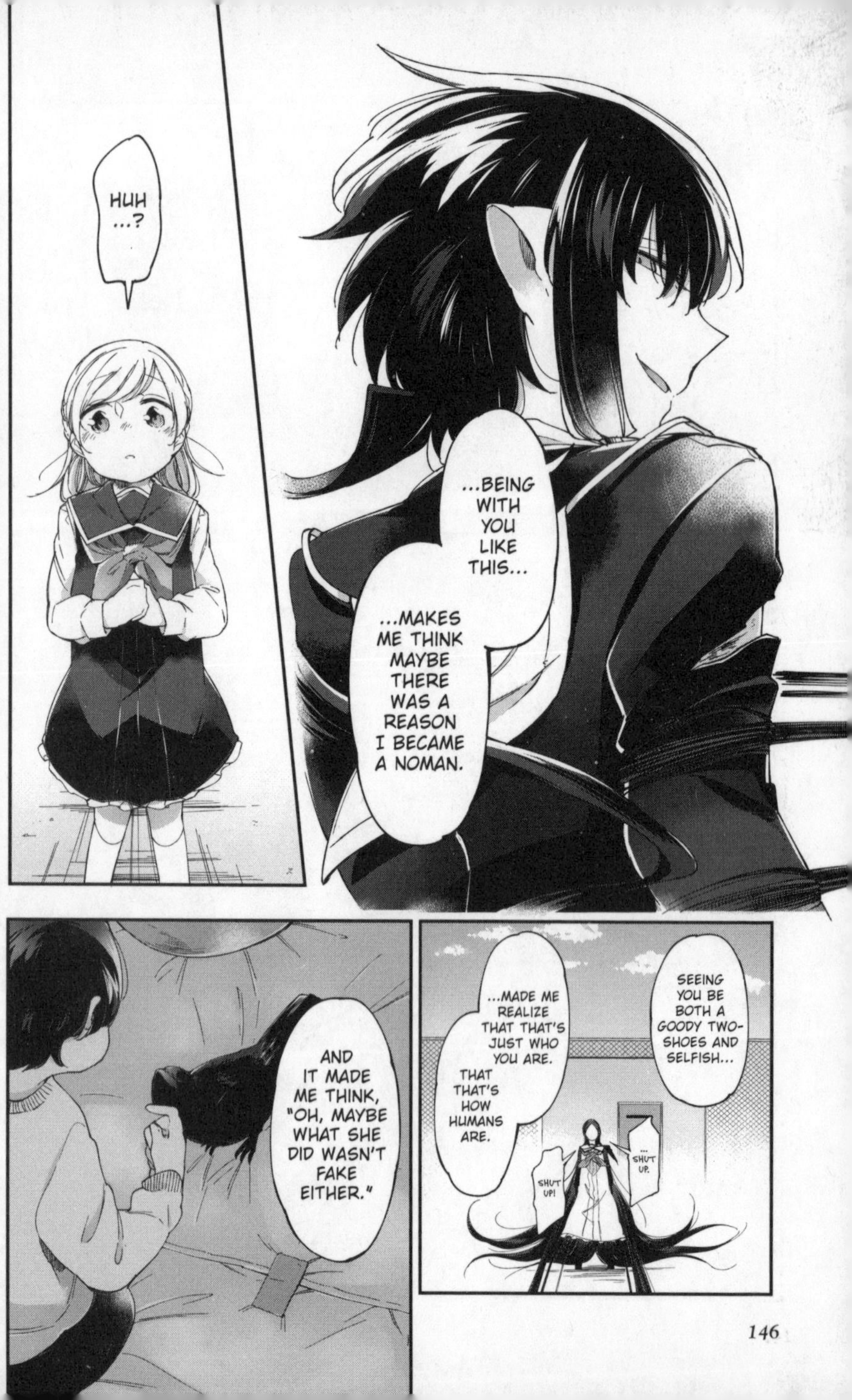
...BEING WITH YOU LIKE THIS...
...MAKES ME THINK MAYBE THERE WAS A REASON I BECAME A NOMAN.
HUH ...?
SEEING YOU BE BOTH A GOODY TWO-SHOES AND SELFISH...
...MADE ME REALIZE THAT THAT'S JUST WHO YOU ARE.
THAT THAT'S HOW HUMANS ARE.
...SHUT UP.
SHUT UP!
AND IT MADE ME THINK, "OH, MAYBE WHAT SHE DID WASN'T FAKE EITHER."

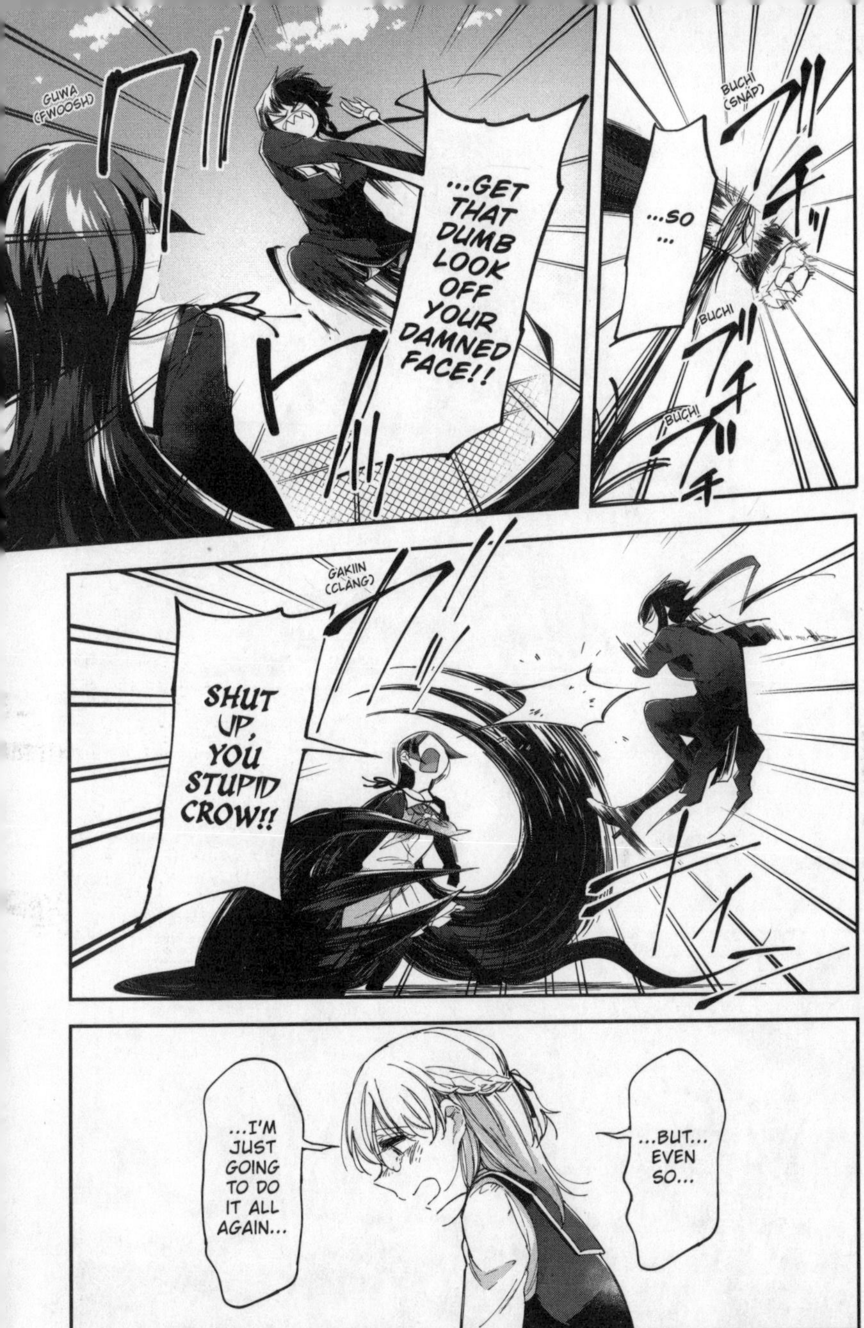
BUCHI (SNAP)
...SO ...
BUCHI
BUCH!
GUWA (FWOOSH)
...GET THAT DUMB LOOK OFF YOUR DAMNED FACE!!
GAKIIN (CLANG)
SHUT UP, YOU STUPID CROW!!
...BUT... EVEN SO...
...I'M JUST GOING TO DO IT ALL AGAIN...

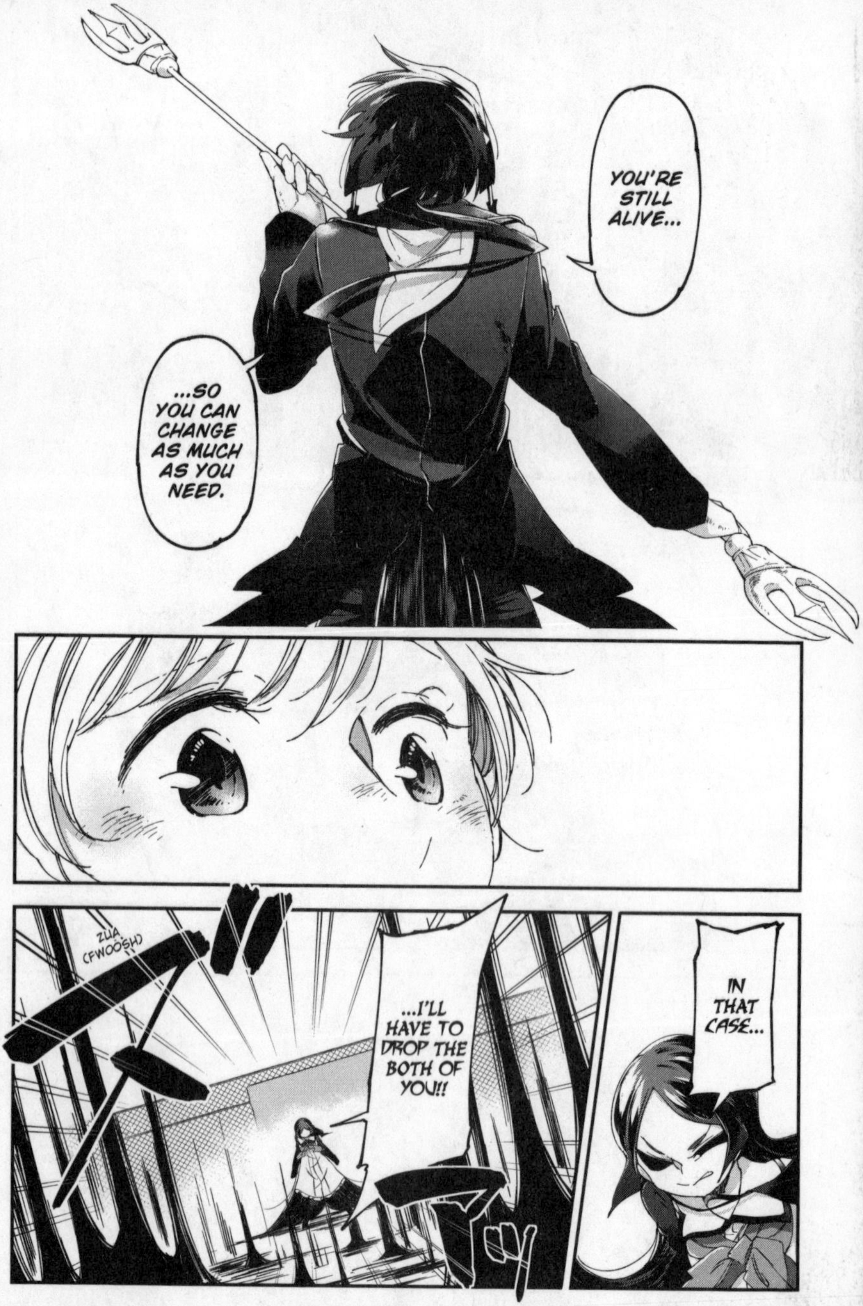
YOU'RE STILL ALIVE...
...SO YOU CAN CHANGE AS MUCH AS YOU NEED.
IN THAT CASE...
...I'LL HAVE TO DROP THE BOTH OF YOU!!
ZUA (FWOOSH)

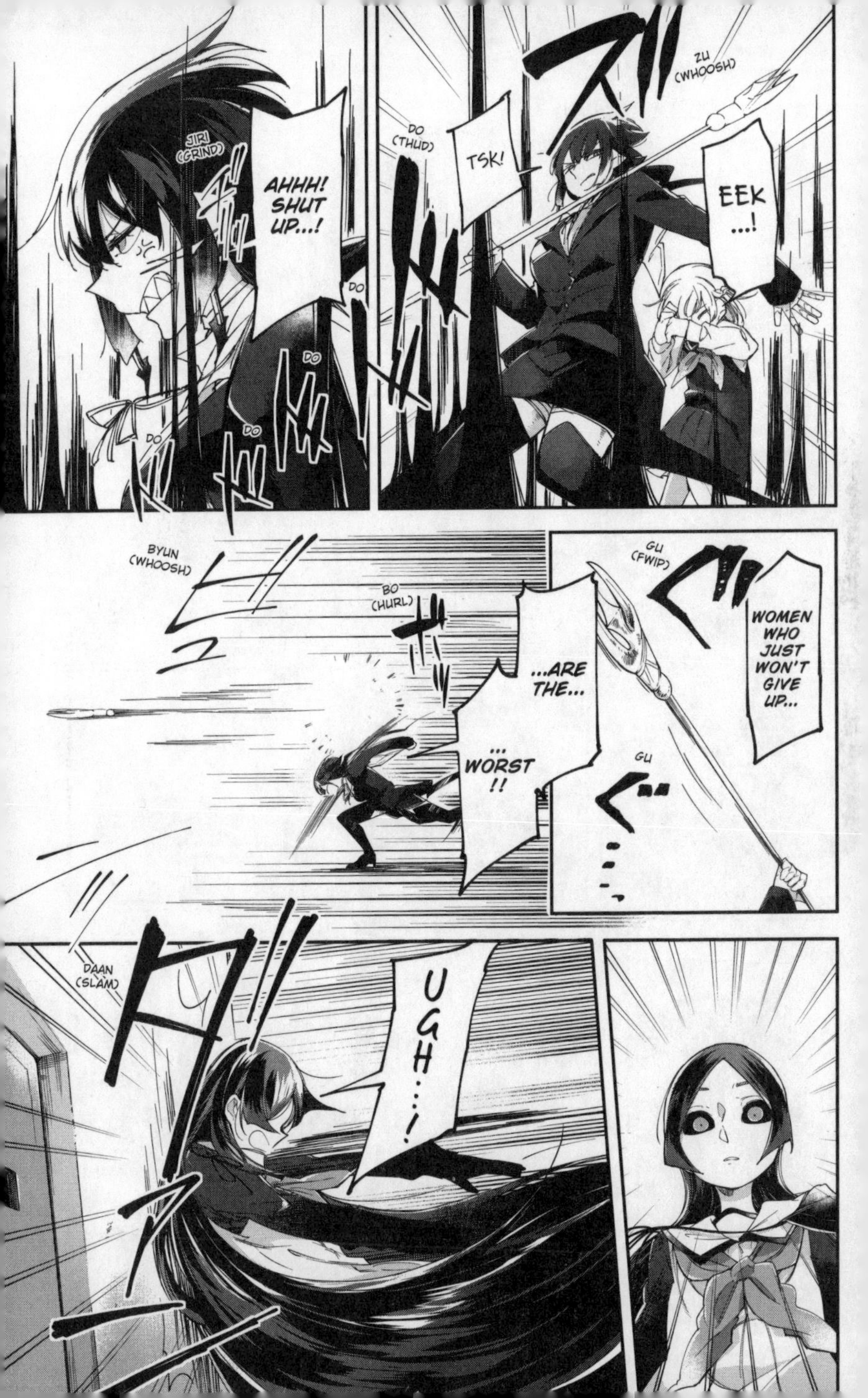
ZU (WHOOSH)
EEK ...!
TSK!
DO (THUD)
AHHH! SHUT UP...!
JIRI (GRIND)
DO
DO
DO
DO
GU (FWIP)
WOMEN WHO JUST WON'T GIVE UP...
GU
...ARE THE...
BO (HURL)
BYUN (WHOOSH)
... WORST !!
UGH...!
DAAN (SLAM)

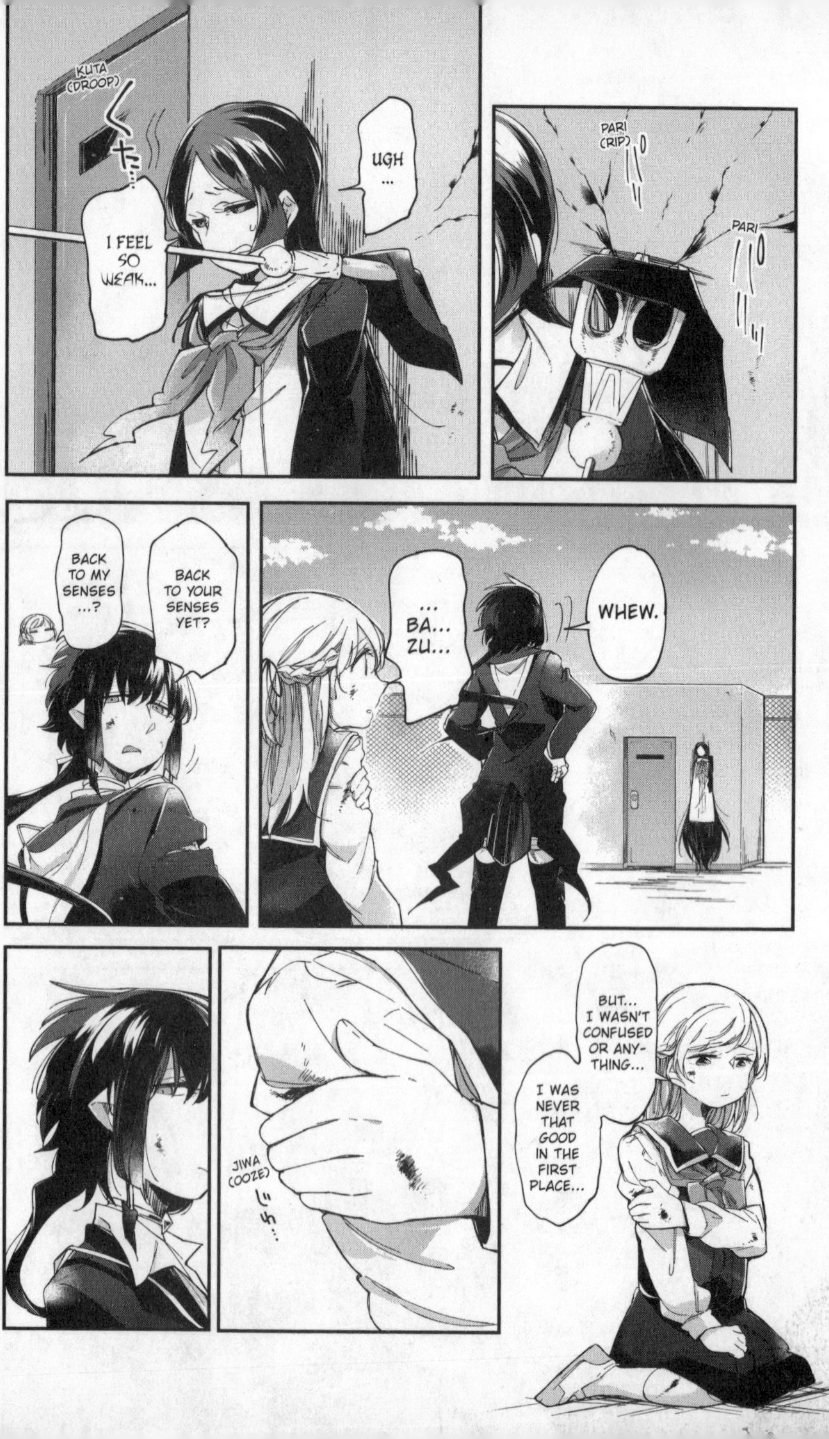
PARI (RIP)
PARI
UGH...
KUTA (DROOP)
I FEEL SO WEAK...
WHEW.
... BA... ZU...
BACK TO YOUR SENSES YET?
BACK TO MY SENSES ...?
BUT... I WASN'T CONFUSED OR ANYTHING...
I WAS NEVER THAT GOOD IN THE FIRST PLACE...
JIWA (OOZE)

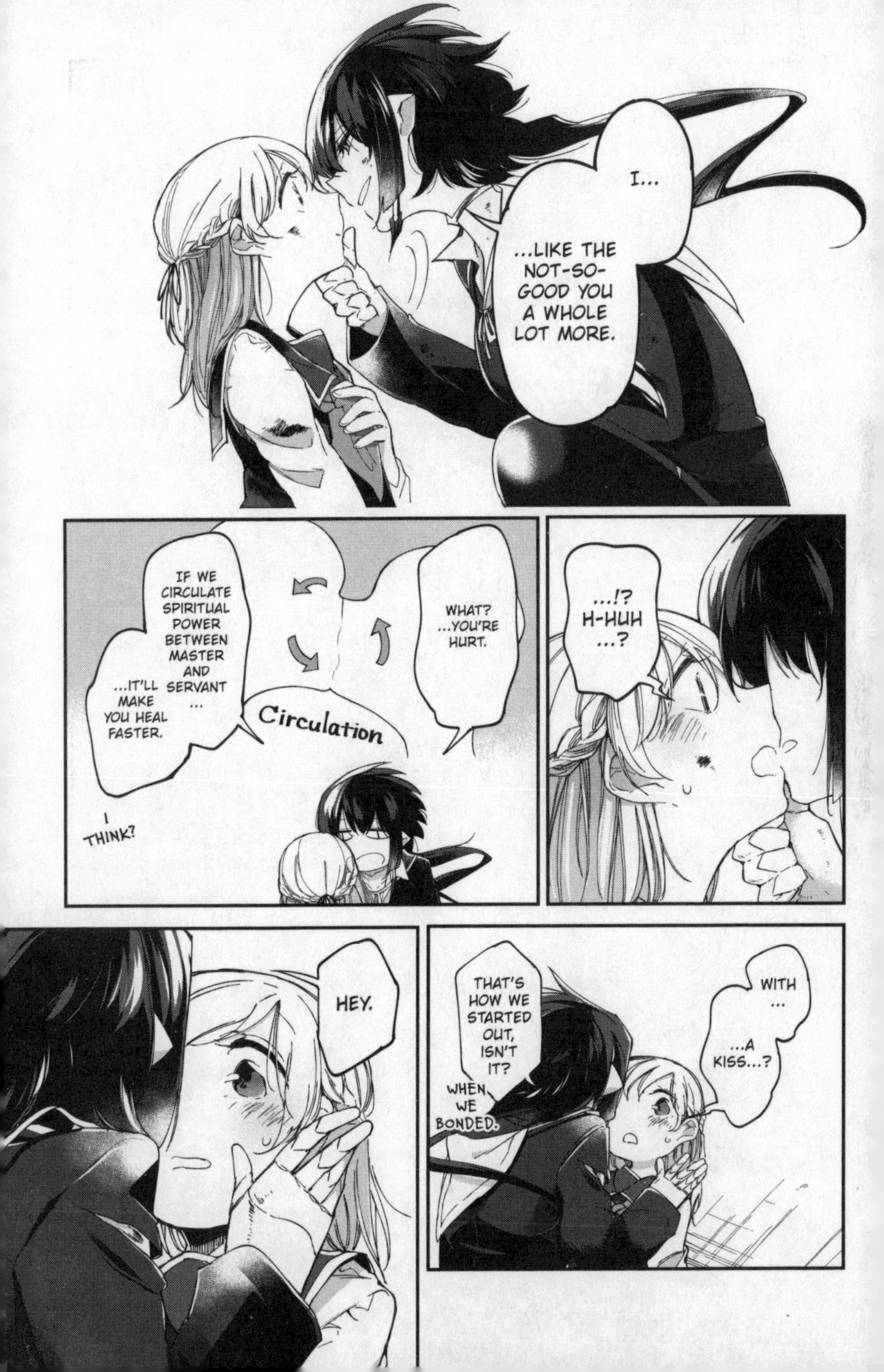
I...
...LIKE THE NOT-SO-GOOD YOU A WHOLE LOT MORE.
...!? H-HUH ...?
WHAT? ...YOU'RE HURT.
IF WE CIRCULATE SPIRITUAL POWER BETWEEN MASTER AND SERVANT ... ...IT'LL MAKE YOU HEAL FASTER.
Circulation
I THINK?
WITH ... ...A KISS...?
THAT'S HOW WE STARTED OUT, ISN'T IT?
WHEN WE BONDED.
HEY.

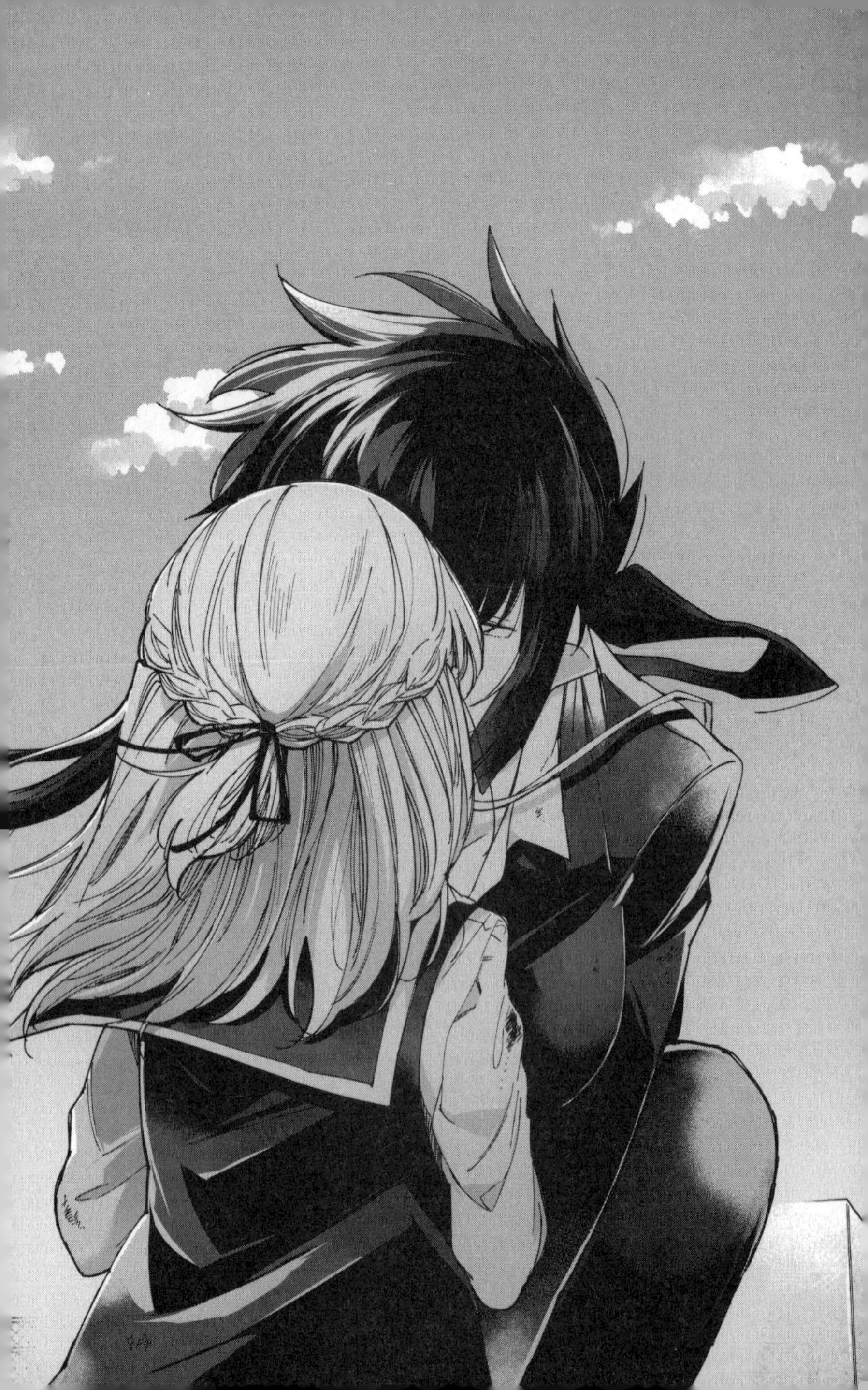

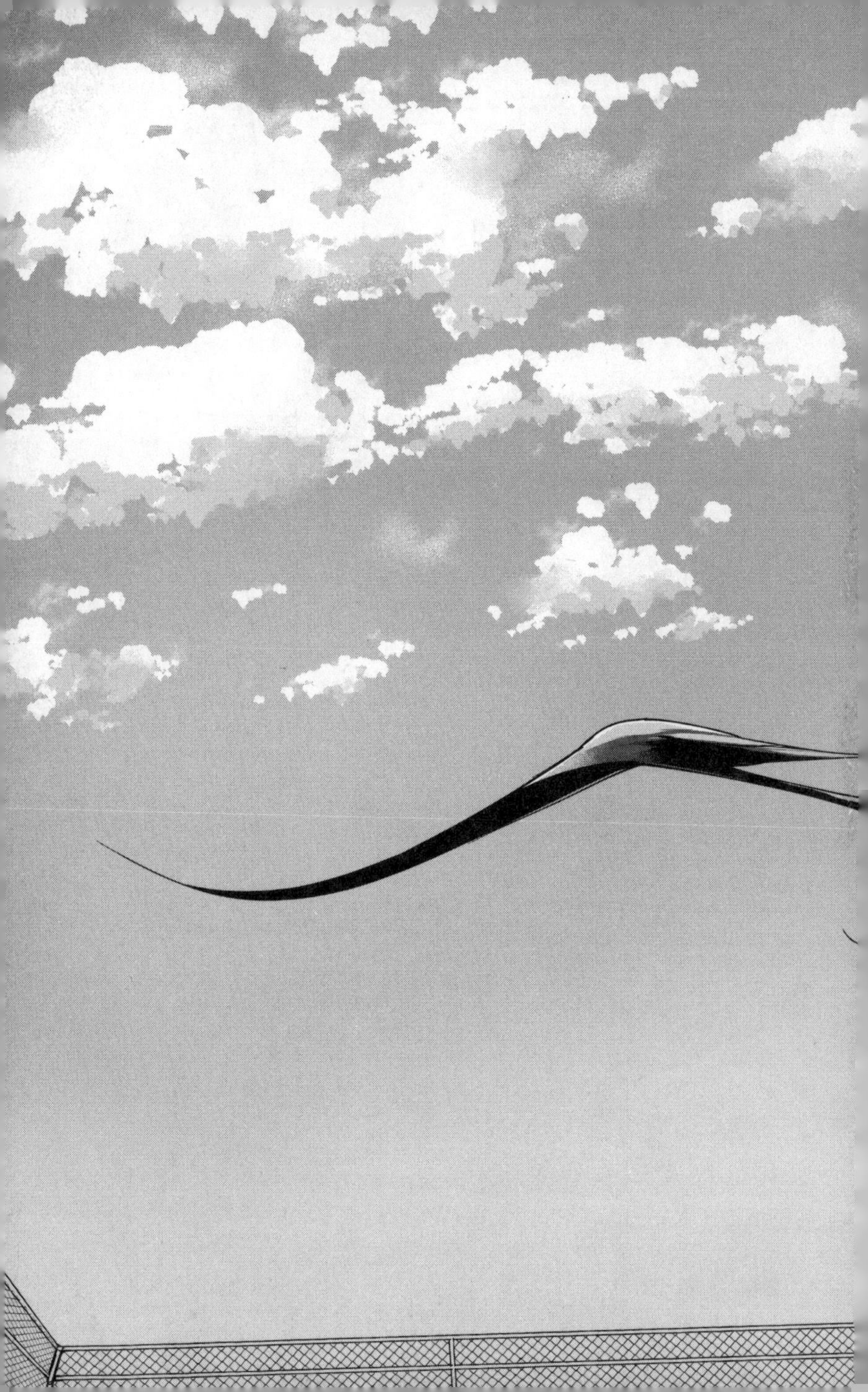

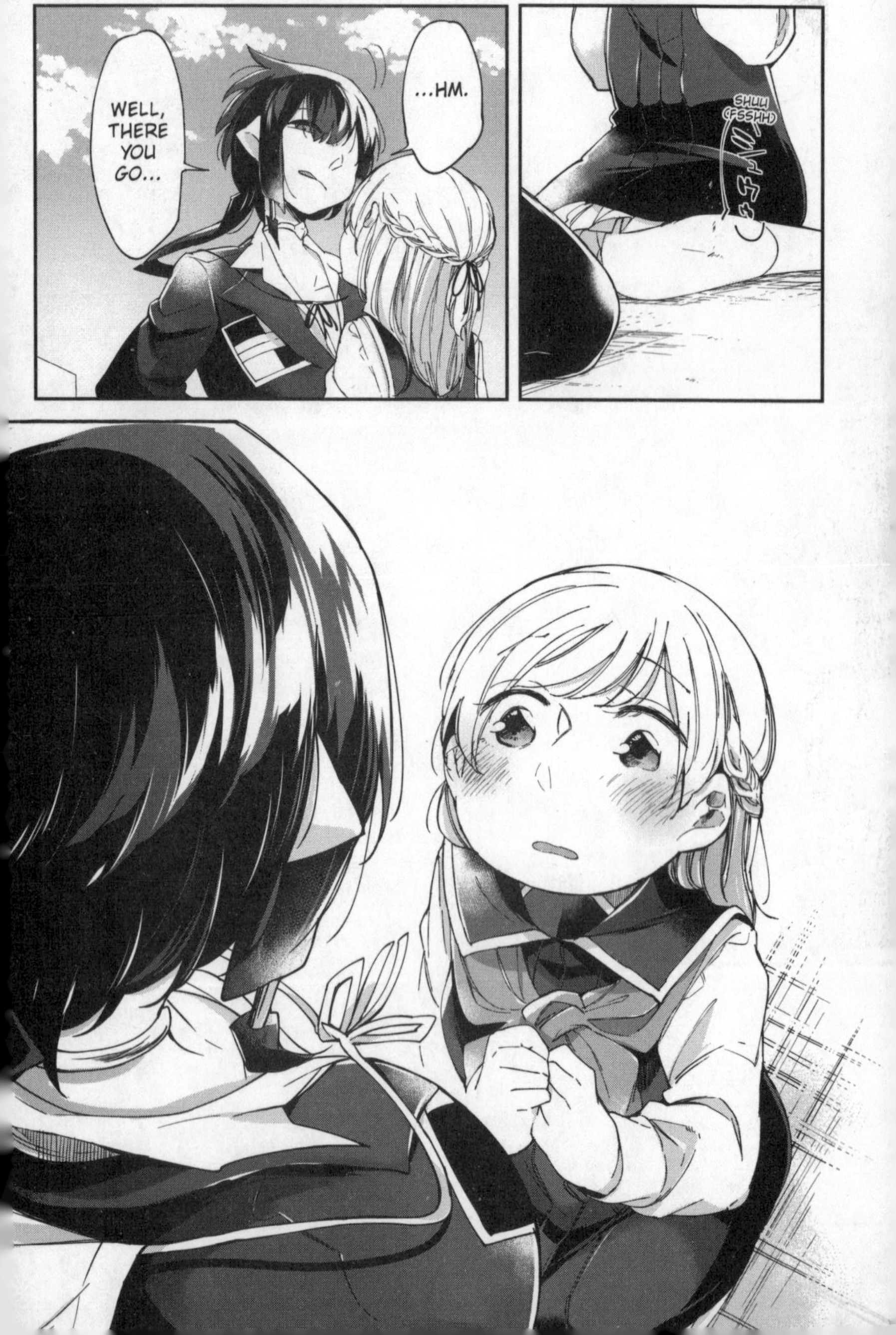
SHUU (FSSHH)
...HM.
WELL, THERE YOU GO...

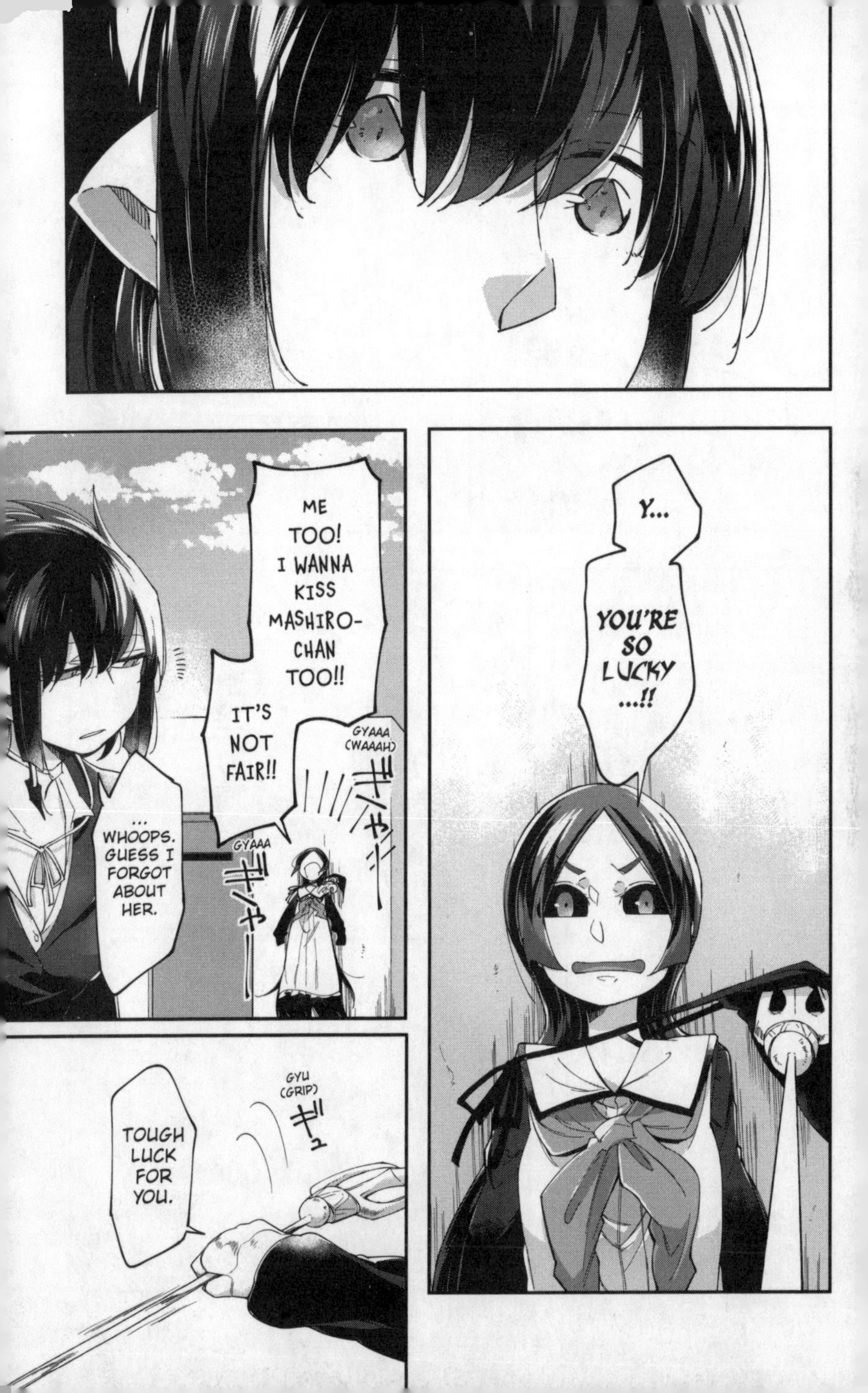
Y...
YOU'RE SO LUCKY ...!!
ME TOO! I WANNA KISS MASHIRO-CHAN TOO!!
IT'S NOT FAIR!!
GYAAA (WAAAH)
GYAAA
... WHOOPS. GUESS I FORGOT ABOUT HER.
GYU (GRIP)
TOUGH LUCK FOR YOU.

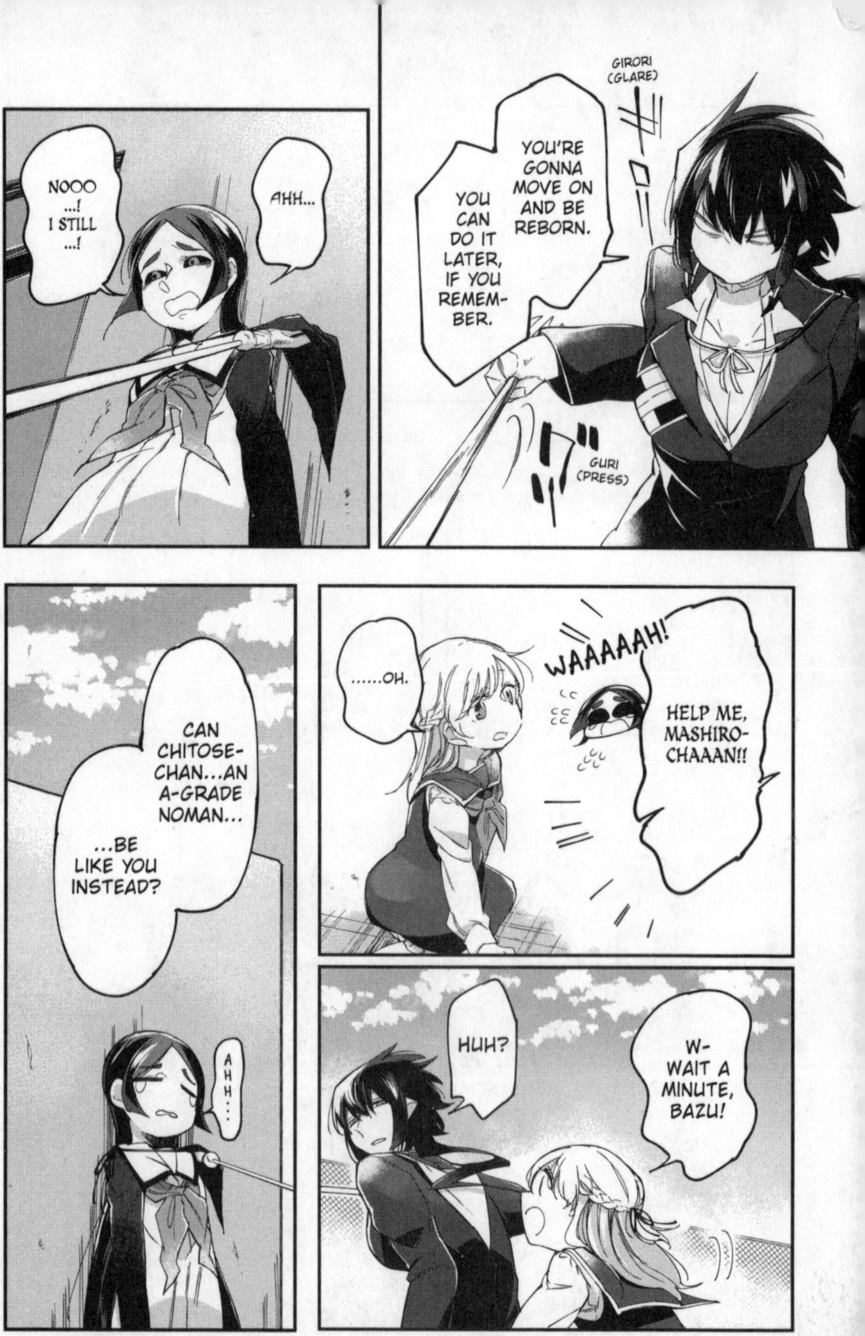
GIRORI (GLARE)
YOU'RE GONNA MOVE ON AND BE REBORN.
YOU CAN DO IT LATER, IF YOU REMEMBER.
GURI (PRESS)
AHH...
NOOO ...! I STILL ...!
WAAAAAH!
HELP ME, MASHIRO-CHAAAN!!
......OH.
W-WAIT A MINUTE, BAZU!
HUH?
CAN CHITOSE-CHAN...AN A-GRADE NOMAN...
...BE LIKE YOU INSTEAD?
AHH...

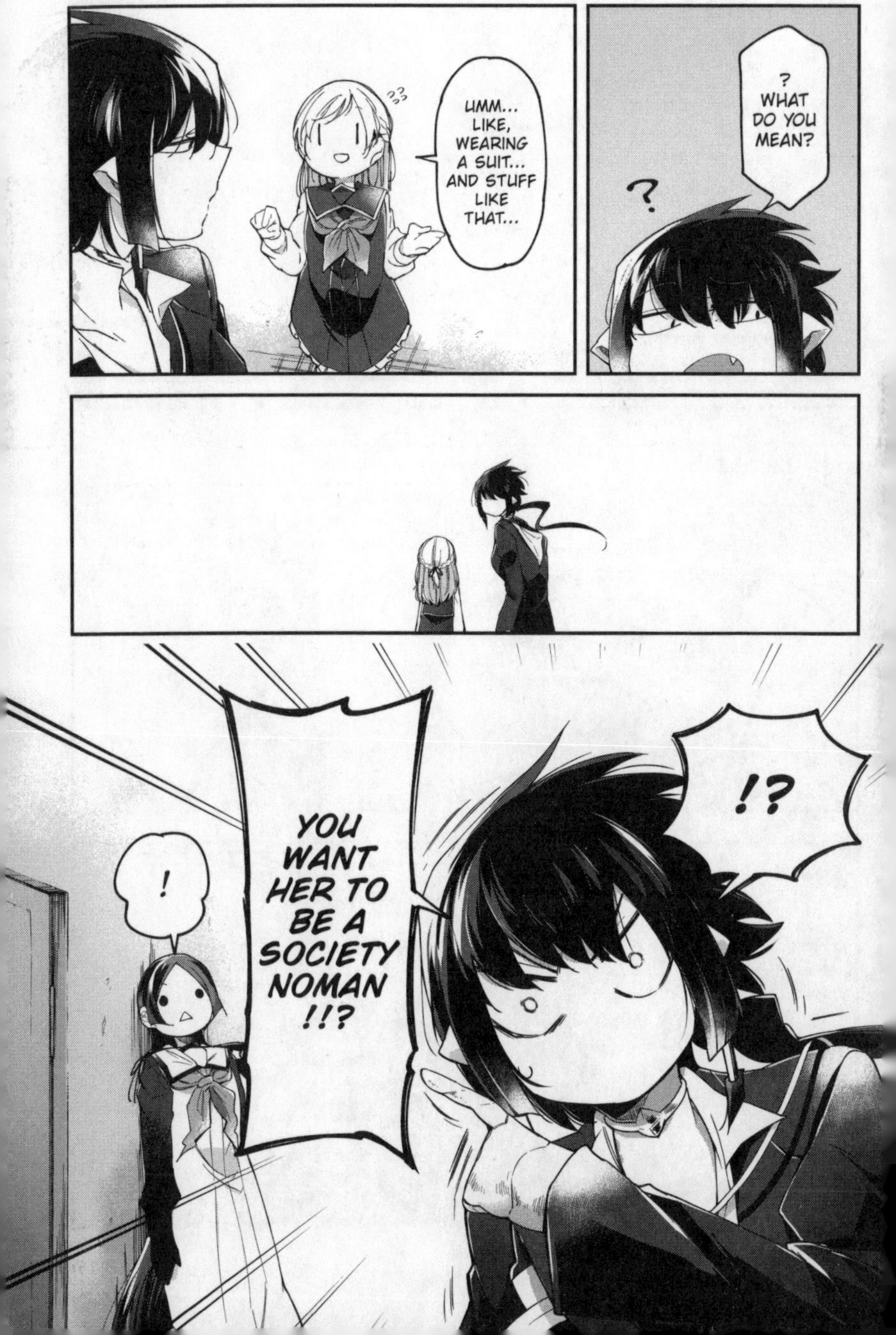
?
WHAT DO YOU MEAN?
UMM... LIKE, WEARING A SUIT... AND STUFF LIKE THAT...
!?
YOU WANT HER TO BE A SOCIETY NOMAN!!?
!

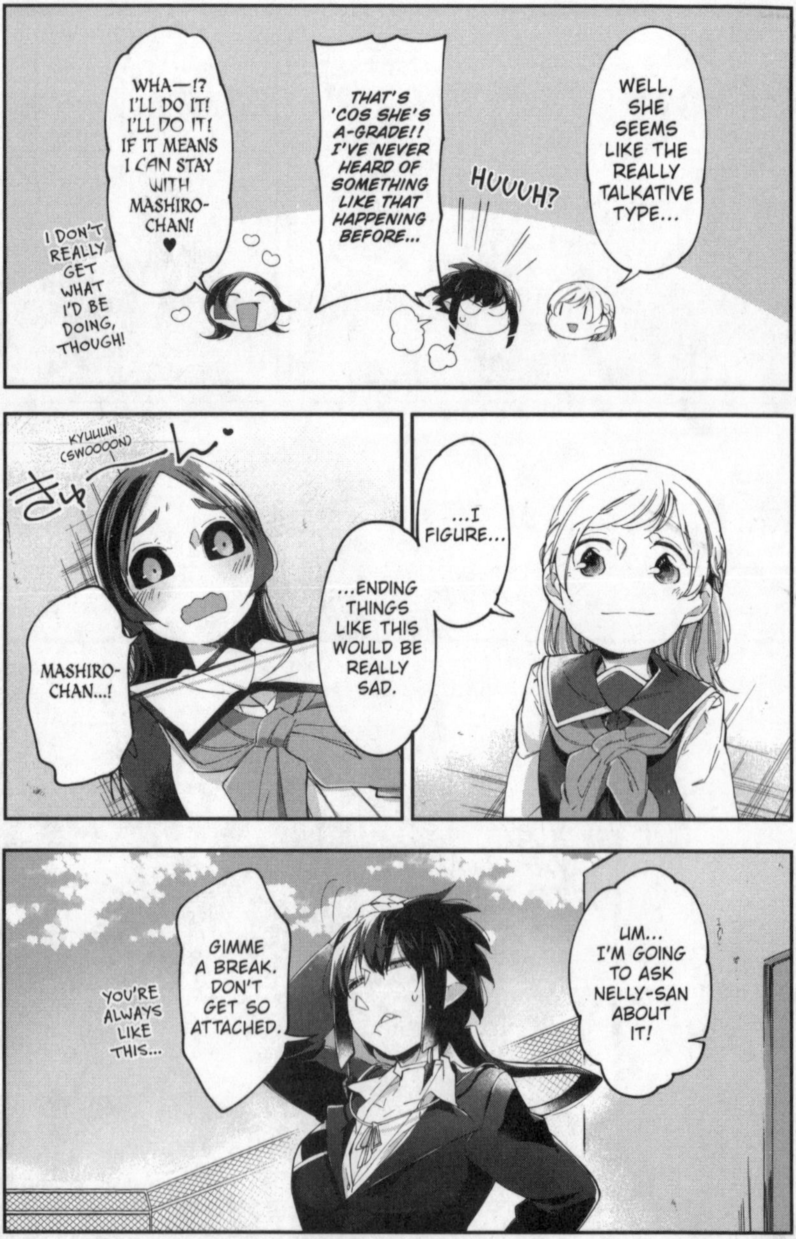
WELL, SHE SEEMS LIKE THE REALLY TALKATIVE TYPE...
HUUUH?
THAT'S 'COS SHE'S A-GRADE!! I'VE NEVER HEARD OF SOMETHING LIKE THAT HAPPENING BEFORE...
WHA—!? I'LL DO IT! I'LL DO IT! IF IT MEANS I CAN STAY WITH MASHIRO-CHAN! ♥
I DON'T REALLY GET WHAT I'D BE DOING, THOUGH!
...I FIGURE...
...ENDING THINGS LIKE THIS WOULD BE REALLY SAD.
KYUUUN (SWOOOON)
MASHIRO-CHAN...!
UM... I'M GOING TO ASK NELLY-SAN ABOUT IT!
GIMME A BREAK. DON'T GET SO ATTACHED.
YOU'RE ALWAYS LIKE THIS...

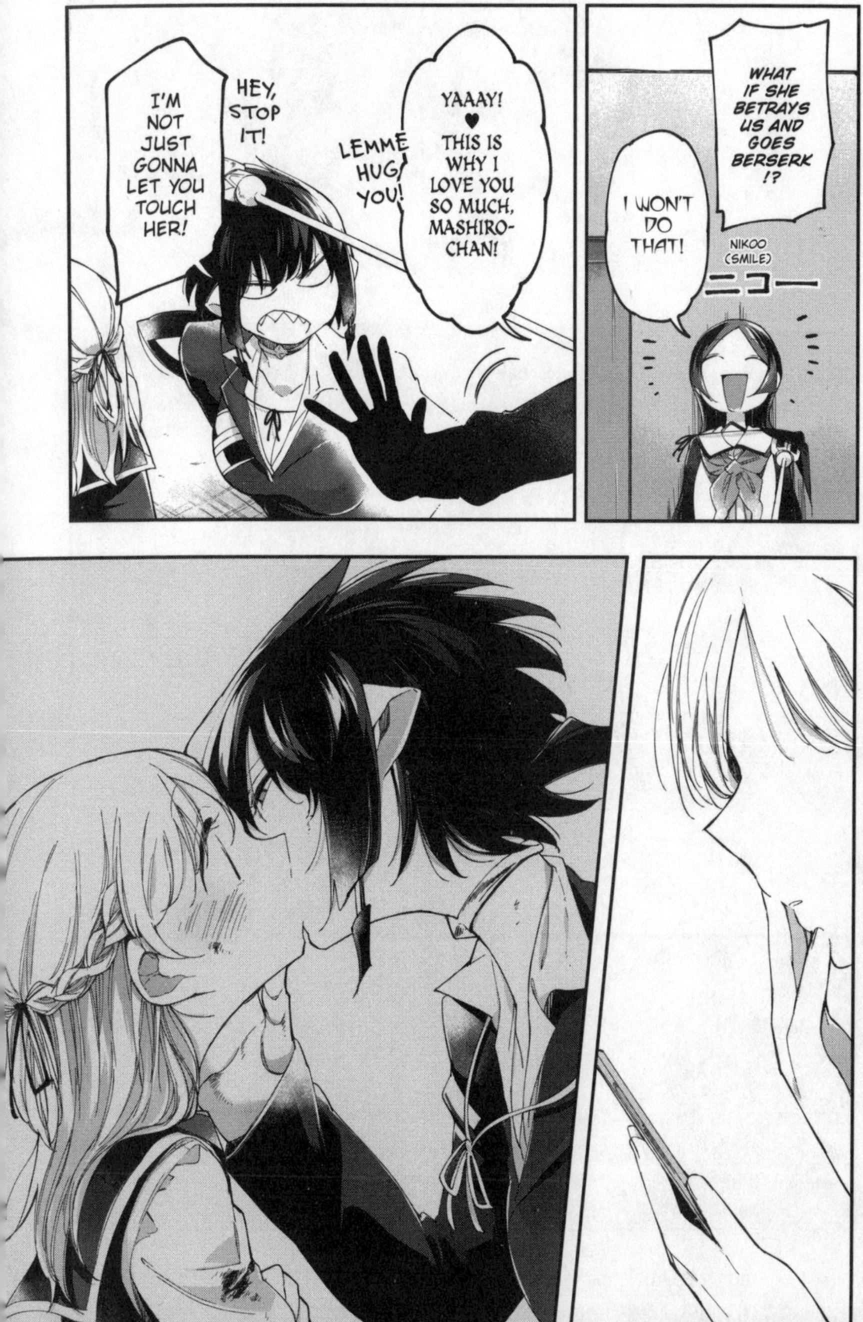
WHAT IF SHE BETRAYS US AND GOES BERSERK!?
I WON'T DO THAT!
NIKOO (SMILE)
ニコー
YAAAY! ♥ THIS IS WHY I LOVE YOU SO MUCH, MASHIRO-CHAN!
LEMME HUG YOU!
HEY, STOP IT!
I'M NOT JUST GONNA LET YOU TOUCH HER!

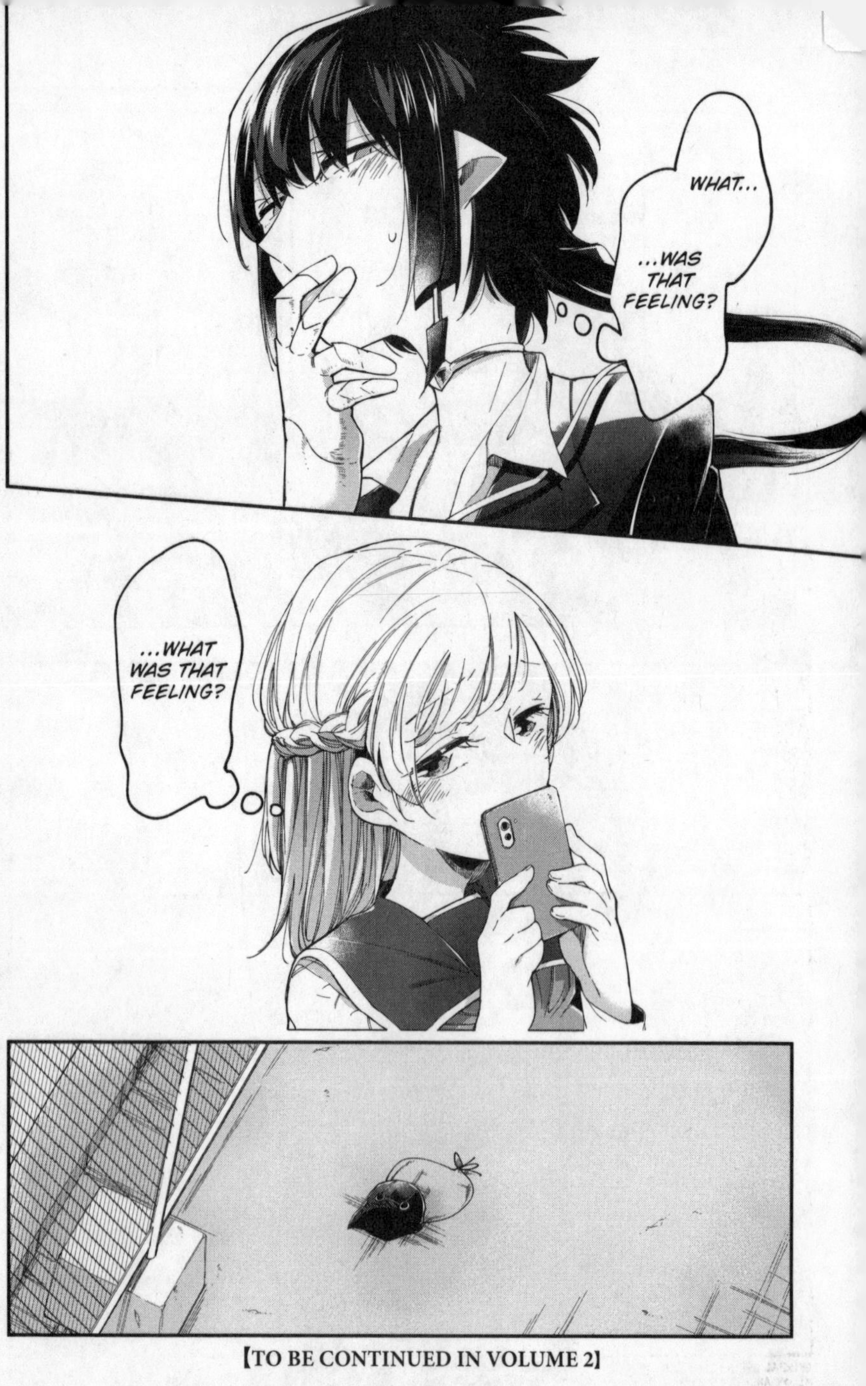
WHAT...
...WAS THAT FEELING?
...WHAT WAS THAT FEELING?

【TO BE CONTINUED IN VOLUME 2】

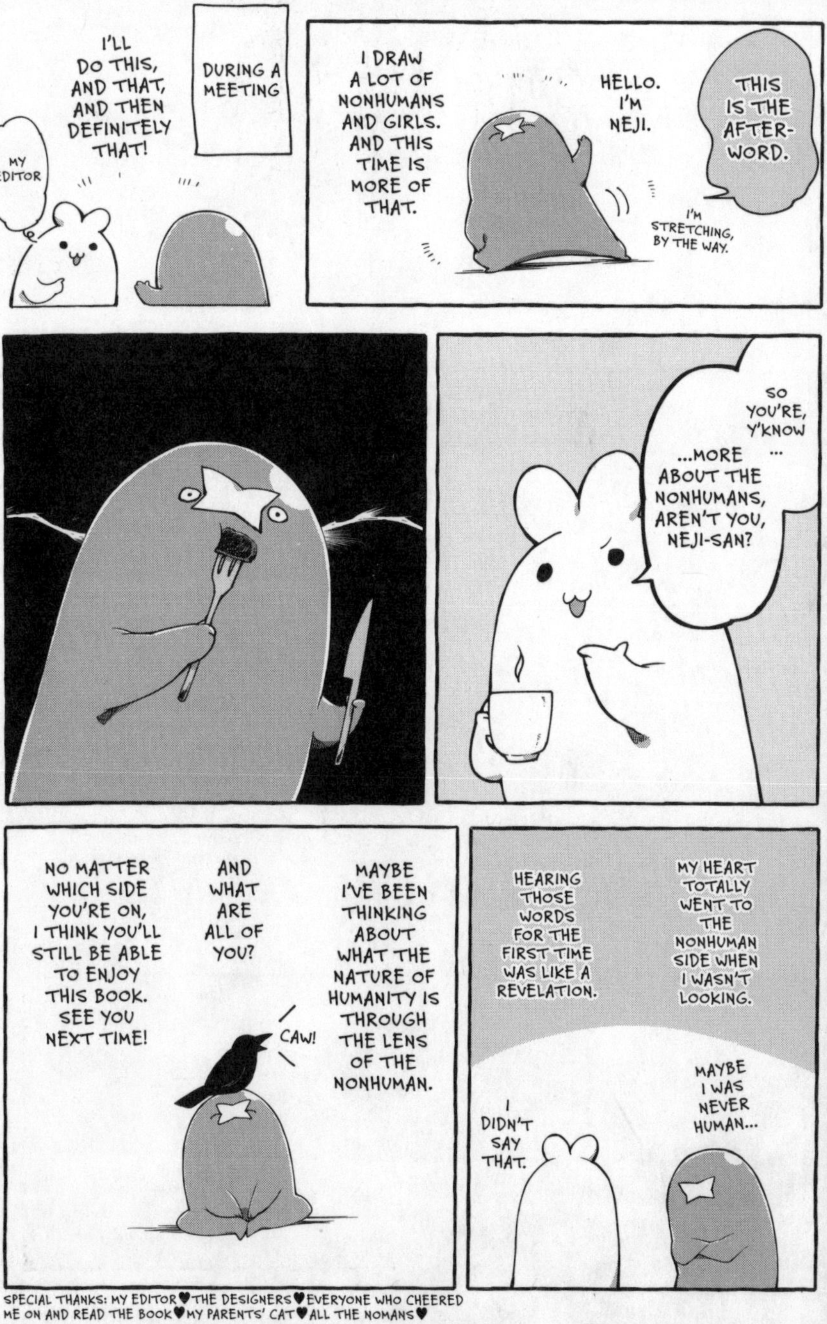
THIS IS THE AFTERWORD.
HELLO. I'M NEJI.
I'M STRETCHING, BY THE WAY.
I DRAW A LOT OF NONHUMANS AND GIRLS. AND THIS TIME IS MORE OF THAT.
DURING A MEETING
I'LL DO THIS, AND THAT, AND THEN DEFINITELY THAT!
MY EDITOR
SO YOU'RE, Y'KNOW ...
...MORE ABOUT THE NONHUMANS, AREN'T YOU, NEJI-SAN?
MY HEART TOTALLY WENT TO THE NONHUMAN SIDE WHEN I WASN'T LOOKING.
HEARING THOSE WORDS FOR THE FIRST TIME WAS LIKE A REVELATION.
MAYBE I WAS NEVER HUMAN...
I DIDN'T SAY THAT.
MAYBE I'VE BEEN THINKING ABOUT WHAT THE NATURE OF HUMANITY IS THROUGH THE LENS OF THE NONHUMAN.
CAW!
AND WHAT ARE ALL OF YOU?
NO MATTER WHICH SIDE YOU'RE ON, I THINK YOU'LL STILL BE ABLE TO ENJOY THIS BOOK. SEE YOU NEXT TIME!

SPECIAL THANKS: MY EDITOR♥THE DESIGNERS♥EVERYONE WHO CHEERED ME ON AND READ THE BOOK♥MY PARENTS' CAT♥ALL THE NOMANS♥

Dear NOMAN 1

Neji

Translation: **Leighann Harvey** Lettering: **Chiho Christie**

Dear NOMAN Vol. 1
© Neji 2020
First published in Japan in 2020 by KADOKAWA CORPORATION, Tokyo.
English translation rights arranged with KADOKAWA CORPORATION, Tokyo,
through Tuttle-Mori Agency, Inc., Tokyo.

English translation © 2021 by Yen Press, LLC

Yen Press
150 West 30th Street, 19th Floor
New York, NY 10001

Visit us at yenpress.com
facebook.com/yenpress
twitter.com/yenpress
yenpress.tumblr.com
instagram.com/yenpress

First Yen Press Edition: January 2021

Yen Press is an imprint of Yen Press, LLC.
The Yen Press name and logo are trademarks of Yen Press, LLC.

The publisher is not responsible for websites (or their content) that are not owned by the publisher.

Library of Congress Control Number: 2020948856

ISBNs: 978-1-9753-2008-9 (paperback)
       978-1-9753-2009-6 (ebook)

10 9 8 7 6 5 4 3 2 1

WOR

Printed in the United States of America